You probably don't want to read this book to read another book—the greatest book authoritative commands, and its head-scra probably don't want to read either book, but you will be glad you did. Anne Kennedy's precise, honest, and piercing commentary is a trustworthy guide for reluctant readers. A myriad of voices purport to examine the Bible honestly, but end up walking away from Scripture's God. *Nailed It* looks hard at the Bible and concludes that God has a perfect right to be exactly who he is. This is not a comfortable book, but it is ultimately comforting. It will make you love yourself less and your Savior more. Which is to say, it's a very good book.

MEGAN HILL Editor at The Gospel Coalition and author of *A Place to Belong: Learning to Love the Local Church, Praying Together: The Priority and Privilege of Prayer in Our Homes, Communities, and Churches,* and *Contentment: Seeing God's Goodness*

This is not the good book. That is, it's not the Bible. But it is a good book, because it might give you an appetite for the taste of the real thing. It could make you laugh; it should make you pray. It will always make you think, if you actually give it a go and read it. But either way, it will look good on your shelf. How many other reasons do you need to buy it?

LEE GATISS Director of Church Society

Using her combination of theological acumen and literary brilliance, Anne Kennedy unites her own personal experiences with biblical truth, enabling the reader to see through the malaise of life's every day circumstances to find freedom and wholeness in Christ.

JULIAN DOBBS Bishop of the Diocese of the Living Word, ACNA

If you're looking for a bland, motivational bit of reading to start your day, *Nailed It* is not for you. If, on the other hand, you are looking for frank and faithful words that insist on pointing you toward the One who afflicts the comfortable and comforts the afflicted, Anne Kennedy's unconventional devotional is precisely what you need. Her wry writing style requires you to pay attention; her deep insight will make you glad you did.

MICHELLE VAN LOON author of *Becoming Sage: Cultivating Maturity, Purpose, and Spirituality at Midlife*

I'm not a devotionals guy. But I love this one, and it's because if Anne Carlson Kennedy wrote licensing agreements, I wouldn't just click "I read and understood." I'd actually read it and love every line of it. Her writing is highly intelligent, funny, Jesus-centered, and completely refreshing.

BRANT HANSEN radio host and author of *The Truth about Us, Blessed are the Misfits,* and *Unoffendable*

Nailed It is a work of art filled with the creative and insightful observations that could only come from someone with a deep affection for the Bible. Anne Kennedy's whimsical yet sophisticated style take the reader on a journey from laughter to sober contemplation, never losing the heart of the biblical text. This is a perfect companion to reading through Scripture in a year.

ALISA CHILDERS author of *Another Gospel? A Lifelong Christian Seeks Truth in Response to Progressive Christianity*

Anne Kennedy has put together insightful and rich meditations and reflections on various passages of Scripture for daily use. Don't use this unless you are ready to think and be challenged.

FOLEY BEACH Archbishop and Primate, Anglican Church in North America; Bishop, Anglican Diocese of the South

There's only one devotional book that I recommend to women—this one. Anne's devotions are not of the sanguine, "everything's awesome" variety that you usually find in this genre. This is a devotional for those who don't fit into the happy-little-Christian box. And it's also for those who think it's okay to have a little humor in their reading reflections. Anne doesn't pick all the easy verses either. She pulls devotion to God out of what may have seemed random acts in history. Our days are kind of like that, aren't they? Circumstances often seem arbitrary and we sometimes question if it really matters how we get through them. This is what I especially appreciated about the book—Anne weaves all the biblical tapestry together and helps the reader see the significance of God's holiness, mercy, and love in Christ working in our own lives now.

AIMEE BYRD author of *Recovering from Biblical Manhood and Womanhood* and *Why Can't We be Friends?*

Nailed It

ANNE KENNEDY

Nailed It

365
Readings
for Angry *or*
Worn-Out
People

REVISED

SECOND

EDITION

SQUARE HALO BOOKS

In Christian art, the square halo identified a living person presumed to be a saint. Square Halo Books is devoted to publishing works that present contextually sensitive biblical studies, and practical instruction consistent with the Doctrines of the Reformation. The goal of Square Halo Books is to provide materials useful for encouraging and equipping the saints.

©2020 Square Halo Books, Inc.
P.O. Box 18954
Baltimore, MD 21206
www.SquareHaloBooks.com

ISBN: 978-1-941106-14-3
Library of Congress Control Number: 2020936819

Printed in the United States of America

For Matt,
whose preaching
keeps me from bashing
in my own head
with my tent peg.

And for Joyce, Paula,
and Allison with whom
I hope one day to wander
around Trebizond,
the four of us together.

Introduction

"WHAT KIND OF DEVOTIONAL DO YOU USE?" a young Christian woman plaintively inquired.

"What do you mean?" I asked. But I knew what she meant. She, like everyone who asks me this question, was tired and overworked and wanted a box she could check to get a grip on her spiritual life. It was so tempting, for me, to name another program, to make it easier. But in the end, I asked the dreadful question: "Have you read the Bible? All the way through?"

"I was going along fine, and then I hit Numbers . . . and the baby got sick, and I can never get anywhere on time, and my mother-in-law is visiting . . ." The voice trailed off.

"You should start there," I always say. "You should read the Bible, all the way through." But given the choice between scrolling through Facebook one more time and struggling through another chapter of ancient people and their ancient problems, the last traces of virtuous resolve inexorably dissolve. That this is true is why a dear aunt bestows on me a scroll-lettered, faux-leather-bound Devotional for Women year after year. Sit in the quiet of your clean kitchen, they instruct. Read the verse, make notes in the lines provided, become a better person and closer to Jesus.

These devotional books provoke my rebellious nature. Whenever the author tells me to do something—stop being angry, pray more, trust Jesus—I know I can't do it. Suddenly, my quiet moment with Jesus (though for me, never quiet) has been folded into my exhaustive to-do list. The devotional itself has become a barrier I have to climb over to get to the Bible.

But the Bible, though occasionally difficult to understand, is not a barrier to knowing and loving God. It is not a list of things we have to do. It is the glory of God's revelation of himself to us. While there is plenty in it that we ought to do and not do, the text itself has the power to cut open and then to heal, to convict and then to restore. As I have read through the Bible, I have come closer to the glory of God, to knowing him and being known by him. I want the same for the people in my church and my life.

365 Readings for Angry of Worn-Out People is my capitulation to the world of Devotionals for Women. It is a collection of sketches of biblical characters and events, a coaxing of the overburdened modern Christian person into particular moments in Scripture to see what they have to do with God's plan, with Jesus, and with one's own circumstances. Occasionally the sketches are funny; often they are sad, because Scripture itself plumbs the depths of human sorrow and sin. Sometimes they are even sarcastic. I have written about Eve and Mary, Jezebel and Jael, the hero and the villain.

I hope these sketches are a way into the Bible itself, a helpful stepping-stone instead of a stumbling block. I hope they create a hunger for Scripture, to know God as he has most mysteriously and perfectly revealed himself.

HOW TO USE THIS BOOK

The best way to use this book would be to buy it, because books are nice to have and it's a comfort to see them sitting around in great stacks all over the house and desk and office and lying around in the car. But then, every time you pick it up and hold it in your hand, drop it and pick up that better book, the much thicker one with the beautiful, leather cover. You will eventually lose this book in all the clutter. That other book, on the other hand, even if you leave it in the pew at church or lose it under your bed, is everywhere. There is your own copy, the grand family copy, the old one you got as a teenager, the heaps of copies carelessly left in your house after study group, the entire text distilled into an app on your phone. No matter where you lay your hand, there is a chance to read it. Therefore, whenever you see the cover of this book, go pick up that book, the Bible, and read a snatch, a few verses, here and there. But then, when you have grown tired, or have come to something perplexing or troubling, you might pick up this book for a moment. Each sketch is so short. It might be just a little respite, a pause before you return to the true riches of God's own Word. That's the best way.

Or, perhaps you are coming up close to the new year, or the new church year, or the beginning of Lent, and you decide to Read The Whole Bible. You are enthusiastic and fresh, and you search around and find a sensible reading plan. Only four chapters a day! It will be nothing for you to read so little! In which case, you can pick up this book after—only after—you have read your four chapters. And then, after you have fallen off your reading plan, because there is one of these for every day of the year, you might use this book to reignite your vigor and enthusiasm for your first love. You might use it to step back up onto your resolution.

Or, as a very last resort, you might use it like a concordance. You can find a chapter and verse and read about a particular person or event that might be needling you. There are a few great themes that run through the whole tapestry of Scripture, some true, perfect colors that emanate from what sometimes feels like a brown or gray confusion. The sketches might act like small bridges that you can walk over from one story to another, from the Old Testament to the New, from the words on the page to your own thoughts and motivations and troubles.

Of course, you might also take this book and a large pie and read the whole thing in one go, but only if you tell yourself that tomorrow you'll restart your diet and your reading plan.

BUT YOU TOOK OUT MY FAVORITE ONE

I read somewhere that in order for a book to be counted as a true "second edition" at least thirty percent of it must be completely new. I don't know if that is the case or not, but you will find that I have made a lot of "adjustments." For example, nearly all the psalms are gone. That is not because I no longer care for the psalms. It is because the psalms will be getting their own book, and so the few left here are only to remind you to rush out and buy it as soon as I've taken the trouble to fling it on the page. All the ones that used to be there are now distributed through the rest of the Bible. I leave it to you to be upset or happy about how different—or the same—this effort feels.

Another adjustment I made was to massacre (that's what it felt like) a lot of the entries I particularly liked, or to edit them so severely that they are almost completely new. I can't remember why I did this, and if you're mad at me, I'm sorry. Some things—even book writing—are essentially beyond my control. Whatever your feelings, I hope you will drop your anger, fatigue, and cutting sarcasm, and go huffing back into the Bible itself.

Which leads me to a final caution. If you have never read the Bible before, and are reading this in order to help you with that prior goal, you must know two things. First, you will need more help. You will need some other books about the Bible, like, *How to Read the Bible for All It's Worth* (Gordon D. Fee & Douglas Stuart), or *What's In The Bible* (R.C. Sproul & Robert Wolgemuth), and maybe a couple of good commentaries. You would certainly also benefit from a good Bible teacher—a preacher or instructor who has the wits and patience to dig down to the meaning of a text. And you would do well to find a group of people—a church perhaps—who trust God and are trying to understand the text just like you are.

Second, and I am sorry to have to say it, you must actually read the Bible. I don't take the trouble to set context, to explain much about what's going on. If this is your *only* help through your first trek through the Bible, you will probably come away more confused, not less so. I am trusting you, the reader, to examine the chapters all around the verse quoted, to ask questions of knowledgeable people, to gain some information about the passage on your own. In other words, I am assuming some knowledge of the Bible itself on your part, so if you don't have any, go get some! It will be the best thing you ever did. —AK

The Beginning

In the beginning, God created the heavens and the earth.
GENESIS 1:1

That's right. Crack open that big, fat, dusty, two-toned, faux leather Daily Devotional Bible and scrape the grime and neglect right off it. It wasn't the Bible you wanted when you stood there in the bad lighting, surrounded by every size and shape of Bible. A child lying on the floor beside you, screaming, your phone buzzing every few seconds, the sudden remembrance of there being nothing for dinner—all these spoiled your concentration. Your longing for peace and calm culminated in the exasperated purchase of another Bible you didn't need and now don't want.

Whatever. It's the one you have in your hands, so pry it open.

Are you irritated and confused by the translation? The little notes and scrolled embellishments, do they cause your soul to chafe? How long has it been since you've heard a decent sermon? As the objections mount, beat back the temptation to close it and walk away.

Long, long ago, in the beginning before all other beginnings, God—for purposes of his own—took the trouble to create not only the vast heavens and the rich earth, but he also began to prepare a place for you. He planned, he measured, he foresaw, he foreknew. He wanted, from before all time, for you to sit here—helpless and exhausted, with this dusty, tiny-print book in front of you—and cast your internal gaze up for a while and consider who he is and what he has done.

2   The Light

And God said, "Let there be light," and there was light.
GENESIS 1:3

So often the introduction of light into a room seems like exactly the wrong thing. Whenever I huff my way into the dimness of the Parish Hall on a Saturday evening—my hands full of Sunday School paraphernalia—it is not a relief to turn on the lights. The light exposes surfaces obscured by clutter: an array of brown tables and cold metal chairs, the gaping maw of the closet jumbled with lost coats and shoes and candy wrappers. It is the ubiquitous stuff that fills up every free space in the cosmos, whether a poor dusty yard in Africa or my own kitchen counter a world away. How can any of this be good?

But God says that the introduction of light into the world is "good." He brings the light himself, and it is good because he is good. All the clutter in the corners of your soul, the vague disappointments of the day and of life, the myriad small failures that build over the week into a mountain by Friday, over it all God casts his light. The Day of his Presence doesn't start out cheerfully. The first harrowing light illumines the sin underneath everything. The soul reels back and tries to apply the dimmer. But God's light is sure and true. Eventually, the eye adjusts. A path is cleared, the dust wiped off, and the big obstacles to trust and love thrown away.

3 In the Image

So God created man in his own image, in the image of God he created him; male and female he created them.
GENESIS 2:27

Everything is in place. The land and sea nestle together. Day and night circle the earth. The trees and flowers array themselves in glory. Everything is ready—perfect and unspoiled. And then, unaccountably, God says, "Let's make man."

And for thousands upon thousands of years we sit around asking why. *Why?* Why did you do it? And not just a man or a woman, but the two, together. Somehow the two reflect something in God. Together they are in the "image" of God.

I look at my gray, harried image in the morning, the flap of my worn-out middle swaying back and forth in the brisk winter breeze, wishing I could have some other image, that the eyes were more cheerful, the nose not so prominent, the tone of the skin brighter. Wishing someone would airbrush me into an image that *I* think is beautiful, that reflects my idea of who God should have made me to be. And then I turn around to look into the face of someone whose eyes look just as tired but who, let's not kid ourselves, looks better every year, more distinguished with every gray hair. The two of us look at each other, as in a mirror darkly. Then we look out at the world and try to do whatever it is we think we've been called to. And every evening, and every morning, I whisper quietly to myself, "Really?" And then I remember the image of the firstborn, naked, hanging out there in the breeze, broken.

4 The Fall

But the Lord God called to the man and said to him, "Where are you?"
GENESIS 3:9

A few years after we dug up the grass in our Edenic little garden and shoved flowers into every scrap of earth, arguing about which overgrown bushes to tear out and what kind of fruit trees to plant (a bitter disagreement, as it turns out—I wanted two apple trees, a peach, and a pear, and he, wretched man, wanted to keep the forsythia), someone torched the playground around the corner in the middle of the night. My dismayed children accosted me, having now no place to play, uttering that useless question we each ask as we scrape and crawl our way back to a vision of life without sin. "Why?" they asked. Why would someone do that?

The word "sin" is impossible to swallow. That primordial bite down on the fruit of the tree of the knowledge of good and evil means that almost all other tastes or experiences make us choke. It shouldn't be like this. The world is meant to be golden. We are meant to be happy. And yet we endure a sickening compulsion to devour, to lie, to break things, to pull things up, to burn things down, and even to kill.

I say "we" because the sin of Adam belongs to each of us. His disobedience is yours. His shame is mine. Each of us, without exception, though we choke over the association—hiding in the dark, running from the truth of who we are.

Look, then, at the kindness of the question. "Where are you?" Come out of your hiding and answer. Open your mouth to tell the truth.

GENESIS 3

5   Lamech

"If Cain's revenge is sevenfold, then Lamech's is seventy-sevenfold."
GENESIS 4:24

Cain killed Abel out of what? Jealously? Disappointment? He picked up a rock and struck his brother. And now we hear about his revenge—*Cain's* revenge? Can Cain have cause for revenge? But the Fall spread out, a rippling wave cursing the uttermost parts of the earth. Cain wandered away from killing Abel—unrepentant, angry with God. Angry that God wouldn't acquiesce, congratulate, or honor him, that God would not bend to his own will. As he goes, he revises the story, the account of the murder. Abel had it coming, Cain says to himself. He finds a wife who bears his children and the story of his bitterness grows with each generation. Evil entrenches itself in the minds of his family as good. They meditate on it, chewing it over, rejoicing in wrongdoing. Cain's descendent, Lamech, calls his wives to honor him, to hear his song of praise to himself. He has killed a man—a child, really—and he is proud.

But God's work is seventy-sevenfold. Forgiveness will be an overpowering tidal wave when compared to the meager, grasping ripple of bitterness and revenge. Lamech's strength will melt in the fire of God's holiness. Take heed. Do not sing a song of honor to yourself for your sin. Hear the blood of Abel crying from the ground and seek mercy from the One who promises to have mercy.

GENESIS 4, 6:1–8

6 Noah

Noah was six hundred years old when the flood waters came upon the earth.
GENESIS 7:6

"I'm not getting any younger," you grumble to yourself as you close the door on yet another unkind neighbor who sat at your kitchen table, as they have all done day after day, criticizing your whole way of life. Criticizing your ancient and faithful husband for following God's excellent but nevertheless bizarre command to build a boat the size of several buildings in the middle of a desert with no water anywhere nearby. Every evening he comes in—your husband, that is—hands all calloused and sweaty, ego cracked and on the edge of breaking, to ask you the same three questions.

"Do you think I'm crazy? Do you think it will ever rain? Do I look stupid out there building that boat?"

And, of course, you have sat there day after day saying, "Of course you don't look stupid, dear. Everything is going to be alright," while secretly biting your nails and imploring God to bring the rain.

So, when the zoo arrives, the added amount of work in no way diminishes your sense of relief and joy. Neither of you, God be praised, appear to be crazy. And then the rain and the stone in the pit of your stomach as you watch all of creation die—and see for the first time that your family alone, in all of creation, is safe.

GENESIS 6:9–7:24

Babel

Therefore its name was called Babel, because there the LORD confused the language of all the earth. And from there the LORD dispersed them over the face of all the earth.
GENESIS 11:9

I used to love the idea of the world living in unity, speaking one language, happy together. Then I got, as they say, my "socials"—Facebook, Instagram, and my favorite, Twitter. Now I would rather be socially distant from everyone.

It's possible, in a primordial yet ever fresh conundrum, that God is enacting both judgment and mercy at the same time. On the one hand, God, in justifiable wrath, strikes the people with confusion (that would either be lots of different languages, or Twitter, you pick). The result of this judgment is tumultuous misunderstanding. No one can follow the tongue of anyone else. The people on the plain of Shinar drift away into tribal factions.

On the other hand, the confusion is divine forbearance. The only thing humanity is ever able to unify around on its own is an entrenched, contemptuous desire to be God. If we continued in this unified desire, we would overthrow the created order. The mercy is that we cannot talk to each other all that well.

A long way off from this disappointing moment a lot of people will rush out of a dim, locked room, not "unified" by an idea, but united by one Spirit, one tongue, one hope, one love. They will spread out over the world, not to teach everyone how to build better with bricks and pride, but being bound together in a strange spiritual body that makes all the sense in the cosmos.

GENESIS 8, 9:1–17, 11:1–9

8 Sarai

And Abram took Sarai his wife, and Lot his brother's son, and all their possessions that they had gathered, and the people they had acquired in Haran, and they set out to go to the land of Canaan.
GENESIS 12:5

There's the folding up of your own tent, the organizing of all your servant girls, the keeping up with all the cattle boys, and the answering of thousands of questions of people who come looking for direction. There are the tents themselves, tied and gathered into a long, imposing caravan. Abram has a faraway, hopeful look in his eyes. He is a changed man, thinking about everything differently, wondering about this God who has commanded him to pack up everything and move. It's not a god anyone else has ever heard from before. Just Abram.

You retie your scarf and survey the accumulated stuff—the stuff you've had a lifetime to gather and treasure. You aren't throwing any of it away. You aren't letting anyone go. You've collected it and it's all going with you. It won't be a fast journey. The livestock will move slowly and methodically into this new land—a land that will be covered, in another thousand years, with the scars and bitterness of tumult and war. You will go as a stranger— the first stranger—your footsteps making a way for the ultimate stranger— God himself—to finally walk the same way. Don't look back, don't fret. Recheck all the bundles and wagons. Inquire of your servant if she has definitely packed the kneading bowl.

9 Hagar

And the angel of the L*ORD* *said to her, "Behold, you are pregnant and*
shall bear a son. You shall call his name Ishmael, because the L*ORD* *has*
listened to your affliction."

GENESIS 16:11

Ishmael means "The Lord Hears." It hasn't seemed like he's been hearing
for ages though. Sarai's bitter grasping anxiety has overtaken the camp.
Everywhere you go and everything you do is an offense to her. "That's
what happens when you solve your own problems and do God's work for
him," you want to lash out. But you hold your tongue. You were obedient
to her, and it profited you nothing.

What do you do when you've done everything you were supposed to,
and it ends terribly? What do you do when you are faithful in your work
and in your manner of life, and you pray and read your Bible and do what
you're supposed to do, but nothing happens? Do you storm? Do you rage?
Do you fix it yourself? What on earth, or in heaven, can you do?

You retreat in sorrow and fear and cry out to God. That's what you do.
You cry out. And when you cry out, God hears you. It may not seem like he
does. You may sit there, crying, wondering how it can possibly be that he
hears you, but he does.

The angel promises a child—not the child of the promise—but a child,
nevertheless. "So she called the name of the LORD who spoke to her, 'You
are a God of seeing,' for she said, 'Truly here I have seen him who looks
after me.'" The Lord heard and saw.

10 Sodom

And they struck with blindness the men who were at the entrance of the house, both small and great, so that they wore themselves out groping for the door.

GENESIS 19:11

Lot settles in the plain. He is going to be "in the world," but, you know, "not of the world." Somehow his life is going to stand out as a model of God-fearing righteousness. "Maybe the people will see me and be saved," he imagines to himself as he buys a house right smack in the middle of Sodom, unwraps his furniture, and inspects the glories of the splendid marketplace. The produce is amazing: the melons, the leeks! His wife and daughters, anxious at first, gradually settle in and make themselves at home. It's not exactly compromising. It's not like they stop worshiping God, whatever that even means.

But God is angry anyway, whether or not Lot lives there. If Abraham can produce ten righteous people, he'll have mercy, but, well, Lot's family consists of himself, his two daughters, and his wife, which makes four, not ten.

None of us really want God to be angry at sin. We don't really want him to judge the world. So we tuck in the delicate filigree crosses that hang on our necks. We meekly suggest to our unsaved friends that if they pray, maybe God will help them.

The world "wears itself out" looking for the door, and we, languishing between righteousness and comfort, have to be caught up and dragged, complaining, to safety.

Isaac

And Sarah conceived and bore Abraham a son in his old age at the time of which God had spoken to him.

GENESIS 21:2

Finally. You've waited longer than anyone waits for anything. It's not like you'd gone out into the desert to look for God: to gaze up at the stars and ask for something. For what? A son? You hadn't even asked. All the women in the camp have had their babies. You stood at the entrance of your tent, painful in its cleanness, troubled in the perfect arrangement of rugs and vessels.

The servants' tents are a jumble of little kids and dirt. Hagar has had a child—your child, you thought. You didn't know how much you would hate to see her hold that baby—bundled, chubby, with perfect fingers and toes. You can't control your sorrow. It is felt in every corner and every place, in everyone's gaze. Past childbearing. Past reasonableness. Past anything.

And then you get sick. And then you become huge. You waddle around, feeling more ridiculous than anything—not a young woman, but an old woman—bearing what a young woman is meant to endure. And then there he is: an actual baby all your own. He nurses and grows and spreads his baby entitlement all over the place. Is there a God? You wondered sometimes, listening to your fanatical and preoccupied husband. But he was right. There is a God, a God who does not grow weary of giving pleasure.

GENESIS 17:1–18:15, 21:1–21

Moriah

And Abraham took the wood of the burnt offering and laid it on Isaac his son. And he took in his hand the fire and the knife. So they went both of them together.

GENESIS 22:6

The mountain is shrouded in silence. Never has such a deafening quiet resounded through your own soul. A wave of ache for the noise and chaos of a camp filled with servants and herds of cattle washes over you—the bleating sheep, the calls of mothers to their children, the bustle of camaraderie and work. So often, just to hear what's going on in your own head you have wandered far out into the wilderness at night in search of a little silence. But here, it is oppressive. The beating of the heart. The regular laboring of the breath. The still air. The even measure of your son's own steps.

You stride on together in silence.

The fire and the knife. The wood. No sound of an animal, no gust of wind, no other living thing to break through and rescue you from this narrow road.

And so, the Father and the Son walk the weary way to death. There isn't anything else to be done. There isn't any other answer to the terrible evil that has overwhelmed creation. The Father will have to sacrifice his innocent Son. They go this way together for the salvation of the whole world.

13 Machpelah

After this, Abraham buried Sarah his wife in the cave of the field of
Machpelah east of Mamre (that is, Hebron) in the land of Canaan.
GENESIS 23:19

Moving house and city and land is one thing—setting up tents and wandering out over the countryside, looking for green pasture and cool water, living as an alien and a stranger. But burying the dead is another. Death is the first possession of the land, a grave the very first holding. The cave is gaping and empty, hewn out of rock: dark, ready for death. Abraham buys the cave and buries his beloved, his companion, his friend. All his wealth won't bring her back.

What do you have to show for the whole substance of your life? Even if you count it all up—the accomplishments, the house, the car, the acclaim, the relationships, the disappointments—at the final moment all you are left with is the grave. We are all going to it, one after another. It claims everyone.

Abraham shrouds his friend, his lover, the one who waited with him, who traveled with him, who tolerated him. He goes in and lays her there. Much, much later, her descendant—the firstborn, the child of the promise, the Rock himself—will walk out into the bright clear sunlight, shielding his eyes, looking around for his friends, death's ownership over us cracked, broken in pieces.

14   Rebekah

The young woman was very attractive in appearance, a maiden whom
no man had known. She went down to the spring and filled her jar and
came up.

GENESIS 24:16

It is possible, on occasion, to be in the right place at the right time. So
many love stories start with being in a place that you wouldn't have thought
significant until later, when you thread the strands together, amazed at
your astonishing good fortune. *If I hadn't gone to the well at that moment.*
If the flock had run into trouble that day. If I hadn't taken three extra minutes
this morning fussing with my hair. I don't usually, but I did, for no apparent
good reason—until you looked back and were able to see that everything
had already been arranged.

Every day as you go to the well of Scripture, as you go to quench your
thirst, to gain strength and hope, you are always going to be in the right
place at the right moment. God himself is waiting there, for you. It is the
greatest love story, the greatest moment of everything coming together,
all the threads weaving themselves into the perfect wedding garment, the
most beautiful cloth for an attractive and beautiful bride. Don't look away
and think that the meeting should have been for someone else, or that
you're not as beautiful as you could be. Go. Fill up your jar. Keep the appointment of your life.

GENESIS 24

15 Jacob and Esau

*And the L*ORD *said to her, "Two nations are in your womb, and two peoples from within you shall be divided; the one shall be stronger than the other, the older shall serve the younger."*

GENESIS 25:23

Rebekah goes to inquire of the Lord. She is exhausted by a painful, difficult pregnancy—one so long desired that she can't imagine that everything is really okay. Other women go along in childbearing with no problem, glowing with joy and expectation. Not Rebekah. Sick, fatigued by a war inside her own body, she goes to discover what is wrong. And the Lord answers her. He gives a real reason. It's not just a child, one favored child, but two. And the two are already divided, already in conflict. And on this answer, she is expected to go forward.

But jealousy will creep in, favoritism even. The discord will be felt everywhere. The boys will grow and compete and draw Rebekah and Isaac into conflict and intrigue and sin and deceit. The days will grow darker for these two babies as they stretch into manhood, wrestling with each other, with their own selves, and, one of them at least, with God. And all the time God's ordered, merciful plan will continue, picture by picture, person by person, until he himself steps in to make all divisions, all conflict cease.

Meanwhile, as your flesh wars against you, as you war in your spirit against everything, cling to the hope that there is an answer, and that the answer is a person.

GENESIS 25:1–27

16 The Stew

Once when Jacob was cooking stew, Esau came in from the field, and he
was exhausted.
GENESIS 25:29

I always think I'm going to die if I don't get what I want, or what I think I need, at the precise moment I want or need it. I stand, furtively, eating or drinking or yelling, sure that if I don't look after myself no one else will, certainly not God. My clamoring need obscures my judgment. My stomach rumbles and I grab whatever on hand is already cooked.

Esau was exhausted—tired past the point of being able to think about tomorrow, tired down to his very bones. He felt like he was going to die from the exhaustion.

And at the precise point of his overpowering weakness, his trickster brother took advantage of him to lay hold of what God could have given if he wanted to, indeed, had already promised to give. Esau lay back, dying, the ambrosial scent of stew wafting in his face. Living is always better than dying. What's the point of being born first if you're not alive to enjoy it? In this way he despised, or hated, what should have been his.

There I stand, tired down to the bone, filling myself. I am hating the God who provides, who would freely give me enough if I would only stop, and wait, and let him.

GENESIS 25:29–26:34

Esau's Wives

So when Esau saw that the Canaanite women did not please Isaac his
father, Esau went to Ishmael and took as his wife, besides the wives he had,
Mahalath the daughter of Ishmael, Abraham's son, the sister of Nebaioth.
GENESIS 28:8—9

Families have all kinds of ways of communicating with each other, of letting each other know what they think and feel. Some use caustic criticism. Others use aggressive hints. Few opt for precise, clear language about expectations, be they reasonable or unreasonable.

If you were only allowed to pick out one great systemic sin of the Patriarchs, you might easily choose terrible communication. Why on earth did Isaac and Rebekah never bother to mention to Esau what kind of wife they both wished he would marry? Why didn't they spend any time sitting around in the evening, the smoldering flames of the fire pushing away the darkness, recounting something—anything—about the kind of God they were all apparently following? That their disapproval should have been news to him *after* all the marrying and being given in marriage is so tragic. That he should fix the first problem by taking yet another wife makes it not just absurd but disastrous.

Between these two men, these brothers, and their parents, there is so much jealous misery. No family gathering measures the raw pain of this group when they gather together. So they don't. They spread out, running away from each other, carrying resentment and strife over into the next generation.

GENESIS 27:1–28:9

18 Leah

Now Laban had two daughters. The name of the older was Leah, and the name of the younger was Rachel. Leah's eyes were weak, but Rachel was beautiful in form and appearance.

GENESIS 29:16—17

Nobody wants to be Leah. Leah with her close-set eyes and her pinched, plain disposition. Leah, wanting the pretty things of her sister. Jealous, dissatisfied, hurt by everyone's silent acknowledgment of her unhappy height and awkward mannerisms. Leah, the lady who walks into the room and immediately understands that everyone wishes she had stayed at home. She stands uncomfortably next to her pretty, easygoing sister, trying to stop feeling the weight of herself for just a few minutes, and failing. She doesn't even need a multimillion-dollar advertising industrial complex to make her feel bad about herself. She had that nailed down from the first time her fluffy-haired little sister toddled from one end of the tent to the other.

Nevertheless, God wanted her. God chose rejected, slighted Leah to be the bearer of life, the mother of the promise. She will have the child that has the Child that saves the whole world.

Even then, she has to wait. Even then, she has to be fine with everyone's displeasure and unkindness. Even then she has to accept that God will be enough for her. "This time," she says, waving her gawky arms up to heaven, practically dropping baby Judah, "this time I will praise the Lord."

The Angel

19

Then he said, "Your name shall no longer be called Jacob, but Israel, for you have striven with God and with men, and have prevailed."
GENESIS 32:28

Jacob takes his wives and his children and his stuff across the ford of the Jabbok. And then he goes off by himself, and God intrudes on his solitude and wrestles with him all night. It's a dangerous place to be: alone with God. You don't know what kind of trouble you might get into. You don't know what kind of wound you will sustain. When the crowd has hurried by and it's just you and God, and you decide not to let go—to hang on no matter what—what will be the outcome? What manner of suffering will you endure? Jacob's hip wrenches out of its socket and he goes, broken, limping into the light.

Can you strive, wrestle with God, and prevail? I ask myself this question all the time as I limp around, my body broken by age and childbirth. My back stoops from bending over laundry baskets, from lifting children splayed out, too asleep to climb into their beds by themselves, from leaning low to pick up another lost sock off the floor.

Have I prevailed over God? Have I won? Yes. The gain is beyond measuring, so says another. The body *you* have broken, God, that same body will rejoice.

GENESIS 31:1–21, 32:1–32, 35:1–15

The Dreamer

But when he told it to his father and to his brothers, his father rebuked
him and said to him, "What is this dream that you have dreamed? Shall
I and your mother and your brothers indeed come to bow ourselves to the
ground before you?"
GENESIS 37:10

Jacob hasn't been a good father. He hasn't stood up to the task of managing the emotional and spiritual futures of so many big, strapping, unruly boys. The ugliness of favoritism is obvious to everyone who wanders into his camp. His young son, Joseph, grows up happy and secure, but every day his big brothers look at him and seethe. How was Jacob to know? Jacob had been favored over his twin brother. Why wouldn't he play favorites among his sons?

Then Joseph dreams a dream: he will be exalted. All his brothers will bow before him. And then he tells the dream, perhaps foolishly. Certainly, his father rebukes him for telling the dream. Except that the dream is true—true words coming down from the Father of Lights, in whom there is no shadow or variation or change. But no one is willing to listen.

Much later a young man will rise up in the midst of his brothers and will tell the truth—that he is the truth, that everyone will need to bow before him willingly or unwillingly—and no one will listen. All his brothers will rise up to kill. But his life will be for them, for you. Why wouldn't you listen to him?

GENESIS 37, 39, 41:25–56

The Brother

"But if you will not send him, we will not go down, for the man said to us, 'You shall not see my face, unless your brother is with you.'"
GENESIS 43:5

Usually when something terrible happens—some ugly sin—after the initial shock and grief everyone picks up and carries on, never speaking of the thing again. Joseph's brothers sell him into slavery and then go home to console their father, pretending that Joseph's disappearance was an accident. And Joseph goes to be a stranger in a strange land. But the thing has been done. Whether anyone speaks of it, or thinks of it, it is always there.

A whole lifetime, then, is lived between the dreams of Joseph and the dreams of Pharaoh. It seems like the past has been buried. But going into work one morning, Joseph looks out over the crowd and sees his brothers. And instantaneously, as if it had just happened, that never forgotten violence washes over him in a wave of nausea. And as the wave recedes, he discovers forgiveness.

Therefore he must maneuver to be able to see his brothers again, to see Benjamin, to see his father. And so he says, and they hear him, "Unless your brother be with you, you will not see my face." And so speaking, his words are for every single person whose life is marred by some ugly stain, some ruinous event that clouds the future and disfigures the past. You can't go in to see the king. You can't come in unless you bring your brother, the Savior, with you.

GENESIS 42, 43:1–15, 45:1–15, 25–28

Moses

> *When the child grew older, she brought him to Pharaoh's daughter, and*
> *he became her son. She named him Moses, "Because," she said, "I drew*
> *him out of the water."*
>
> EXODUS 2:10

A new, forgetful pharaoh ascends the throne—one who doesn't bother to pour over the hieroglyphs. It is always easier to blame others, and then to oppress them. It's what we all do, only most of us aren't kings. We can only do it in small, petty ways, letting bad temper be a shelter from another person's complexity.

Pharaoh enslaves the people of Israel. And then, to control their numbers, he orders that all the baby boys should be thrown into the Nile. Many babies are wrenched away from their mothers and drowned. But some mothers manage to shelter their infant sons. Thus, a young girl finds herself standing around watching her baby brother rocking gently in the rippling river. He is strategically placed, hidden in the rushes close to the favorite bathing spot of the Princess of Egypt. The baby cries, and then coos and sucks his toes and smiles a great winning smile at the enemy. His sister pokes her head out and offers to find the baby a nurse. In this way, the child goes comfortably back to the arms of his own mother, and the princess names him Moses, because she drew him out of the water.

Complexity itself, therefore, moves into those gracious halls. Moses, moving fluidly back and forth between two languages, drawn out of death to save his own people, is a foretaste of another, walking seamlessly between perpetual light and our enslaving darkness, rising up out of the river dripping with sin-soaked water.

The Darkness

They did not see one another, nor did anyone rise from his place for three days, but all the people of Israel had light where they lived.
EXODUS 10:23

You rise up from your bed and run your hand along the wall, trying to feel your way into something familiar, something that will instruct your mind as if you could see. The darkness is so complete it seeps into your pores. You pause and consider, lest your hand or foot encounter a scorpion, or snake, or some other catastrophe. After a while you light a lamp, but it is not strong enough to illumine even a small circle. It only intensifies the power of the darkness around you.

This is the darkness of sin. This is the darkness that settled into the hearts of Adam and Eve and Cain and Lamech and every single person after. There isn't anything you can do about it. You try various small lights to push it back, but they only show you how powerful it is. You try and fill up its deep confusing silence with a cacophony. You keep busy. You look at your phone every few minutes, the relief of the bright screen giving you rest from the black that is always pressing in.

And so it might always be, except that on the third day the Light overpowered the darkness forever.

24 The Passover

In this manner you shall eat it: with your belt fastened, your sandals on your feet, and your staff in your hand. And you shall eat it in haste. It is the LORD's Passover.

EXODUS 12:11

It always seems to me—as I'm scrubbing my house for the next holiday, planning menus, figuring out what the children are going to wear, wondering if I need to cook extra food for anyone who might just appear, so tired at the end of the day I can't think straight—that if I were God and I was planning a crucial theological moment, I wouldn't include any material work. I would consign my soul to an enlightened, gnostic rest.

But God works out the salvation of his people in the dust and the details. "Fasten your belt," he says—which means you have to have one. "Put on your sandals." Which ones? Not the sparkly ones that will trip you up as you run the length of the Red Sea. No, the good solid ones that won't wear out for the next forty years. The ones that you will love every day you wear them, and wearily loathe so much as you strap them on one more time for another day of walking. "Eat in haste," God says. "Which is well-nigh impossible," you think to yourself, standing over your pokey child as he twirls his unleavened bread and now room-temperature lamb around on his plate.

Lamb—freshly slaughtered. Its blood smeared over the doorway of your empty, swept house. The table and the hearth you will never see again. Your bundles are stacked by the door, ready to be tied on your beast of burden as you flee into the night.

EXODUS 11, 12

The Exodus

Then Moses stretched out his hand over the sea, and the LORD drove the sea back by a strong east wind all night and made the sea dry land, and the waters were divided.

EXODUS 14:21

I imagine this is what everyone means when they say that they are stuck between a rock and a hard place. Between death by drowning and death by arrows. God commands you to fly, Pharaoh finally chucks you out, and so you go. It's not like you insisted on staying in Egypt. But instead of being allowed to go the reasonable way, over the land, you are smack up against a great body of water. And so you stop, and sit down, and search through your bundles for something to eat. But you are interrupted by the terrifying rumble of chariots and horsemen—the entire Egyptian army. And you and your family and everybody else are supposed to "Trust God"—whatever that even means.

You break off pieces of bread for all the people sitting around you and join them in the general muttering about what an incredibly bizarre situation you're all in, and who is God anyway? But then you swallow your complaint as you watch a wall of fire move between you and the Egyptians. The lady next to you stops her grumbling and hoists her bundle on her back and grabs a little kid; and you follow because the sea has opened up in front of you, and everybody is hurrying through—water on either side, dry ground underfoot.

You'd heard that God was going to get glory over Pharaoh. You quietly hope he won't decide to get glory over you.

26　The Manna

When the people of Israel saw it, they said to one another, "What is it?"
For they did not know what it was. And Moses said to them, "It is the
bread that the LORD has given you to eat."

EXODUS 16:15

Long gone is the dribbling stain of forbidden juice from that fallen fruit—
the fruit that was grabbed, was stolen, the fruit that produced suffering
and sorrow. Now the Lord has given you something to eat. The whole
house of Israel looks around—exasperated, hot, disappointed. The exodus has turned out not to be a lovely holiday along the Mediterranean
with the cool sea breeze and a luxurious lunch of leeks, roasted with just a
hint of garlic, and a little pleasant glass of wine. Rather than that you have
your life—but not much else besides sweat, thirst, and a few thousand
other quarrelsome children and women with their irritating husbands.
Evidently, you explain to yourself, the Lord has brought us out here to
suffer and die. And, apparently, you're not supposed to complain about
it either.

So, even though your terrible attitude has made Moses and God thor-
oughly angry, the Lord sends food anyway. As the morning light falls over
the dry land, compressed between quiet and forgiving layers of dew, there
is a manna—bread—from heaven.

It isn't what you want. You get tired of it almost immediately. But it's
what God has given. Can you accept it from his hand? If you can say yes,
then you also can praise the Lord.

The Rock

And he called the name of the place Massah and Meribah, because of
the quarreling of the people of Israel, and because they tested the LORD by
saying, "Is the LORD among us or not?"
EXODUS 17:7

I regularly turn on the tap in the church kitchen and face a yellow-ish-brown stream of water flowing out to fill the basin. I humph, waiting for the liquid to run clear before I fill my glass.

But the clearest thing is that my mind and body are so connected, *and* so disjointed, that I mistake the thirst of the soul for the thirst of the body. I misunderstand the thirst of my body and think my soul is desolate. When I find myself on the edge of tears—despairing, unable to deal—sometimes it's because I need to drink a glass of water. Other times I melt down because I've opened the fridge and there is only water to drink. The tongue thirsts, and the soul blames God. He must not love me. He wants me to die.

"I will stand before the rock," says God, "and you shall strike the rock. And out of the rock will flow water." The people drank and were bitter in spirit, even as they drank. This moment is a byword in all the rest of Scripture. "Don't be like the people at Meribah." But the people couldn't help it. I can't either. I stand by, hard and angry, as the rock is struck, as a stream of living water flows from his side. Will I even drink of him? Will I stop my complaining mouth with the only water that can quench my thirst?

28 The Sabbath

"Six days you shall do your work, but on the seventh day you shall rest;
that your ox and your donkey may have rest, and the son of your servant
woman, and the alien, may be refreshed."
EXODUS 23:12

Not that long ago, when my children were young and we lived next door to the church, on Sunday mornings my children would toddle over—hair bows askew, shoes on the wrong feet, squabbling with each other—and spread over the parish hall like a gentle wave, dis-ordering the chairs and riding a horrible, pink, plastic bike back and forth and back and forth. They would drink chocolate milk and eat cookies while I made coffee and swept up after them and checked over everything I forgot to do during the week. Then late on Sunday afternoon I would unstrap my high heels and collapse on the couch, all rested out.

Six days you shall do all your work, but on the seventh day you shall rest, you and everyone. You shan't go out to the field or begin building your next bigger house or anything. So, of course, in trying to figure out what it meant not to work, we exhausted ourselves, and broke the law.

There is one place of perfect rest, though—the tomb. The quiet of a body broken, wrapped, still. No breath disturbs the air. No voice, no crying out. The body lies silent over the whole Sabbath, the perfect Sabbath. The women sit still, in an agony of rest. And then the sun breaks forth, the tomb bursts open, and all the work is finished.

The Tabernacle

"There I will meet with you, and from above the mercy seat, from between the two cherubim that are on the ark of the testimony, I will speak with you about all that I will give you in commandment for the people of Israel."

EXODUS 25:22

All the tents of Israel sit dotted around the base of the mountain. The camp is well organized but loud and dusty. It's impossible to get a tent properly clean, no matter how hard you try. Thousands of little fires, their smoke and ash ascending in the early morning, light up as everyone gets up and goes about the business of the day. Anyone lifting up his eyes can see that the mountain itself blazes with a consuming fire. And yet Moses, there in the middle of the cloud and flame, is not consumed. There, in the belly of the furnace, he is with God, and God is with man.

Not anymore a young spring chicken, Moses would climb up and up, and there would be God, and they would speak to each other. And then Moses would climb back down, hauling the heavy burden of the law along with him. And there would be all those little fires at the bottom of the mountain, and sometimes very big ones.

It's safer when God is up there, the fire contained. It's going to be complicated and intrusive, to have God down here, wandering around looking at everyone and listening to everything. So there will a tent, a place for God to sit down and Moses to go in and stand before God's mercy.

EXODUS 25:10–22, 31:1–11, 40

The Golden Calf

And they rose up early the next morning and offered burnt offerings and brought peace offerings. And the people sat down to eat and drink and rose up to play.

EXODUS 32:6

Forty days is an awfully long time—more than a whole month. The great lesson of the exodus is that God takes his sweet time. Who can wait around for the day of his coming? Almost no one. He ought to make allowances for the boredom and frustration of wilderness living.

Aaron hears the rumbling of the people and decides, like practically everybody in human history, to take matters into his own hands. A little gold, a little fire, a little waving of the hands in prayer, and there you are. A standard golden calf. Not too big, nor too small—just right.

The people sit down to eat and drink and rise up to "play." Most unsuitable. But nobody's sensibilities are offended, and no single internal moral compass signals a warning. It's just a good time. *Everyone* is having a good time.

And so, while Moses stands under the burden of God's mercy and love—listening to him and learning about what sort of God he is and what kind of way he expects his people to live—the people have a party for themselves. They sing and dance and express themselves. They do everything the modern person is taught to do.

But the light and heat of their good time filters up the mountain and ignites God's wrath, and Moses has to run quickly back down the mountain.

EXODUS 32, 33:1–6, 12–23, 34:1–9, 29–35

The Ash Heap

". . . all the rest of the bull—he shall carry outside the camp to a clean place, to the ash heap, and shall burn it up on a fire of wood. On the ash heap it shall be burned up."

LEVITICUS 4:12

I am often hearing about how much God longs to be with his people, if only they would decide to be with him. He does everything for them, and they need only turn around and realize how greatly he loves them. After all, he made them in his very image. They just don't realize their own worth. Once they do, they will rush headlong back into his arms. Indeed, I have probably said this myself sometimes.

The trouble is, the way back is through the Ash Heap.

My town doesn't even have an ash heap. Nor is there some imposing structure where I must go in order to be forgiven of all my lawbreaking. Neither tabernacle, nor ash heap—it is just me, quietly in my own house, having to live within the vortex of my own spiritual feelings.

Nevertheless, back in that long-lost day, when the people would break the law, sin if you will, they had to go first to the tabernacle where the priest would lay his hands on the head of the bull so that all the sins of all the people would be transferred onto that innocent animal. The bull would be killed and hauled out of the camp to the ash heap and there burned, all of it.

It is rather an unusual journey to make to be with someone. Funny that it was God going out there and not me.

Nadab and Abihu

Now Nadab and Abihu, the sons of Aaron, each took his censor and put
fire in it and laid incense on it and offered unauthorized fire before the
LORD, *which he had not commanded them.*
LEVITICUS 10:1

Despite making an actual golden calf for the people of Israel to worship
instead of God, Aaron survived the just wrath of the Lord and has now
been ordained and consecrated as priest. The mercy of God is everlasting
and new every morning. His love never fails, though it is not the kind of
love any of us are expecting. This being so, you would think that Nadab
and Abihu, Aaron's own sons—ordained now themselves—would have noticed the resulting carnage of that fiasco and satisfied themselves with
obedience.

But, well, when you see God's merciful action in the world, do you turn
around and obey him? Do you swallow your biting anger? Avert your eyes
from that which you should not see? Forgive when it is clearly your place
to forgive? Make allowances for those who are weaker than you? Speak
charitably about the one who always has it in for you? Count others as
more significant than yourself? Or do you take up your own plans in your
own hands and carry them out, even when your own destruction looms
over you?

Nadab and Abihu take up their censors and do something strange and
abominable—something completely idolatrous. And God swallows them
up. Take the warning. At some point the fire of his just judgment will consume the whole earth.

33 It Shall Be Clean

"Thus he shall cleanse the house with the blood of the bird and with the fresh water and with the live bird and with the cedarwood and hyssop and scarlet yarn."
LEVITICUS 14:52

That's a curious assortment of objects. A bird, fresh water, cedarwood, and scarlet yarn.

Anyway, I seriously wish this were just about sorting out a cluttered house. As in, I needed help picking up all the books and crayons off my dining room table. Also, the strange smell lurking in the basement. And maybe the apocalypse that is the boys' room. I go from one pile of junk to the other and wish I could afford a professional cleaning service.

Alas, no. The everyday clutter and tracked-in dirt of a house is apparently the least of my problems. It's the "leprosy" inside the very walls of the structure that's the trouble. Weird how the priest had to look at the house and shut it up for a while and then go back and look at it again, and if it wasn't clean the whole thing had to be torn down. I feel like that's going to come up again in a few centuries—the going in, clearing everything out, even perhaps turning over a few tables with a touch of anger, leaving, seeing how it gets on, coming back again, cursing the whole edifice and then it actually gets pulled down, so that not even one stone is left upon another.

I'm pretty sure we're not just talking about houses anymore.

34 The Atonement

"And this shall be a statute forever for you, that atonement may be made for the people of Israel once in the year because of all their sins." And Aaron did as the Lord commanded Moses.

LEVITICUS 16:34

If you were unclean you couldn't go near the tabernacle, the place where God put his peculiar presence. And you were unclean. At some point, no matter how hard you might try to avoid it, you would become unclean. The natural ordering of your body and the necessities of life required that you regularly acknowledged that you were not clean. Only the good, the beautiful, and the pure could come into the presence of God. And such were—are—none of you. Not good: because you have not loved God alone but have mainly and completely loved yourself. Not beautiful: because your body shows and bears the ravages of sin and age and death. And not pure: because your body cannot be kept wholly clean and your mind is awash in every kind of evil.

But a perfect bull and a perfect lamb and a perfect goat are slain in your place. And the blood runs out onto the altar, and down the sides. Your blood isn't acceptable. Your life blood courses through your veins in sin. And so true innocence is slaughtered, flayed open, and the blood runs down. And then you can come in for a few brief moments of fellowship and communion with God.

Sitting in your clean, bright pew, your eyes alight with beauty and peace, don't forget the blood.

Not Really What I Long For

You shall be holy to me, for I the LORD am holy and have separated you
from the peoples, that you should be mine.
LEVITICUS 20:26

I've always disliked that song, "Holiness, holiness is what I long for,"
mainly because the construction of the opening line is so awkward. Why
repeat it? Also, whenever I have to sing it, there's a nasty little backchat-
ting voice in my head. Really? Holiness? This song ending is what I really
long for.

Honestly, neither did the people of God way back in the day long for
holiness. They seriously recoiled from God's hallowed name and resisted
strenuously every opportunity he took to make them holy as he is holy.
Nevertheless, with little to no cooperation from them, *he* set them apart.
He made them his. *He* made the holy. And all the time, they did *not* sing
this song.

Because holiness is not a soupy, lovely, schmaltzy feeling. It is a deeply
uncomfortable, alien, othering perfection that characterizes God in himself. He is holy. It's who he is, it's who he is, it's who he is (just to poke at
another song I don't love). And who he is, in spite of what we might say
about it, is vaguely repellent to all of his willfully unholy creation.

To make the idea more palatable to themselves, some people try to imagine that they are already "holy," that what they long for is, in fact, holy,
and so God should give up and be happy already.

36 The Arrangement

"The people of Israel shall camp each by his own standard, with the ban-
ners of their fathers' houses. They shall camp facing the tent of meeting
on every side."
NUMBERS 2:2

The best way to get a handle on the pileup of disorder, the junk that ac-
cumulates on every surface, is to decide to rearrange the living room.
Rearranging the living room sets off a chain reaction, culminating in the
decluttering and ordering of all the other rooms in the house.

The arrangement of the camp of Israel won't be jumbled and confused
or haphazard. God arranges each family, each clan, each tribe by standard, facing the tabernacle. If there is any clutter, disorder, or confusion,
it will be in your own tent and in your own mind. Whenever you step over
your own threshold, you will behold the wide-open pathways between the
rows of tents leading always up to the place God has chosen to live.

In this way the arrangement of the camp in the wilderness reflects
God's own ordered nature. His mind and character are not a jumble. He
never loses anything he once set down. He doesn't start something and
then forget to finish it. He does not wonder where to put something, or
how two things might best fit together. He doesn't wake up in the morning
confused about what he should do first and then second. And you might
be given he own mind when you become the place where he lives.

Human Flourishing

> *So they brought to the people of Israel a bad report of the land that they*
> *had spied out, saying, "The land, through which we have gone to spy it*
> *out, is a land that devours its inhabitants, and all the people that we saw*
> *in it are of great height."*
>
> NUMBERS 13:32

It's usually only after the fact—after whatever dreadful consequences have unfolded—that you can go back and see the roots, and before that the seeds, of where you went wrong. For that, of course, we constantly go back to the garden where the seed of distrust was planted deep inside the human soul. But in the long, winding road away from the garden there are lots of other bad beginnings. In the camp and tents of Israel, since the moment they first complained to Moses before passing through the Red Sea, the people have been nurturing and watering and tending the seeds and vines of rebellion. The first flowers of it are bursting forth—the fruit is visible on the vine.

Here they are, at the very threshold of the place they have so longed to be. They can paddle their toes in the Jordan River and look out over the lush countryside. A short walk across the river, a little flinging of an arrow here and there, and then to settle down and enjoy the secure provision of God.

But the men, the spies went into the land of God's promise, they looked around, and they came back and gave a bad report. They looked at it, and said it wasn't good.

38 The Serpent

And the people spoke against God and against Moses, "Why have you
brought us up out of Egypt to die in the wilderness? For there is no food
and no water, and we loathe this worthless food."

NUMBERS 21:5

The people saw the goodness of the land they'd been promised and thought to themselves, "God must really hate us to bring us all this way just to show us what he can't give us. Not only is he small, he is unkind and evil." Somehow God could part the Red Sea and deliver water out of a rock and rain down bread from heaven, but he was going to prove much, much too weak against some big, strong men.

And so, poisoned by this wrong, terrible picture of God, the people became impatient. They hated the manna so much they didn't even count it as food. They moaned and grumbled. God was, not surprisingly, very angry.

Therefore, the Lord killed many of them—though certainly they all should have been killed.

Just as I, standing at my sink grumbling about the endless gray sky, look up at the heavens and shake my fist. God must really loathe me to give me a big house and some healthy children. He has given me life, but he is too small to give me whatever else I think I want.

And yet he stays his hand. His mercy matches his judgment. The serpent that Moses lifts up in the wilderness, the snake that the people must look upon to live, is the Son of Man cursed as their grumbling mistrust and sin. When they look at him, the Lord will forgive them.

Balaam

And when the donkey saw the angel of the LORD, she pushed the wall and pressed Balaam's foot against the wall. So he struck her again.
NUMBERS 22:25

Poor Balaam, minding his own business, rousted out of his comfortable chair by Balak, king of Moab, made to climb on his wretched donkey and lumber off to a place where he could stand overlooking the sprawling camp of Israel. There he was supposed to rain down imprecations upon the people of God, in the hopes of forestalling Balak's certain demise.

Except that Balaam couldn't. In the first place, he couldn't because God told him not to go at all. Then, for reasons not vouchsafed, God said he *could* go but he had to be awfully careful about what he said—as in, no actual cursing. And then, while he was on his way, an angel appeared to further jolt him out of his peace of mind. Well, rephrase that. The angel didn't appear to Balaam. The angel appeared to Balaam's poor donkey.

I sometimes wonder who is hearing and seeing what God is doing right now around me while I carry on in metaphorical—though spiritually real—blindness. I curse and bang into furniture, busy with my own plans and my own desires and my own agenda, and it may be that God is right there, watching me, possibly even tripping me up, ready to enlightenment me about what constitutes real blessings and real curses.

40 The Lord Will Forgive Her

"But if, on the day that her husband comes to hear of it, he opposes her,
then he makes void her vow that was on her, and the thoughtless utter-
ance of her lips by which she bound herself. And the LORD will forgive her."
NUMBERS 30:8

So, just to recap, the guy gets to make any kind of vow he wants? But if he hears that his daughter or wife has made some similar kind of promise or whatever and he doesn't like it, or thinks it is "foolish," he can just cancel it, basically, without too much ceremony? "Not Fair!" you cry, clicking away from the Bible so fast the mouse lights on fire.

Remember that none of this is really about you—not directly, though in every possible way, indirectly. There is one person who has the right to "cancel" the vows made by the one he loves. But it costs him rather a great deal to do it. There she was, selling her actual soul to the devil, or snake or whatever, and there was no remedy once she had done it. The price of this "foolish" vow was her own life. And the devil was happy to collect his prize. But the bridegroom happens along and offers his life in place of hers. The devil can't have her. Her vow to him is nothing.

All those "thoughtless utterances" "by which she bound herself"— gone. The Lord forgave her. And continues to, every day that he hears of it, because that One, that bridegroom, what was his name . . . he took that wretched vow onto himself and destroyed it in his own blood.

Gods of Wood or Stone

"And the LORD will scatter you among the peoples, and you will be left few
in number among the nations where the LORD will drive you. And there
you will serve gods of wood and stone, the work of human hands, that
neither see, nor hear, nor eat, nor smell."

DEUTERONOMY 4:27—28

God is not surprised by who you are and what you do. There isn't astonished amazement in the mind and heart of God when you do something
that he told you not to do or when you fail to do something that he clearly
told you to do. There is no wringing of the divine hands in shock and horror over the sins of his people.

How do I know? Because hundreds and hundreds of years before Israel
and Judah were sent into exile, God saw, knew—predicted even—that they
would reject him and that he would vomit them out of his land.

Nevertheless, knowing it in advance doesn't make it better. The sin—
when you commit it—is truly offensive. Just because God saw long beforehand that the people would set up wooden images, carved figures with
faces and hands and noses and eyes, didn't make it less abominable the
moment the little figure went up on the little altar. "Are you kidding me?"
says God. "A figure? A carved, mute face? Sitting there immobile, unable
to hear and smell and see and touch and speak?"

The people will grow weary of God. You will fall into sin. His eyes have
seen it from a long way off. His voice of warning cries out. His hand of
mercy extends from everlasting to everlasting.

42 Too Difficult

"You shall teach them diligently to your children, and shall talk of them
when you sit in your house, and when you walk by the way, and when
you lie down, and when you rise."

DEUTERONOMY 6:7

Except you won't. I mean, you will tie them around your head and onto
your arms—for a while. And you might remember to scrawl them over the
door posts of your house, but your eyes will look past them after a while,
and you won't bring them up with your children. When you sit down in
your living room you will chat about how well they worked in the field and
admonish them to stop arguing all the time.

But when the words come up to your lips about who God is, and what
he has done and the love he has already shown for you, you will swallow
them down and glance out of the window at the sky. And when you are
walking along the way and you pass a pile of stones, and your child points
and says, "What's that?" you will say, "Ask me later." And all the time you
will feel harried and guilty, and the words just won't be forced out from
between your lips.

And so the children of Israel fell away, and slid into idolatry, and did
not love God and each other. And so the Lord had to open his own mouth.
The saving Word came himself—to say what needed to be said.

43 Blessed

"Blessed shall be your basket and your kneading bowl. Blessed shall you be when you come in, and blessed shall you be when you go out."
DEUTERONOMY 28:5—6

We spend a lot of time assuring ourselves that there is no correlation—not a direct one anyway—between the things we do and the catastrophic circumstances that beset us. If I sin, I won't therefore get cancer. If I lie, I won't then get hit by a bus. But we do want it to go the other way. If I'm awfully nice and good, then everything should be easy for me. I should never discover that my taxes are way too complicated and that I don't have the money to pay them. Or that the dryer has broken at the same time that the car needs new brakes. Because I'm good. Things ought to be easy. But frequently they are not, and sometimes I carry around anger because God hasn't aligned himself with my expectations.

How can I be blessed and not cursed? How can I be blessed even in the circumstances of my life, not just the quietness of my mind? Maybe I can try really hard. I can perfectly follow the law.

"No, you can't," says Moses, and he sings a long, long song about how you won't. I won't. We won't. We won't love God. We won't flee from idolatry. We will occasionally lie. We will covet so many things, big and small. Sin will be with us in the field, and in the kitchen, and in our baskets and kneading bowl, when we go out, and when we come in.

DEUTERONOMY 11, 28:1–14

44 Cursed

"Cursed shall you be in the city and cursed shall you be in the field.
Cursed shall be your basket and your kneading bowl. Cursed shall be
the fruit of your womb and the fruit of your ground, the increase of your
herds and the young of your flock. Cursed shall you be when you come in,
and cursed shall you be when you go out."

DEUTERONOMY 28:16—19

And because of sin pervading everything, tucked into every corner of the house, found at the end of every lane, every transaction, every plan, God promises curses rather than blessings. He promises trouble rather than ease, poverty rather than wealth, isolation rather than familial companionship, death rather than life.

Is this an unkindness? A cursed, forsaken existence for each person who wanders the world, like Cain, ruined? Should we just try harder? As the curses spread out and overtake everything? As all the things that can go wrong do go wrong?

No. The harder you try to follow the law, the worse it will be, because you'll just try to organize your own way rather than turning to God and trusting him to be good. So eventually you will, maybe, stop trying. And there will be another One who comes and absorbs all the curses in himself. He will gather them, each one, out of the basket and the kneading bowl and the womb, out of the field and the flock. He will carry them and bury them. And sometimes you will still grumble because it wasn't exactly what you were looking for.

DEUTERONOMY 28:15—68

45 The Land

And the Lᴏʀᴅ said to him, "This is the land which I swore to Abraham,
to Isaac, and to Jacob, 'I will give it to your offspring.' I have let you see it
with your eyes, but you shall not go over there."
DEUTERONOMY 34:4

Moses didn't go around sinning. He was the meekest man to ever live. He hated to speak out loud. He was willing—though he didn't like it—to endure every trouble. So God waited and waited. And just at the right time, when Moses had finally had enough and his temper got the better of him, he, Moses, disobeyed. When the people needed water, Moses struck the rock instead of speaking to it. And then, in anger, he struck it again. But God himself is the Rock, and the living water, and he is also patient. It was the moment He was waiting for.

"You won't go into the land, Moses," said God, "because you struck the rock."

Moses argues. He frets. To have worked so hard and then not to see what all the work has been for? It was too bad. He toils up the mountain. He shades his eyes and looks out over the inheritance of his people: the good, good land. And then he lies down and dies.

But really, he steps out of the shadow and into the real thing. He puts one foot and then the other over the threshold of God's perfect mercy.

All things work together for your good, someone will say later, if you love God. Even the bad things, even the disappointments and sin. All of them will be made into something good.

DEUTERONOMY 33–34

46 Jericho

> "Behold, when we come into the land, you shall tie this scarlet cord in
> the window through which you let us down, and you shall gather into
> your house your father and mother, your brothers, and all your father's
> household."
>
> JOSHUA 2:18

A scarlet cord—a long bright ribbon the color of blood—hangs as a sign, a streak of mercy. Gather those you love, Rahab. Bring them into your house and console them against the immanent loss of everything they know and love. Tie the wind-whipped cord from the window and see your deliverance.

It's not going to come from on high, angels descending to rain down sulfur and fire. Nor will it spring up from the ground, a terrifying well of water. No, it's just a bunch of sinners walking around the city once every day, blowing their useless trumpets, and then going home again. What are they doing in between? Eating chocolates? Sharpening their spears? But on the last day they go round and round . . . and then it's all over.

The thing that seems the strongest—the vast towers of power that array themselves against God, the principalities and authorities and wicked-ness of the earth—crumble before the might and power of God. They will not stand strong before his righteous and holy strength. And yet, He gives a single blood-colored cord, whipped and bleeding in the sun. He gives it for you, that you might be saved and dwell secure and peaceful in the land the Lord your God gives you.

47 Achan

> *But the people of Israel broke faith in regard to the devoted things, for*
> *Achan the son of Carmi, son of Zabdi, son of Zerah, of the tribe of Judah,*
> *took some of the devoted things. And the anger of the LORD burned against*
> *the people of Israel.*
>
> JOSHUA 7:1

Jericho was conquered—by God. The battle was won entirely *by* God. The strongest fortified city for miles crumbled because the people of Israel blew some horns and walked around a bit. No one is really confused, especially those buried under the rubble. It's not as if it is unclear who God is or what he expects from the people he called, delivered, and set apart for Himself. Nor, for that matter, how strong He is and what He can accomplish. But Achan sees a shiny cloak from Shinar, that gorgeously idolatrous plain where all the language was confused. "They make great stuff there," he mutters, snatching a handful of silver coins and a gold bar.

For so little—a pittance—Achan throws away his own life, his future, the land he would have inherited, and the lives of his children. He just chucks it away. How foolish.

But the thing never seems small when you're looking at it, when you're reaching out your hand toward whatever it is you're sure you have to have. All the little things you say to make it okay, the little justifications, they seem rock solid and sensible. I should have this. I deserve it. God wanted to give it to me, or he would have *if* he was good.

food

So we risk death: for a handful of nothing.

JOSHUA 7, 8

Gibeon

So the men took some of their provisions, but did not ask counsel from
the LORD. And Joshua made peace with them and made a covenant with
them, to let them live, and the leaders of the congregation swore to them.
JOSHUA 9:14–15

The Gibeonites, like all of us, don't want to die. They are numbered among the many who have sinned so much—whose sin has become a full measure, pressed down, shaken together—that God is spitting them out of the land. It's not that the people of Israel are so good that God is bringing them in and giving them all these good things. It's that the people of Canaan are so bad.

The Gibeonites watch the destruction of Ai and Jericho, consider their options, and gather up their worst-looking ragged clothing, their old stale bread, their shoes that they should have long ago thrown away. They set out from their own small city and arrive, panting and exhausted, to see Joshua, insisting that they are not from just around the corner, but have traveled from a far-distant country, *not* anywhere nearby. Joshua should be nice to them and not kill them.

Joshua hears them out. He looks over their bread. He pokes at their shoes. They look pretty tired. Their story makes pretty good sense. He "does not inquire of the Lord." Instead, he makes peace with them.

Really? He couldn't stop for a few minutes and shoot up one of those nothing prayers, "Oh God, please help me to know what to do?"

Prayer: it's good for practically everything.

49 The Springs of Water

She said to him, "Give me a blessing. Since you have given me the land
of the Negeb, give me also springs of water." And he gave her the upper
springs and the lower springs.

JOSHUA 15:19

All the land is divided up clan by clan, tribe by tribe, family by family. It really is a matter of ask and you shall receive. Caleb asks for a certain piece of real estate, marries off his daughter, and gives her land as a present. And, because she asks, he gives her the springs to go with it.

It's not that God doesn't want you to have nice things. It's not that he wants you to sit hungry and thirsty and tired in a corner. That you have to rush out and get what you need because he isn't good, and he doesn't love you, and he just wants you to suffer. No.

But sometimes, when you're standing in Target, your fingers hovering over some bright and shiny object, evil springs up and whispers, "You'd better just get it, because God won't give you anything." And so you shell out your hard-earned cash and feel like you've won, you beat God.

But God doesn't hate you. He's not holding everything in reserve so that you'll starve and die of thirst. Come to the living water. Ask. Keep asking. Do you have a need or a desire? Ask. Once in a while you will ask for something good, and he will be delighted to give it to you.

JOSHUA 14:1–15:19

The Cities of Refuge

He shall flee to one of these cities and shall stand at the entrance of the gate of the city and explain his case to the elders of that city. Then they shall take him into the city and give him a place, and he shall remain with them.

JOSHUA 20:4

You definitely did not mean for that guy to die. You were just rolling your logs down the road—how could you have known he was going to step out in front of them all like that? People should be lots, lots more careful. Then his giant brother came flying out of the woods after you. What could you do but run? And by run, I mean faster than you have in ages. It's super disappointing because those logs would have made a great house, if you'd been able to actually build it.

Fortunately, the guy at the gate of this town, seeing you running head-long, gave a signal, and when you careened into him, collapsing and out of breath, he took you in and you explained what happened, and he gave you some water and let you sit down. Fifteen minutes later that huge guy arrived, but they didn't let him in. I mean, no lie, it's still super stressful. You have your trial to look forward to, and it could go either way. No one saw what happened. But for now, as long as you stay *inside* the city walls, you don't have to die.

What was that line? "My refuge and my fortress, my God, in whom I put my trust." Imagine there being a place you could go for safety even if you *were* guilty.

Ehud

And the hilt also went in after the blade, and the fat closed over the blade,
for he did not pull the sword out of his belly; and the dung came out.
JUDGES 3:22

I feel like this section of Judges is God's love letter to teenage boys (and even some girls). In Bible charades, it was my favorite. I insisted on doing it every single time. It's the thrusting motion with your left hand that gives it away. Although, if you always do it everyone stops guessing and groans. If you're not up for charades, the grotesque thrill, "and the fat closed over the blade," electrifies every performative reading. And people try to tell me the Bible isn't relevant.

Now, of course, I do shudder. It's not particularly amusing to read about a powerful group of people oppressing a less powerful one, nor about God letting subjugation, injustice, exploitation, or just the general hassles of life go on unchecked. So what if "the people of Israel again did what was evil in the sight of the Lord?" It's important to keep the good (Ehud, clever left-handed judge of Israel, dexterous with a sword) marked out from the evil (Eglon, shockingly overweight king of Moab, notorious enemy of Israel).

It's nice, too, how God keeps raising up these barely consequential heroes, admired only by the middle school blood-lusty, who come in and stab the evil fat guy and free all of the oppressed. Helps swallow down the hideous "nuance" of why the evil bad guy appears in the first place.

Maybe "swallow" wasn't the best word . . .

Jael

> *But Jael the wife of Heber took a tent peg, and took a hammer in her*
> *hand. Then she went softly to him and drove the peg into his temple*
> *until it went down into the ground while he was lying fast asleep from*
> *weariness. So he died.*
>
> JUDGES 4:21

Some days my tent is swept and put in order, my vat of warm milk ready for anyone who needs a drink. I would be happy to loll in the shade reading a good book while the men keep things going in the war. The pegs at the corners of my dwelling are meant to keep it up, to keep me cool and happy. War is supposed to stay far away, out there.

But then other days I find that I am wandering around with a tent peg in my hand, facing down an enemy, whether I'm ready for him or not. I didn't ask for it. It wasn't on the list of things I imagined to be necessary. Exasperation and bitterness crouch at the doorway. "Let the men do what they are supposed to do," I protest behind the smile. But at least the tent is swept, and the milk is warm. The peg at the ready.

When the men won't go to war, every woman must sweep her floor and steady her hand against the enemy. She must not fuss and complain about how bad she has it. She must take up her courage and her peg—but softly, carefully, with judicious reserve. And not drive it into her own head.

Gideon

So Gideon took ten men of his servants and did as the LORD had told him.
But because he was too afraid of his family and the men of the town to do
it by day, he did it by night.

JUDGES 6:27

Salvation belongs to the Lord. Which is great because if it were up to Gideon where would any of us be?

Salvation from running after false, wrong, inadequate, brutal gods that sit there—lumps of clay and wood. They must be torn down, pushed over, their oppressive presence expelled from the land. "Why," you ask, "are they there, after Israel swore so faithfully to follow the Lord, to serve him only for all their generations?"

The same might be asked of me. Why do I lug around my own ego, like some precious tiny tin-pot dictator, forcing everyone to accommodate my whims and plans?

If ever there was a picture of the Christian, the modern lover of God, it is me creeping around in quiet lest someone discover my true obedience. When it *is* discovered I try to convince myself that it doesn't signify much. It's no big deal.

Fortunately, salvation actually does belong to the Lord. And He sees, even in the darkness of night He sees. A few hundred trumpets blown, some jars smashed, and the enemy runs away as if perused by an actual army. Even when I obey in terror and darkness, the Lord delivers me out of the hand of all my enemies—most especially when that enemy is myself.

54 # Jephthah

So she said to her father, "Let this thing be done for me: leave me alone
two months, that I may go up and down on the mountains and weep for
my virginity, I and my companions."
JUDGES 11:37

Let what be done for me? Let me go off into the mountains? Let me travel
a way off to be with women who will console me for all I am about to lose?
I won't lose just my life, but my respectability, the peaceful future hoped
for the world over.

That's the call. Whenever God gets involved in the mess of your life—
in your expectations and the promises you make to yourself—it means a
horrible letting go of everything you thought you were owed and thought
should happen to you and for you. It's completely acceptable to retreat for
a bit to "mourn," or at least wrap your mind and heart around whatever it
is God is going to do to, or rather with, you. It can almost be compared to
something another young woman says hundreds of years later: "Let it be
to me according to your word."

In this tale of woe (Jephthah had only to read the law to see he didn't
have to carry through with his hasty and injudicious oath), it is not *you*
going off to die, to sacrifice your life as some act of martyrdom that dec-
imates you, that annihilates you, that sends you down into Sheol forever.
But it certainly points to the One who goes all the way down into the grave
in your place, so that your death, when it comes, is only a shadow, the
merest sorrow, forgotten the moment you behold His astonishing mercy.

55 Samson

Then Samson called to the Lord and said, "O Lord God, please remember
me and please strengthen me only this once, O God, that I may be
avenged on the Philistines for my two eyes."
JUDGES 16:28

It's a pity that vengeance is so out of fashion in modern society. Not that
we were ever supposed to avenge ourselves. That was always God's job.
But back in the good old Bible days at least we were allowed to pray for it,
as Samson does here. And he is so far from being pure as the wind-driven
snow. So, so far. Nearly everything he did was wrong. And his attitude was
terrible. And his parents didn't properly govern him. What a horrendous
mess of a family and a person. I always turn to Samson when I want to feel
better about my own life choices. I haven't committed adultery or disobeyed the Lord with such showy, tragic consequences.

But God did use Samson. God had plans and accomplished them
through the bad, terrible, freaky choices of Samson. The bawdy, tawdry
appetites of Samson.

Is it so difficult to consider that God might be involved in the outworking of your life? That your inclinations, good and bad, are not beyond the reaches of His will? Even your death, your sin, your questionable
longing for justice is providentially arranged. Don't be surprised when
the Lord inserts Himself into the picture from time to time as you stretch
and strain against the pillars of your life, dysfunctioning yourself to death
but saved unto life.

JUDGES 13–16

56 The Concubine

And when he entered his house, he took a knife, and taking hold of his
concubine he divided her, limb by limb, into twelve pieces, and sent her
throughout all the territory of Israel.

JUDGES 19:29

And here we come to another cruel moment, reminiscent of that arche-
typal garden failure: the violation and abuse of an abandoned woman so
that she dies with her hands thrown across the threshold of the house
where she was a guest. This is the ancient horror film, the suspense
building scene by scene.

Her affectionate father doesn't want her to leave his house yet with
the Levite; they are not even married—she is only his concubine. The father implores them not to go. So, they stay a while longer, but finally they
leave and arrive late at night in an unfriendly town. They set up camp in
the main square until someone takes them in. The men of the city come
and demand to be given the Levite, the stranger, to abuse and violate, but
their host gives the young concubine instead. It is practically modern in
its brutality and horror.

The Levite, in the morning finding her dead, takes her up, completes
his journey, and then cuts her dead body into twelve parts and sends her
broken, divided flesh to the twelve tribes of Israel. So shocked by this
wicked thing, Israel rises up and fights a civil war against the tribe who
murdered her. Death reigns. Even so, every such death is surely a prefig-
uring—a foretaste of the final death of the one whose body is broken, who
falls to the ground in that epic and brutal war against Satan, won in blood
so that you might live.

JUDGES 19, 21:25

Ruth

But Ruth said, "Do not urge me to leave you or to return from following
you. For where you go I will go, and where you lodge I will lodge. Your
people shall be my people, and your God my God. Where you die I will
die, and there will I be buried. May the LORD do so to me and more also if
anything but death parts me from you."

RUTH 1:16

Three women stand bereft in a field. Death has stolen everything they
have, everything they desired. Hope has gone down into the grave. No
children, no grandchildren, no men to protect and provide for them.
Childless, alone, forsaken. So today stand many women—tall and desolate—choosing between various kinds of loneliness and despair.

"Don't leave me here," says Ruth. "Let me go with you. Let your God
be my God."

Naomi takes the name bitterness. She can't see into the future. It
seems she is going backwards, into the past, back to the land where God
has already failed her. Why would she take anyone with her?

"Don't leave me here," says Ruth. Somehow, in this barren field, she
fixes herself to the Lord. "Let me go with you."

Orpah makes a show of grief and goes away. She doesn't see the peril.
Death is just another part of life. She will pull things together and make
a go of it.

"Don't leave me here," says Ruth, and Naomi relents. What can she
do? The one who loves the Lord will go even unbidden. Ruth and Naomi
tie their ways together and the Lord adds another thread to the tapestry
of salvation.

58 Hannah

"He raises up the poor from the dust; he lifts the needy from the ash heap
to make them sit with princes and inherit a seat of honor. For the pillars
of the earth are the Lord's, and on them he has set the world."
I SAMUEL 2:8

There you are, year after year, going up to worship the Lord at the tabernacle. Your rival, the other wife of your husband, is resplendent among
her children. She strides on ahead, making sure that you can see her, that
you are fully aware of her children and her glory. You trudge along behind
in depression and shame, though—amazingly—your husband is always
there with you, trying to help you out of your despair. He gives you a double portion of the feast—because he loves you.

Still, it's your own grief. Your husband can't really understand. He
can only stand by and watch you and sometimes be frustrated by his own
helplessness. He will suggest ways to fix it. And you will smile, because he
is being awfully nice about everything.

No, he can't help. And you can't help yourself.

Instead of endlessly complaining or running farther and farther
into the blackness of your disappointment and sorrow, you could, like
Hannah, turn to God. You could go into the courts of the Lord to plead, to
weep and cry out. If you tried it, God would listen to you. But even if you
don't bother, He still hears.

Ichabod

*And about the time of her death the women attending her said to her,
"Do not be afraid, for you have borne a son." But she did not answer or
pay attention. And she named the child Ichabod, saying, "The glory has
departed from Israel!" because the ark of God had been captured and
because of her father-in-law and her husband. And she said, "The glory
has departed from Israel, for the ark of God has been captured."*
1 SAMUEL 4:20

It is a bleak moment to be hearing the words "Do not be afraid," not from
an angel bearing good news, but from the women—the women who cluster around in the moment of grief and calamity. "Do not be afraid, for you
have borne a son." Nobody says it that way anymore.

What is there for her to be afraid of? She is already slipping out of life.
Her grief pulls her into the roots of the earth. She does not answer or pay
attention. As her soul goes down to death, to Sheol, she names the child
Ichabod, which means, "The glory has departed from Israel." The Lord
has gone, as surely as her own breath is gone. Ichabod: a tiny imprint of
despair and hope. Despair because Israel is under such devastating judgment, and not just Israel, but every person, family, and nation who persists in idolatry and wickedness. Hope because he is a shadowy type of the
Savior. The announcement of his birth—that the glory of God will be taken
outside the camp by the enemies of Israel to die—is the foretelling of not
your death, but his. Do not be afraid.

60 Agag

But Saul and the people spared Agag and the best of the sheep and of the oxen and of the fattened calves and the lambs, and all that was good, and would not utterly destroy them. All that was despised and worthless they devoted to destruction.

I SAMUEL 15:9

Samuel comes pattering along and says to Saul, "?!" "What is this sound of sheep, bleating in my ears?"

But Saul doesn't get it. "What's the big deal? So I didn't do exactly what God said to do. Who cares? So what if I didn't kill this man? It would have been such a waste to slaughter all these sheep. Not considering the hassle of blood and death, is it even kind to kill people and animals? Everyone here thinks God is good but he's not," thinks Saul.

It is so tantalizing to indulge bewitching, half-baked empathy when disobedience is less of a hassle. Like a good economy, or less killing, Saul's internal moral sense seems more reasonable to him than what God actually said. But Samuel is not as clueless as Saul. He knows that God isn't interested in less killing. He is interested in true goodness.

"Put everything to death that is evil and selfish and wrong," says God.

The word eventually spoken is Die. Die to yourself. And do it right away, as a first fruit, instead of waiting around for a better offer. Don't be tempted by Saul's disobedient fake compassion when eventually you will die anyway. Samuel hacked Agag to pieces and Saul's sensibilities were offended. Don't you be offended. Not by the Lord. He is good. All the way down to the blood.

61 Goliath

Then Saul clothed David with his armor. He put a helmet of bronze on his
head and clothed him with a coat of mail, and David strapped his sword
over his armor. And he tried in vain to go, for he had not tested them.
Then David said to Saul, "I cannot go with these, for I have not tested
them." So David put them off.

I SAMUEL 17:38

When David comes into the camp, he is scandalized that everyone is
standing around biting their fingernails, wondering what to do about
Goliath. You know, like when you walk into a room that's been completely
trashed and all your kids are standing there, not sure what to do. You ask
them what on earth is going on and they just stare at you, blankly, like
you're not speaking a language they know. The obvious thing, cleaning
up—or in this case, killing Goliath—seems to have escaped them.

Saul, meanwhile, is sweating in his tent. When David comes along,
incensed about the general helplessness of the entire army of Israel, Saul
doesn't leap up to face Goliath himself. Instead, he tries to stuff David
into his own clothes—garments heretofore shrouding inadequacy, futility, laziness, and even rebellion. But David is impatient and frustrated
with the defeatist spirit of this moldering camp. He plunks Saul's armor
down and stalks off with his five smooth stones and his sling.

Don't clothe yourself with futility and vanity and fear. Don't ignore
the obvious thing—that God is powerful and real, and that he has real
plans to destroy all the evil in your life. Even the evil you love. Especially   4-23-22
the evil you fear.   PTL

The Commander

And everyone who was in distress, and everyone who was in debt, and
everyone who was bitter in soul, gathered to him. And he became com-
mander over them. And there were with him about four hundred men.
I SAMUEL 22:2

David is on the run from Saul. There, in impossibly disappointing circumstances, he gathers strength and courage to claim what God has promised, which is to be king of Israel. He finds refuge in the wasteland. He settles in for the interminable wait. He gathers to himself the needy and downcast.

That should mean everyone, but then—as now—only those so painfully aware of their need that they actually come. The distressed, the indebted, the bitter in soul, the ones who have reached the end of themselves, who look around and don't see a way out. Their troubles have mounted into a great heap that cannot be moved. Their souls are already in Sheol. Yet David welcomes them, leading them out of their hopelessness and into the wilderness where suddenly they find comfort in the stronghold of their commander.

Much later, another man will walk through that same land, and every-one will gather to him for healing. The blind and lame and sick will seek him out. He will welcome them all, rallying them, feeding them, strength-ening them.

Are you bitter in soul? Does your great debt tower over you? Gather in the stronghold and let the Lord be your commander.

A-23-22

63 Abigail

Then Abigail made haste and took two hundred loaves and two skins
of wine and five sheep already prepared and five seahs of parched grain
and a hundred clusters of raisins and two hundred cakes of figs, and
laid them on donkeys. And she said to her young men, "Go on before me;
behold, I come after you." But she did not tell her husband Nabal.

I SAMUEL 25:18—19

A wise woman, as they say, builds her home. She thinks and acts in moments of crisis and evil. She preserves the life of her husband and all those in her sway.

When Abigail hears the awful news—that Nabal had no interest in or time for a man of power and grace, who had done good and not evil, who had looked not only to his own property but to that of others, who had been his brother's keeper—when she hears this dreadful truth, she doesn't sit back and wring her hands. She doesn't blame Nabal. She doesn't go down to the local lawyer's office to see if she can leave him and take with her some of the vast wealth presently at her disposal. She doesn't even get on Facebook and ask all her friends what they think. No, she gathers her wits and assembles an enormous lunch—bread, raisins, cakes of figs, roast lamb, and wine. She packs it all up and bundles it onto the donkeys hanging around her dusty courtyard. She makes haste. She hurries. She throws herself into David's way. She intercedes for her worthless husband.

That he, her own husband, doesn't deserve it, makes it all the more a matter of love.

64 The Witch

*Then the woman said, "Whom shall I bring up for you?" He said, "Bring
up Samuel for me."*
I SAMUEL 28:11

There you are hiding in your clandestine hovel, engaged in all the works
of the devil, trying to eke out a living at what you do best but mainly trying
not to be found out. But everybody knows about you anyway. When someone wants to acquire some forbidden knowledge, in that same primordial
way that humankind has always done, you know how to provide the apple,
the vision, the knowledge of evil.

But then one day the person who made you an outlaw comes creeping
in. You, not suspecting the worst but always ready to accept any little bit
of money, do what he asks. You conjure up a dead person. It shouldn't be
a big deal—until you find yourself gazing upon the servant of the Lord:
Samuel, the one who was always bringing evil into the light. Samuel, who
from a child stood in the presence of God and heard his voice.

God is everywhere, and nothing can be hidden from him.

Saul collapses on the floor and you—in the midst of the fear of death—
slaughter an animal, cook a bowl of something fortifying, and coax him
to eat it.

But will *you* repent and turn away from evil? God sent his servant,
even from the dead, for judgment and for salvation. Let it be for salvation.

I SAMUEL 27, 28

65 Uzzah

And the anger of the LORD was kindled against Uzzah, and God struck him down there because of his error, and he died there beside the ark of God.

II SAMUEL 6:7

Uzzah is carrying on in apparent obedience, for all anyone around him can see. David, his new king, wants the ark brought up: that holy and terrifying box upon which the Lord of heaven and earth will place his feet as a sign of his favor and mercy. David loves the Lord and wants to be near him.

Uzzah and his companion contemplate the box: a box they have been trained, from childhood, to carry in a certain way, to never touch with their own hands, their sinful and grimy and deceitful hands. Then, instead of handling it the way they have been taught, they cast about for a cart. Are they afraid? Or so lazy that they cannot slide the long, smooth poles through the rings and lift the ark, suspending it between heaven and earth, to carry it to its dwelling? They get the cart; they maneuver the ark—somehow without touching it—onto the cart. The cattle strain and lumber forward. Surely the king will be pleased. Surely the Lord will understand. The cattle stumble, the ark tips, and Uzzah stretches out his hand—his faithless, rebellious, wicked hand—to steady the presence of God.

Come into the presence of the Lord. Draw near and see the glory and goodness of the Most High. But don't touch. You cannot touch until, sometime later, the Glory of the Lord looks at a man—a foolish, faithless man—and says: "Put your hand here."

II SAMUEL 5:1–6:11

Michal

> *As the ark of the* Lord *came into the city of David, Michal the daughter of*
> *Saul looked out of the window and saw King David leaping and dancing*
> *before the* Lord, *and she despised him in her heart.*
>
> II SAMUEL 6:16

Like a man reborn, David makes merry. God has given back so much that was lost—all the time that he endured running for his life. It's like the restoration of the years that the locusts had devoured. He praises God as if nothing and no one sees him. He and God, together. The way you collapse into the arms of your mother after a great trial, falling with relief into safety and comfort. The person who loves God, whose heart is after the Lord, will praise with abandon when the Lord does what he says he is going to do.

But the world will mock and despise such love. Michal, the daughter of Saul who rejected the word of God, recoils. She takes offense.

It's just as if you sit and explain to someone the great tidal wave of God's steadfast love for you, and how it covers over everything and makes your steps sure and your heart fixed—and the expression in your eyes causes that person to seize up and push back from the table to escape. Your love of God is a thing of horror, an offense. The dry heart of Michal is reflected in her barren flesh. There is nothing more for the person who despises God except to go down into Sheol, alone.

But not David. The ark is in his city. All of Solomon's gorgeous temple could not house David's joy.

II SAMUEL 6:12–7:29

Mephibosheth

So Mephibosheth lived in Jerusalem, for he ate always at the king's table.
Now he was lame in both his feet.

II SAMUEL 9:13

David is established in Jerusalem. The Lord has built for him a house and a name and now David has a moment of rest from all his enemies that surround him. And so, because the Lord has fulfilled all his promises, David longs to keep one of his own. Jonathan, whose soul David loved, whose life had been lost along with his faithless father Saul, whose obedience to his father was measured by his risk for his friend, has one single descendent left: Mephibosheth. David sends and brings this one to his own table. He restores Mephibosheth's lost inheritance. He comes with mercy and goodness to honor the child of his friend. Mephibosheth is lame and helpless and honored.

It is so easy to pass by, to dishonor, to break promises—to leave aside the weaker member for the sake of ease and comfort. But you and I are like Mephibosheth: the child of a child of an enemy. Lame. We deserve for the curse of our father Adam to be carried on to our own children. But surely the Lord's mercy and goodness brings us to his table, where there is always a place set out, meal after meal, day after day. And there the cup runs over.

68   I Will Go to Him

He said, "While the child was still alive, I fasted and wept, for I said,
"Who knows whether the LORD will be gracious to me, that the child
may live?' But now he is dead. Why should I fast? Can I bring him back
again? I shall go to him, but he will not return to me."
II SAMUEL 12:22

That is always the question: "Who knows whether the Lord will be gracious to me?" We ask it a hundred ways as we go about our lives, doing the
things we know will make us happy, taking the things we think we need.
What was David thinking when he looked out and saw Bathsheba, the wife
of Uriah the Hittite, one of his own Mighty Men? What led him to think
that the Lord had not been gracious, had not given him all that he needed,
so that he reached out and took the life and future of another? We don't
know. Except that he was lingering around Jerusalem looking for something, but not for God.

We all fall into it. We all, in the midst of richness and blessing, go to the
farthest point to satisfy our hunger for everything that God hasn't given.

Even then the Lord is gracious. David's sin is so redeemed by God's
gracious mercy that a perfect good for the whole world comes out from it.
Who knows whether the Lord will be gracious? You know. You know when
you look up at the One who did not go up, but who came down. It's not that
you go up to him, but that He came down to you.

69 Tamar

And Tamar put ashes on her head and tore the long robe that she wore. And she laid her hand on her head and went away, crying aloud as she went.
II SAMUEL 13:19

It is an age-old conundrum that parents who sin grievously and feel bad about those sins have a hard time disciplining their children for the grievous sins that *they*, the children, commit. If David hadn't committed adultery with Bathsheba—scratch that. If David had only taken one wife and been faithful to her—never mind. The "ifs" can go all the way back to the beginning. They are awfully useful when you are trying to figure out why you are so unhappy all the time, but they don't tell you much about how to stop and do something different.

Sorting out generational sin and trauma is a perplexing undertaking. You can be the person on the outside, explaining how if only David had done things differently, his sons could have been less awful. Or you can be on the inside—Tamar deliberately tearing her long, graceful sleeves, putting her hand on her head and wailing as the law demands. Or you can be like Amnon, "hating with a very great hate," petulant, wicked. You can even go from being one to the other over the course of your life.

Or you can notice that there is yet a God who doesn't forget anything that happens to anyone.

Absalom

> *Thus Absalom did to all of Israel who came to the king for judgment. So Absalom stole the hearts of the men of Israel.*
>
> II SAMUEL 15:6

Apparently Absalom had great hair—thick, glorious, perfect for a man-bun. Not that that had anything to do with it. I'm sure it wasn't his hair that won the hearts of the men of Israel away from David and to him. Just like it was not the windswept, photogenic coiffure of Jesus that helped him save the world.

Pride and a teaspoon helping of truth will go a long way to ruin everything. The key is to flatten something out in the meatgrinder of half-credible soundbites. Amnon rapes his sister, Tamar. David doesn't do anything about it. So far Absalom, Tamar's full brother, is justified in his wrath, and he could very well have cried out to God to judge the wicked; he could have pled for justice for Tamar. Instead, he takes that true thing and subverts it to his own purposes, demonizing everybody who doesn't leap to his cause all along the way.

In the end, you have "good" Absalom against "bad" David—the two tribes of humanity, me against you, or us two against everyone in the world. Unfortunately, it's just not that clear. There are no true "good" against the clearly defined "bad." There is you, the sinner, and me, the sinner, both of us sometimes wrong and other times right, both of us needing Jesus.

Who Cares How Many

Again the anger of the LORD was kindled against Israel, and he incited David against them, saying, "Go, number Israel and Judah."

II SAMUEL 24:1

On Sundays during the sermon, I like to stand at the back and silently jot down the names of the all the people who came to church in a little notebook I keep for the purpose. In one column, I write down the names of those who are there, and in another column, I write down the names of those who are missing. I tot them up and, when the service is over, write it all down in the big, red book in the sacristy, while at the same time I am searching through my purse to see where my keys are, and if I have lost my cellphone again. It's okay that I do this, because if I didn't do it, how would anyone know?

It's not that counting things up is bad. It's not that looking at your life and measuring it, examining it to see what it is, is evil. Counting is a kind of organizing and organizing is almost always a good thing.

But what is the purpose of having that knowledge? What is it about knowing how much there is that will be useful to you as you go on? The Bible itself is a careful accounting of the people of God so that you and I can be astonished by God's mercy. But David wanted something else. He wanted to know for himself how strong he was.

It's a dangerous spot, seeing what you have and what you can do with it. Looking at God afterward and trying to fit him in along the edges.

The Prostitute

And the king said, "Bring me a sword." So a sword was brought before the king. And the king said, "Divide the living child in two, and give half to the one and half to the other."
I KINGS 3:24—25

There you are, scraping out a wretched existence in sin and depravity. For whatever reason, you are living in exactly the wrong place, with the wrong kind of people, doing the wrong thing. Daily you give yourself to evil and are a victim of the evil of others. And then you have a child. In the greatest possible mire of sin, a life springs forth—the comfort of a baby, a moment of relief from the grief and burden of guilt. The woman near you is caught in the same place, but death steals her solace in the night. In envy, she takes your child and you wake in the morning joyless, empty, and alone.

"Bring me a sword," says the king. A sword that should pierce your soul. A sword of justice and righteousness. A sword that opens up the expanse of grief and loss forever. Except that the sword is for another. Another woman will watch her child die in the wrong place, with the wrong people, for the right reason. Sorrow and love will flow mingled down.

Are you caught in grief? Are you in the wrong place doing the wrong thing? Let the sword strike your heart. Let the One who died be a comfort—a relief from sin and guilt and grief.

The House

And in the eleventh year, in the month of Bul, which is the eighth month,
the house was finished in all its part, and according to all its specifica-
tions. He was seven years in building it.

I KINGS 6:38

Solomon did what his father, David, longed to do. He built a house for the
Lord. In seven years, Solomon caused its walls, its smooth courts, its immense columns and pillars, its many rooms to be fashioned and adorned
in gold. When it was complete, the presence of the Lord descended and
filled the whole place.

You, far away from Jerusalem, could work—tending your vines and
your crops and your small house, struggling along to keep body and soul
together—and then, at least once a year, make the journey to come to the
house of the Lord. Your sacrifice in your hand, a song in your mouth, you
could climb up the steps to go into the great court to have your sins atoned
for. And then, in the presence of God, for a moment, you could rest.

But as Solomon wandered away into the imaginations of his own
heart—and Israel after him—the temple stood crumbling into ruin. Long
after, a man would walk in and be angry about the filth and corruption. He
would turn and go out, the presence and glory of the Most High leaving
that once beautiful place.

And now you are the temple of the Lord, if he lives in you. He builds
you and fashions you and adorns you with his grace. So far from you
climbing up all those steps to ascend to his presence, he has descended
low to build his rest and presence in you.

74 Solomon

And the Lord was angry with Solomon, because his heart had turned away from the Lord, the God of Israel, who had appeared to him twice and had commanded him concerning this thing, that he should not go after other gods. But he did not keep what the Lord commanded.

I KINGS 11:9—10

The wisest person on earth can't keep the commandments and love of God. Having the ability to think a problem through and see it in every possible light, to read and understand what he is reading, to see into the future and predict what troubles may befall the human person, to reason and use the mind to its fullest potential—this wise person cannot walk close to God any more than any other person can. This is surely a discouragement to those of us of average to mediocre intelligence. I, possessing none of Solomon's wealth and wisdom, wander around the internet seeking something to distract myself. Or I drift through the day trying to avoid reality. If Solomon couldn't love God and do what God commanded, particularly in the matter of worshiping God only and not himself or something glittery, is there any hope for me or you?

Yes, there is hope. But only if you wander away from Solomon and his wisdom and toward a person whose wisdom is described as foolishness to the world. The foolish one—alone, beaten, broken, holding heaven and earth together by the power of His will. For the person perishing, maybe you, he will be the wisdom that cannot fail.

75   # The Lion

*And when the prophet who had brought him back from the way heard
of it, he said, "It is the man of God who disobeyed the word of the LORD;
therefore the LORD has given him to the lion, which has torn him and
killed him, according to the word that the LORD spoke to him."*
I KINGS 13: 26

Here is another sordid little tale. A prophet is carrying on, doing what
God has called him to do, pronouncing judgment on Jeroboam and not
eating or drinking for the amount of time the Lord has commanded him
not to eat or drink. But then *another* prophet comes along and, for reasons
not vouchsafed, lies to the first prophet.

"Oh no," says the second prophet, "God talked to me also and told me
to tell you to eat and drink at my house." And so the first prophet, for who
knows why, even though he had been obedient, now disobeys.

We do this too, practically all the time. We putter along in the Bible,
half knowing what it is that God is trying to say. But the minute anyone
comes along and says, "Oh no, God would never say that," we run to eat
and drink and be happy—unwilling to pause for a single, tiny moment to
check one word against another.

And then we are in terrible danger, because God is not tame. He will
rend you, as an angry lion, and you will find yourself, as you are perishing,
wishing you had paid better attention to and stuck to what you did know.

I KINGS 12–13

Something Pleasing

> *Arise therefore, go to your house. When your feet enter the city, the child*
> *shall die. And all Israel shall mourn for him and bury him, for he only*
> *of Jeroboam shall come to the grave, because in him there is found some-*
> *thing pleasing to the Lord, the God of Israel, in the house of Jeroboam.*
> I KINGS 14:12—13

The Lord sees everything there is to see. The inmost parts of the earth, the smallest insect that lives and dies in a day, the hidden devices of the human heart. I, on the other hand, don't see quite so comprehensively. I have to judge by the expression of a face, by circumstances, and by how I feel at any particular moment. I may or may not have a true perception of the way things are, though invariably I count my own version of events as objectively and unerringly true.

Given the chance to be king of Israel, in the face of God's judgment of Solomon and Rehoboam, Jeroboam decides to trust his own judgment rather than consulting the person (God) who elevated him. Indeed, he goes so far into evil and sin and wickedness that God cuts off his whole house. No one will go in peace to the grave.

Save one—a child. A child in whom the Lord found "something pleasing." What is it that he finds? Why only a single child? Sometime, much later, there will be a single person in whom *we* may be found pleasing. He alone will rescue us and save us from the sorrow and judgment of Sheol.

77   The Widow

And she said, "As the LORD your God lives, I have nothing baked, only a
handful of flour in a jar and a little oil in a jug. And now I am gathering
a couple of sticks that I may go in and prepare it for myself and my son,
that we may eat it and die."

I KINGS 17:12

Your small house is spare and clean. Your worn clothes are mended, your thin hands shaky, your mind consumed with anxiety, your heart resigned to death. No husband, no rain, no crops. The obvious choice is to stir up your fire and cook what's left—a handful of flour, and the last drizzle of oil from the jug. You hold the jug a long while over your kneading bowl, eking out one last drop. And then to die.

Maybe a lot of times you have the wrong expectations, wanting what you cannot have, being dissatisfied with an overabundance of stuff and a poverty of spirit. But once in a while, you look around and see the desert encroaching, the barren land yielding nothing at all, the mute, hungry look in your child's eye. You see it as it is, and despair—this is the obvious thing. You cannot get good out of evil.

Gather the sticks. Pour the flour and oil together. Bake the bread. Break it in half. Tithe the dusting of grain spread sparsely at the bottom of your jar. Measure out the poverty of your heart, your helplessness, your hopelessness. Because the Lord is a provider. He gives life. He gives enough. He gives himself. The Lord meets your need with Himself, His own body, broken in half and given for you.

I KINGS 16:29–17:24

Prophets of Baal

And Elijah came near to all the people and said, "How long will you go limping between two different opinions? If the LORD is God, follow him; but if Baal, then follow him." And the people did not answer him a word.
I KINGS 18:21

If you wanted to be a true worshiper of God in Israel during the time of Ahab and Jezebel, you had to be really quiet about it or they would find you and make things unpleasant. It was safer not to believe in God at all.

But Elijah waves his arms and thunders, gathering all the prophets of these ridiculous, mute, savage gods and challenging them to a contest. The prophets of Baal build an altar and slaughter a bull and all they need is for a little fire come down from heaven and burn up the sacrifice. They dance and pray and cut themselves while Elijah stands by. Maybe your god is in the loo, he jokes. Then it's his turn, and he builds his altar and slaughters his bull and pours water all over it. Water and blood everywhere.

Then he prays and asks God to burn up the sacrifice. And fire comes down from heaven and consumes everything. Fire. Water. Blood. Judgment. All the people of Israel who were hanging around, waiting to see who would win, feel sort of bad for limping between their two opinions. Elijah spurs them on down the mountain, urging the people to kill the prophets of Baal along the way.

7/18/22 1/25/22

79   Elijah

Then he was afraid, and he arose and ran for his life and came to Beer-
sheba, which belongs to Judah, and left his servant there.

I KINGS 19:3

Elijah, that great and mighty prophet of God, at whose call the rain stops
and by whose hand the prophets of Baal are brought to nothing, finds
himself threatened by the power of a shrewd and wicked woman. She is
ruthless. She is vindictive. She, with her painted eyes, is what the world
loves—rebellion, strength, self-determination, pragmatism, someone
who can get things done. But Elijah has just seen the power of God. He
has obediently carried out the bloody and difficult will of the Lord. Surely
he can keep the love of God and the glory of the Lord as a banner over his
heart and mind, withstanding evil and temptation. But no, even the great
Elijah succumbs to the ordinary and overwhelming fear of death—and the
power of other people.

Are you afraid? Are the powerful and the wicked arrayed against you?
Can you not succeed in keeping the Lord always before your face? Does
your anxiety stack up like a wall to keep you alone and trembling?

It's not up to you to win, or to have the right perspective, or to trust
God the way you should. There, in your fear, the Lord will feed you, will
talk to you, will strengthen you. For when you are weak, then he is strong.

I KINGS 19, 20

Jezebel

> *But Jezebel his wife came to him and said to him, "Why is your spirit*
> *so vexed that you eat no food?" And he said to her, "Because I spoke to*
> *Naboth the Jezreelite and said to him, 'Give me your vineyard for money,*
> *or else, if it please you, I will give you another vineyard for it.'"*
> I KINGS 21:5

Jezebel is a good wife. Her poor husband is cast down, his heart in the dust because he wants another man's idyllic vineyard—the cool, green vines; the lovely curve of the low, stone wall; the pleasing situation of the watchtower; the grapes full, rich, abundant. His kingly heart grows sad. He wanders, listless, along the smooth courts of his ancestor's palace, his footfalls echoing along the marble courtyards. What is the point of all this if he can't have that?

His wife, attentive to his every whim, ruthless in her pursuit of power and glory—for him, for him—runs her fingers along his petulant brow. She coaxes and soothes and promises him every good thing.

Are you dissatisfied with the riches of God's grace? Do you feel sad in the face of all that God has given you? Do you help others along in their sin, coaxing them to covet what isn't theirs?

But the watchtower is manned. When the blood of Naboth spills out on the ground, the Lord sees. There is no wickedness, no injustice, no evil that he does not see. The blood cries out to him and he answers: blood for blood, drop for drop. Wipe the makeup off your eyes, the red from your lips, and repent. It may be that God will have mercy if you yet turn.

81   Elisha

And Elisha saw it and he cried, "My father, my father! The chariots of
Israel and its horsemen!" And he saw him no more.
II KINGS 2:12

A double measure of blessing. A greater amount of power. Elisha wanted
the blessing and glory that God had put on Elijah to fall on him. Elisha
follows after Elijah, running after the Lord's strength, the Lord's word,
keeping up, breathless. "If you see me caught up," says Elijah, "if you see
me as I go up before your eyes, then what you long for will be yours. Keep
your eyes fixed." So Elisha runs, he watches and runs.

Does your gaze sometimes waver from your Lord? Do you sometimes
find yourself out of breath and lost, having stumbled in the way? Lift up
your eyes. Lift them up to the help that will surely come.

Elisha watches as the chariots of the Lord, the horsemen of his might
and glory, catch Elijah up in a whirl of fire. "My father," he cries. Again,
"my father." Another will stand, much later, suspended between heaven
and earth, crying "My Father," but no horsemen will come, no chariot.
And the fire of the Lord's great wrath will consume him.

Elisha catches up the mantle of Elijah and his blessing and strikes out
to go back into the wickedness and sin of the world. But his eyes have seen
and beheld the glory of the Father, and he will not get lost or lose his way.

II KINGS 1, 2

82 The Room

> *"Let us make a small room on the roof with walls and put there for him a bed, a table, a chair, and a lamp, so that whenever he comes to us, he can go in there."*
>
> II KINGS 4:10

Elisha discovered a hospitable place to stop in all his various ministry travels. He passed by and the Shunammite woman "urged him to eat some food" so that whenever he came there, he visited her. She looked after him. Her house was a place of rest and restoration.

Every once in a while, in the travails and duties of life, you might happen upon someone who is a rest rather than more work, whose company is a balm for your soul and whose house is a rest for your body. You work, pushing past the point of exhaustion. You constantly rush through to the next thing. But then, someone urges you to stop, to eat food, to sleep.

The Shunammite built a room for him. She prepared a place for him. It was a refuge. It had a lamp, a light that pushed away the darkness. It had a bed, for the rest of his body. She ordered in a table and chair, for the quiet meditations of the soul. In her house there were many rooms, but this one was for him.

Are you going back and forth and up and down, working hard for the Lord? Stop for a moment and sit in the chair of his mercy. Lie on the bed of his providence. Lighten your darkness with the light of his word. Do not rush past him in your hunger and weariness. Turn aside into the place he has already prepared.

II KINGS 3, 4

83   The Girl

Now the Syrians on one of their raids had carried off a little girl from the
land of Israel, and she worked in the service of Naaman's wife.
II KINGS 5:2

You wake up one morning to discover that your leprous, mighty husband acquired some new help for you. You brace yourself to face down a battered and broken picture: a little girl wrenched from her home, swept away in the political devastations of the moment. Syria is on the rise. Israel is weak. This girl, once sheltered by the comfort of home and family, has only her own loss and herself to offer. She might easily be a persistent source of bitterness. You don't let yourself consider what she might have endured. What part can a little girl play in the rising and falling of nations and of kings?

If she mourns for herself, you don't see it. No, in your anxiety and despair over your husband, her captor, she comes to advise you. "There is a God," she says, "who can heal and save." How can this be? How can a little girl, a child, know God? How can she set aside the bitterness of abuse and loss? But her firm gaze wins you over and you tell your husband.

Are you overwhelmed by the suffering of the world? By the sweeping injustices that rise and break over your news feed? Much later another girl will step out, alone, with news, not just in her mouth but in her womb, with her eyes full of the hope of the world. She will sing a song of praise for the One who came to cure every disease, and to raise up even the broken from the ashes.

Enemies

So he prepared for them a great feast, and when they had eaten and
drunk, he sent them away, and they went to their master. And the Syri-
ans did not come again on raids into the land of Israel.
II KINGS 6:23

There you are, toiling away in the Syrian Army, an ordinary foot soldier who'd rather be doing anything in the world other than lugging around your armor, defeating all the enemies of your king. It's not completely terrible. You're fed decently, and you haven't died yet because your king always wins. But lately everyone is stressed because it's clear there's a traitor somewhere in the ranks. Every time you go up against the king of Israel it's like he knows you're coming before you get there.

Then comes the most extraordinary rumor. It's not that a person is betraying you to the king of Israel, rather, their God is whispering to their prophet, who goes and tells their king.

Your commander tries to quell the cries of unbelief when you all discover that the entire army is now dispatched against a single man, the prophet of God.

You march down the long road. You arrive. And then you are struck blind, and in the weirdest turn of events you ever lived to tell, when you regain your sight you find yourself seated at a great feast.

But these are our enemies, you think. Yes, and God is your enemy, but while you were yet at war with him, he prepared a table for you, a table at which he feeds you with himself.

II KINGS 6:1–7:2

Economies

In the fifth year of Joram the son of Ahab, king of Israel, when Je-
hoshaphat was king of Judah, Jehoram the son of Jehoshaphat, king of
Judah, began to reign. He was thirty-two years old when he became king,
and he reigned eight years in Jerusalem.

II KINGS 8:16—17

Congratulations—seriously—on making it this far. The fact that you didn't
peter out in Leviticus is momentous, and you deserve a chocolate. I would
stop now and have one because there's a long slog ahead.

The first thing to note—as you read this verse over and over trying to
figure out which king is being described—is that God hasn't put it here
because he hates you and knows you're tired and figures you'll give up any
day now which will mean that he won. He's not trying to trip you up. In
his providence, for reasons known only to him, the books of Kings and
Chronicles are characterized by an Economy of Names. There are only a
few names, and sometimes they are held by different kings at practically
the same time. The thing is to not give up. Keep reading.

When you come out on the other side you will know that: 1. Most of the
kings were really bad. Only the highlights are in the text, and they may be
considered as low as you can go. 2. God's plan is never destroyed by any of
them. No matter how hard they tried, his scarlet thread of salvation was
never cut, nor broken, nor destroyed. So sit back and see the strange and
wicked details unfold.

86 Bones

So Elisha died, and they buried him. Now bands of Moabites used to invade the land in the spring of the year. And as a man was being buried, behold, a marauding band was seen and the man was thrown into the grave of Elisha, and as soon as the man touched the bones of Elisha, he revived and stood on his feet.

II KINGS 13:20–21

There you are, burying your husband who shouldn't have gotten sick and shouldn't have died, wretched man. He could never do anything right. You had to go buy a veil for mourning and all the relatives descended on you and ate absolutely all your food. It was a crazy and insane week and you haven't had a moment's peace.

And then, to top it off, just as you're finally getting to the point of being able to bury him, wretched man, a band of Moabites is spotted up the hill. Can nothing go right! You throw up your hands in exasperation at the never-ending string of tragedy. Weirdly, your very own dead husband is being buried next to Elisha—who died just long enough ago that his bones are lying around in the grave. The band of marauders descends, and, in a panic, the burying men throw your husband into the grave of Elisha. His body falls, falls, you stare as he falls. Will he ever reach the . . . *thud*. He hits. And then, because nothing can ever go right for you, he stands up and climbs out, because the bones of Elisha were what, radiating with power? With the presence of God?

You give him a dubious kiss and start mentally calculating how much a resurrection lunch will cost.

Humility

He restored the border of Israel from Lebo-hamath as far as the Sea of Arabah, according to the word of the LORD, the God of Israel, which he spoke by his servant Jonah the son of Amittai, the prophet, who was from Gath-hepher.

II KINGS 14:25

Jonah gets to have a book all his own; a perfect little tome for helping yourself and others to know that the Bible is really and truly real and true. Because if I, as your esteemed devotionalist, were going to set about writing some little vignette of my life, I would not, for great sums of money, paint such a ghastly portrait of myself as you will find of Jonah in the book bearing his own name. He comes across as so bad, and everyone else as so good, that he must have endured a divine shove. And it is likely that he wrote all four of those perfect chapters himself, having been the only one there when all those strange events were happening. Humility, I feel like someone somewhere said, is being able to accurately articulate your own abilities. So that's sort of discouraging.

Anyway, in the middle of 2 Kings, we discover that Jonah was prophesying in Israel and getting to say nice things, like, in this case, that the borders of Israel would extend as far as the Sea of Arabah—because God wasn't going to totally blot out Israel. He, God, was busy having mercy all over the place. Except that Israel didn't repent, and the people of Nineveh did. And Jonah was really mad about it.

Consequences

Manasseh was twelve years old when he began to reign, and he reigned
fifty-five years in Jerusalem. His mother's name was Hephzibah.
II KINGS 21:1

For real. There is a woman in the Bible whose name is Hephzibah. You may have heard of it with the hearing of your ear, but now your eye has finally beheld it. Anyway, all that you get to know about her is that she is mother to Manasseh who was A Bad King.

His father, Hezekiah, had been a reasonably good king as far as it goes, even praying for help when he got into a tight spot. But he was disobedient in the matter of showing all the wealth of the temple to a Babylonian envoy. Actions have consequences—if you touch a hot pan, your finger will be burned. If you bang into the corner of the coffee table, you will get a bruise. If you show all the wealth of the Lord's temple to a far distant king, that king will sit up and take notice. Just because you love God and are trying to do what he says, doesn't mean you have to indulge in rank foolishness, expecting that he will save you. He *will* save you, but the bruise will smart.

Hezekiah didn't spend enough time with baby Manasseh because Manasseh turns out to be awful. Really, really awful. Filling up Jerusalem from one end to another with innocent blood *awful*. And yet, in a strange turn of events, of all the bad kings of Judah, it is Manasseh who turns around and tries repenting. Actions have consequences, but so does repentance. When Manasseh said he was sorry, God forgave him.

Josiah

And Hilkiah the high priest said to Shaphan the secretary, "I have found
the Book of the Law in the house of the LORD." And Hilkiah gave the book
to Shaphan, and he read it.
II KINGS 22:8

Hilkiah rummaged around one afternoon in one of the back rooms of the
temple of the Lord. The room was dim and dusty. He kept sneezing, shoving furniture around and trying to think through the mental list of what
it would take to whip the whole thing into shape. The outside needed re-
pairs—stones replaced that had just fallen away—but maybe the inside too
could do with a good cleaning.

So many rooms. So much discarded furniture and scrolls and cover-
ings. He turned over a tightly woven cloth and his hand fell onto a scroll.
He picked it up and walked over to the light—the light filtered through the
filth of never-washed windows—the dust dancing in the air. He unrolled
a portion and read. And read and read and read. And then his legs crum-
pled under him, and he fell to the stone floor in horror and awe.

So is the upsetting experience of many a poor soul cracking open the
Bible for the first time. It's so awful. The death, the violence. The despair.
The running away from God of every single person ever.

Rend your garment. Pour ash on your head. Sit and weep over the loss
and the sin and the neglect. Then dry your tears. Lift up your head, for
your salvation is near. It is behind the narrow lines of words swimming
before your watery, dust-filled, horrified eyes.

Exile

And the king of Babylon struck them down and put them to death at Riblah
in the land of Hamath. So Judah was taken into exile out of its land.
II KINGS 25:21

"What's the worst that could happen?" That's the question that's been nagging at the back of everyone's mind as the kings get worse and Babylon's storming presence builds over the horizon.

Well, now everyone knows. The worst is that many in Judah and Jerusalem are killed, brutally. Those that aren't killed are carried away captive to that great, wicked empire. The city is utterly destroyed. The temple's enormous basin—the bronze sea—is smashed and carried away. The gold and silver vessels, the bowls and tongs and cups and plates are gathered up and carried to a foreign land. The temple itself is burned with fire. The only people left are the very poor, looking out over devastation and ruin.

What's the worst that could happen? God could do what he said he was going to do. Just because it seems unbelievable doesn't mean he's not going to do it. "You're not going to die," someone once said to the Son of God—but that does not stop him from going, on purpose, to die. And so "we won't ever be spewed out of the land" doesn't keep God from spewing them out just as He he said he would.

What's the worst that could happen? That you look on the One who always does what he says he is going to do and believe in him? That you trust him in the death you will surely face no matter what?

A Great Many Names

*So all Israel was recorded in genealogies, and these are written in the
Book of the Kings of Israel. And Judah was taken into exile in Babylon
because of their breach of faith.*

I CHRONICLES 9:1

I know, nine chapters of only names is kind of a drag. And there's more
coming. You've already waded through them in other books and now here
they are again, only all together, with no stories in between to relieve
the tedium. Did your eyes glaze over as you read them? You should feel
guilty if they did, because every other living Christian has carefully read
through all the genealogies—because of being really holy already.

The names are there for a reason. They're not just stumbling blocks
placed there to make it hard for you to love God. God isn't being deliberately unkind because he doesn't like you. The names being listed once,
and then again, and then again, are there for a reason. As so much violence and bloodshed and disobedience has overtaken the world, God
has never been overtaken or surprised. He knows each name. He preserves his promise. He is saving the world—name by name, clan by clan,
family by family, until suddenly one name will appear in the list, and the
name itself will mean salvation. When you see it for the first time you can
breathe a breath again, as you have done here, only of relief and wonder,
rather than exhaustion and boredom.

Not by Might

Now these are the chiefs of David's mighty men, who gave him strong support in his kingdom, together with all Israel, to make him king, according to the word of the Lord concerning Israel.

I CHRONICLES 11:10

God gave David some Mighty Men, men of courage and renown, who gathered around him and secured the land of Israel, building it into a strong kingdom. There were the Three and the Thirty. In battle the thirty fought valiantly, distinguishing themselves and strengthening David. Above these were the three, led by Jashobeam "who wielded his spear against 300 whom he killed at one time."

These mighty men were a support and comfort to David. Many of them came to him while he was in the stronghold in the wilderness, on the run from Saul. Later, as all of Israel and Judah gathered itself to him, he organized chiefs and officers over his army. And all that time the mighty men were there, in courage and renown: a shield, going before and behind David in battle. They would do anything for him, heedlessly risking even their lives to do whatever he asked. But he looked after them. He would not risk their lives to no purpose. Their bravery and courage and skill he did not take for granted or throw away.

If you look closely though, you'll find Uriah the Hittite, listed among them. So that's awkward.

93 Join the Choir

*"Blessed be the L*ORD*, the God of Israel, from everlasting to everlasting!"*
*Then all the people said, "Amen!" and praised the L*ORD*.*
I CHRONICLES 16:36

David—mighty warrior, lover of God, king, husband, father, sinner, singer, songwriter—is also pretty organized. The ark is brought into Jerusalem and placed in its tent and all the musicians are arranged by family and task and instrument and voice. It's a marvelous church moment. Not David by himself, but everybody together, standing in their proper places, ready to play and sing in the arranged way, at the correct moment. If you're looking for organized religion, this is it.

Even if you're not looking for organized religion, the plain picture is that God brings order and beauty to the arrangement of worship. We all gather to praise Him, we all play the part we've been given, caught in the rush to be in the right place, in tune with everyone else. No one has to hold a microphone all by himself, wailing away. We don't even have to take turns, one by one by one. No—everyone together, after a lengthy rehearsal, all sings and plays at the same time. The music swells and rises up, the incense is swung, the hands are lifted—accordingly, as it has been practiced beforehand—and God's beauty and order and presence surprises and stuns everyone. Not each one of us doing our own thing, but all of our disparate voices singing his praises as one.

Have I been too obscure? Too vague? Join the choir. The literal, actual church choir. Join it. Or at least sign up to be an usher or pass out water bottles to the people who are singing.

I CHRONICLES 15, 16

Blueprints

He shall build a house for me, and I will establish his throne forever.
I CHRONICLES 17:12

Standing on his gracious balcony, surveying his bright new city, David rubs his hands and turns his inward eye to heaven. He's grateful everything turned out so well. All the years in the wilderness, running for his life, and then the delicate work of uniting a fractious kingdom under his rule made him wonder if he would ever be able to rest, to be established as king. But here he is, so thankful for so much richness and blessing. God built him a house, a throne, a kingdom. After such a long wait, it's glorious to spread out and enjoy all the comfort of a settled peace.

But there is God with no settled place. God ought, at least, to have a house, to have something grander than a dusty tent. David will build him one. His mind wanders out over the whole land, mentally calculating stone, timber, gold, silver, fine-twined linen. He goes to bed and lies awake, thrilled, thinking it all out, planning the glory.

And during the night, God says no. David can't build a house for God. God has built a house for David, and will build it—a house that lasts forever. A house that will look for many chapters and books like it is crumbling into ruin, desecrated, a house that seems like it can't possibly survive but, even in the darkest days, never quite disappears.

You can't build God a house. God will be the one to build his house in you.

95 Strangers

"But who am I, and what is my people, that we should be able thus to offer willingly? For all things come from you, and of your own have we given you. For we are strangers before you and sojourners, as all our fathers were. Our days on the earth are like a shadow, and there is no abiding."
I CHRONICLES 29:14—15

When I was small, a group of Americans came to put a roof on the local school. They were excited to be in Africa for a month and, smiling broadly, shook hands with everyone and ate all the food and took loads of pictures. At the end of two weeks, they climbed on a big bus and drove away. A friend wandered by in the cool of the day. "Oh," he said, "those strangers, their eyes were wide open, but they didn't see anything."

God, as far as we are concerned, is the ultimate stranger. We are the ones at home. God just drops in an out, we tell ourselves. Perfect and holy and good, and what does he really know about our lives? He isn't anything like us.

The truth is, we go around like ghostly shadows, trying to get a handle on reality, trying to hold onto the things we think we see. If God were to come, walking around, talking to us, we would look at him and smile, and scratch our heads, and not understand the strangeness of his words and ways.

And yet, being strange one to another, need we be enemies? All good things come from his hand. We don't have anything to give that he hasn't already given first. Strangers first, but then, at just the right moment, friends.

Love Endures

When all the people of Israel saw the fire come down and the glory of the
LORD on the temple, they bowed down with their faces to the ground on the
pavement and worshiped and gave thanks to the LORD, saying, "For he is
good, for his steadfast love endures forever."
II CHRONICLES 7:3

The temple is finally completed. Solomon and Hiram have collaborated to
do everything in order and beauty. All that could be required is in place:
the dishes, the ark, the altar, the choir, the priests, the Levites. The whole
nation, the family of God, gathers for one perfect moment to rejoice, to
consecrate themselves and the building, to be thankful.

And God comes. He descends. His glory fills the temple. He sends fire
to burn up the sacrifice. The cloud and the fire finally rest over this great,
beautiful court. And you, gathered with all the people, are overcome with
the presence of God. You sing the line of music that runs through the
whole book—not just this one, but all 66 of them—"For he is good, for his
steadfast love endures forever."

It has to be sung here in the presence of God, because as you wend
your way from this wide open court, your mind clouds with care and worry. You begin to try to solve your own problems and organize your own
life. You wonder if God is really good. You turn over and examine the idea
that maybe he doesn't love you.

But you can return to this place in his presence, and you can sing these
words, remembering the cloud and the fire. You can always return and
know that he loves you.

You Had One Job

And the king answered them harshly; and forsaking the counsel of the
old men . . .
II CHRONICLES 10:13

Perhaps it was just the busyness of life, his compulsive accumulation of so much wealth, the need to cope with his many hundreds of wives and children that finally got to Solomon. If every wife had a child, and every child had a problem, and he personally had to think out a solution for each one, he would never have had time for a quiet evening spent gazing out over the beauty of his great city. So in the end he just didn't have time to attend to the education and wisdom of his son and heir.

I totally understand. Here I am, writing all these little whatchamacallits, while my children rage, and scream, and sort out their own way. There are so many important things to do. Interfering in the foolish ways of the child to make him more wise, or at least less foolish, often falls to the bottom of the to-do list. A list which includes items like Clean the Whole House, and Call that Person Back.

Perhaps Solomon could have just required that young Rehoboam read his own book of Proverbs. Or, having once written them out, he could have read them to the child at night, along with a song and a prayer. History might have taken a different turn.

Under the idea that You Only Had One Job, no matter what that job is, every one of us will fail—whether it is to teach our children wisdom, or to act with wisdom ourselves. Wonderfully, though, God isn't surprised by our foolishness and neglect, and has the capacity to properly finish off the job with success rather than total failure.

II CHRONICLES 9:29–11:23

98 Athaliah

Now when Athaliah the mother of Ahaziah saw that her son was dead,
she arose and destroyed all the royal family of the house of Judah.
II CHRONICLES 22:10

It would not be an overstatement to say that things are going badly in the kingdoms of Israel and Judah. Though once united under David and Solomon, now they have split apart, and each successive king of both nations is slightly worse than the last. Ahaziah, king of Judah, has been killed by Jehu, the son of Nimshi, who drives like a madman. This is the moment that Athaliah, queen mother and strong female lead of whoever bought the rights to the movie, has been waiting for. She kills everyone who might have a chance at the throne and makes herself queen. Everyone is afraid of her. She is ruthless and wicked.

But Jehosheba, princess in her own right, married to Jehoidah the High Priest, also with a backbone of steel, takes her courage in both her hands and steals away a tiny child—the king's last heir. For six years she hides him—keeping him safe, biding her time.

How terrifying, that God's plan of saving the world should come down to one child, hidden in a room by a brave woman, against a terrifying evil force. This is not the only time we find ourselves anxious, as everyone is rounded up and killed—everyone but the one that matters. He slips through the net and lives. God must enjoy the suspense. Although, being God, I suppose there isn't much cause for anxiety. But Jehosheba might not have known that, cuddling the baby in the rooms of the temple, praying for a miracle.

99 Forgetting

Thus Joash the king did not remember the kindness that Jehoiada, Zechariah's father, had shown him, but killed his son. And when he was dying, he said, "May the LORD see and avenge!"

II CHRONICLES 24:22

Joash carried on with life doing the good works that Jehoiada the High Priest prepared for him to walk in. The temple was restored and repaired. The people were, basically, encouraged to worship God. Joash wasn't a complete failure—until the death of Jehoiada. Then everything came off the rails. His short and long term memory both flew out of the window on the wings of the dawn.

This not remembering is particularly tragic because, if you've survived reading the last many chapters, you know that Joash was essentially raised by Jehoiada in the temple before the violent and spectacular death of his grandmother, Athaliah, who didn't even know he was alive. The fact that he survived infancy was a miracle. And then Jehoiada stayed next to him, advising him, and helping him to do good and not evil.

It's too bad. But it's not that unusual, chapter by chapter, or even day by day. A king cannot do good alone, nor can the ordinary Israelite tending his vine or beating his donkey. The prophets' words fall constantly on deaf ears—stopped up, bent on evil. Violence grows heavy over the land.

Blame

But Amaziah would not listen, for it was of God, in order that he might give them into the hand of their enemies, because they had sought the gods of Edom.

II CHRONICLES 25:20

It's so awkward, to my western twenty-first century ear, when God himself takes the blame, when he causes it to be written, "for it was of God." I am always trying to make God palatable, to myself and to the world, and that means that God should be completely removed from violence and sorrow, from anything "bad." My definition of "bad," of course, is the measure. God should only be ready to rush in—like me—to make things "better."

But whoever is sitting in the dark cavern of the temple, carefully writing down all the words that God wants him to write down, doesn't seem to mind that God himself takes the blame, nor how unflattering he is being to his own king. He writes the words, and there they stay for every succeeding generation to smack into, like sheep hitting barbed wire.

But, if you set aside your inclination to assign blame for an anguishing hour, it does make sense. It is not irrational of God to deal out a healthy measure of violence when his creatures give in to idolatry—saying that they are worshiping him, when in fact they are steadfastly worshiping themselves. That we, or anyone really, chose to misunderstand the jealous, loving anger of God is not his fault.

Uzziah

But when he was strong, he grew proud, to his destruction. For he was unfaithful to the LORD his God and entered the temple of the LORD to burn incense on the altar of incense.

II CHRONICLES 26:16

Here we are again then—back with another king who starts out good and then, with complete predictability and unutterably boring certainty, veers sharply off course into the foolishness of his own pride. He wakes up one morning, climbs out of his rich, comfortable bed, and gazes benevolently over his realm. The sun is shining, and he's greeted by the roofs of so many houses sloping away from his palatial vantage point. Life is good. Everything is going well.

And so he thinks, for real, "You know what would be great? Me going into the temple and taking the censor and slinging incense around, because I'm so awesome!"

Just like how I, when I wake up in the morning, arrange my day according to all my own specifications, imagining that what the world needs more of is my own self-expression, my own discovery of myself.

And everyone around him, all the priests, and his household, and everybody, rushes around in trauma and woe because the reason everything was ticking along so nicely was not because of him, but because of God. Like so many, Uzziah mistook the peace and bounty of God's provident care and credited it to himself.

The Angel of Death

And the LORD sent an angel, who cut off all the mighty warriors and com-
manders and officers in the camp of the king of Assyria. So he returned
with shame of face to his own land. And when he came into the house of
his god, some of his own sons struck him down there with the sword.
II CHRONICLES 32:21

The clamor of innumerable heavy pieces of armor cast off in relief after a long day's march rises up in the shimmering heat. There are so many tasks facing each soldier pitching his tent before the cool of evening. The valley collects all the heat and noise. Not far off, the city of Jerusalem huddles, bracing for the worst. A few soldiers pace along the wall, watching. Dusk falls and the cooking fires of Assyria's vast army light up the night.

The Assyrians are the most powerful army in the world. Their weapons are strong, their soldiers resolute. They have come prepared to win. The people on the wall know they haven't a hope.

But their king prays. Their king, in wisdom, cries out to God. And then, apparently, he goes to sleep. So everyone else must lie down and try to do likewise.

When they rise up, they strain their eyes over the mist burning off in the sweltering morning sun; they look out and see that not a single enemy solider remains alive. Every single one is dead. The Assyrian king goes home alone and is murdered in his own capital. And the whole world draws in a breath of wonder.

103 The Dirt

. . . to fulfill the word of the LORD by the mouth of Jeremiah, until the land had enjoyed its Sabbaths. All the days that it lay desolate it kept Sabbath, to fulfill seventy years.

II CHRONICLES 36:21

Remember long ago, a young man named Uzzah stretching out his hand to steady the ark of God? He assumed, wrongly, that he was clean and holy, that his hand was worthy to touch the place God had said he would sit, that God needed his help. God struck him down, preferring that the ark should touch the ground rather than Uzzah's sinful flesh.

The fact is, people are wicked, idolatrous, and filthy. We look at the dirt on the ground and try to protect ourselves from it—thinking that the dirt is the problem. But the dirt on the ground is not the problem. It is our internal moral filth, our wickedness, that spoils the very ground we walk on. Our disobedience has consequences all over creation.

So the land, the earth, the dust and the trees and the vineyards and fields, they all get to have a rest. A perfect rest—the complete accumulation of Sabbaths and Jubilees.

Whenever you wash the mire off your hands, remember that it's really you that needs to be washed clean of yourself. The dirt's not the problem. It's you.

The Returning

> *But many of the priests and Levites and heads of fathers' houses, old men*
> *who had seen the first house, wept with a loud voice when they saw the*
> *foundation of this house being laid, though many shouted aloud for joy,*
> *so that the people could not distinguish the sound of the joyful shout from*
> *the sound of people's weeping, for the people shouted with a great shout,*
> *and the sound was heard far away.*
>
> EZRA 3:12–13

Has it ever been, in human history, that a people carried away captive to a strange and foreign land have be able to turn and come back to their own? The whole purpose of captivity and genocide is to destroy, as completely as possible, the people who are your enemy.

And we are the enemies of God. Whatever we may think to ourselves, one way or another, God is our enemy. He isn't like us. He doesn't do anything the way we would do it. He is the great king over all the earth, and rather than bowing to him and serving him, we commit little treasonous acts to make our own small kingdoms all over the place. It should be no surprise that we are carried away captive by trouble and evil. By all rights we should be forever enemies and strangers.

You can see how strange God is, that he would bring his people back. That he would let his house be rebuilt. The sound of weeping mingles with the shouts of joy so that the one cannot be distinguished from the other, and the sound can be heard afar off. Which is how it is when you get to go home after all.

Darius

> *"Also I make a decree that if anyone alters this edict, a beam shall be*
> *pulled out of his house, and he shall be impaled on it, and his house*
> *shall be made a dunghill."*
>
> EZRA 6:11

In case you were wondering about how seriously Darius was taking the project of sending the people of Israel back to their own land and rebuilding their temple, he has the old decree, made by Cyrus, dug up from the archive. He reiterates it in detail to the governor of the province, announces that he will be paying the costs himself—"whatever is needed," which includes all that's required to resume temple sacrifices—and then, to round it off, he adds this ominous curse. Anyone who tries to change these instructions will suffer a gruesome fate.

So the temple is finished and dedicated. Passover is celebrated for the first time in ages, and all the enemies of Israel simmer down for a bit, because it's kind of disappointing to win but then, as the winner, be forced to let the vanquished go home and have all their stuff back.

Incidentally, this is why I do not enjoy praying for my enemies. It muddies the emotional waters. I don't want to care about them. I don't want them to have nice things. I want them to go down in sorrow to Sheol—maybe not impaled on the beams of their own houses, but certainly not having all the wine and oil and grain flow down like it's a party. If I'm still mad, they should still suffer. Gosh it's annoying when the villain does good things sometimes.

EZRA 4, 5, 6

For Shame

Now there were found some of the sons of the priests who had married
foreign women: Maaseiah, Eliezer, Jarib, and Gedaliah, some of the sons
of Jeshua the son of Jozadak and his brothers.
EZRA 10:18

This has to be one of the worst reasons to have your name recorded in the
Bible. Like having your name printed in the paper for scamming the bu-
reau of disability, as my local mayor once did. Except not quite like that,
because at the beginning of the chapter, all the people whose names are
recorded were part of the "people" who "wept bitterly," who said, "We
have broken faith with our God."

But what is the big deal anyway about marrying a foreign wife? It
sounds bigoted, racist even, to object. And certainly, if you take the more
current categories of inclusion and diversity, this is a horrible thing for
God to make the people do—to separate themselves from wives they have
already married.

Marriage, though, is tricky because it casts a dark shadow on the human imagination of what it is like to have a relationship with God. You
can't have other gods alongside God—any other gods, none. Back in the
day, marrying a "foreign" wife was a spiritual act of adultery against the
God who had chosen you for himself. You weren't just marrying her; you
were bringing Dagon and Molech and Baal in—no lie. You had literally just
been thrown out of the land for doing that. It was kind of a big deal. Like,
you had learned nothing at all from the experience of exile.

The Wall

Then I said to them, "You see the trouble we are in, how Jerusalem lies in ruins with its gates burned. Come, let us build the wall of Jerusalem, that we may no longer suffer derision."
NEHEMIAH 2:17

It is sort of weird to me that Nehemiah is so many people's favorite book, especially for leadership principles. As if by doing whatever it was he did, you can "do better" in your job or church or ministry or whatever. Also, churches—not to mention countries or businesses—aren't supposed to be about walls. If you must build a barrier, you should do it sort of apologetically, making as little fuss about it as possible.

The thing that most impresses me about Nehemiah is how frustrated he is, and how small the wall is that he builds. I always thought it must have been huge and impressive, but the excavations have shown it to be quite modest. If you blinked, you might think it was just part of the hill.

And yet, the little that he did cost him a great deal, and much heartbreak—all the derision of his neighbors heaped up around him the whole time the building went on. I think if you had been one of those exhausted guys, not getting enough sleep for fear of attack, lifting rubble all day and trying to piece it back together, you wouldn't think, "Wow, this is really going help my megachurch get to the next level!" You might not even remember to mention to your grandchildren that you were there when Nehemiah built his famous wall.

NEHEMIAH 1, 2

How Inconvenient

Those who carried burdens were loaded in such a way that each labored on the work with one hand and held his weapon in the other.
NEHEMIAH 4:17

"Those who carried burdens were loaded in such a way," might as well be the motto of the millennia, as well as being the most discouraging possible way to work. I always hated trying to chop an onion while holding a baby, or folding laundry while holding a baby, or working on this book while reading a kid's very thrown-together-last-minute-writing-assignment. Building with a weapon in one hand is the ancient form of multitasking: you can't just do one job well, you have to do two jobs badly.

God, unfortunately, is not particularly interested in your productivity. You may be keenly interested in how much you can get done in a day, or in how much you can avoid doing, but God is not terribly impressed. There were two jobs that needed doing at the same time. The wall had to be built, and the enemies had to be repelled. You couldn't do one and then the other, you had to do them both. They both pressed down, heavily, on you when you woke up in the morning, and when you took turns going to bed at night. It was terribly stressful, and at the end, you didn't have the Eiffel Tower (or any tower) to show for it.

"Come to me," said a guy later, walking around the city and the wall, "all you who are weary and heavy laden." Why? So you can load me up with more work I can't do?

No, so you can rest.

The Preaching

They read from the book, from the Law of God, clearly, and they gave the
sense, so that the people understood the reading.

NEHEMIAH 8:8

The work is multifaceted. Nehemiah has to organize the rebuilding of the
wall by the men with a tool in one hand and a weapon in the other. He
has to arrange for the food and lodging of the workers. In between times,
he must beat back of the evil Tobiah and the meddlesome Sanballat. He
suffers care and anxiety aplenty. And shouldn't that be enough? To bring
the people back and count them? To make them safe. To encourage and
strengthen them?

And that's usually where we feel like we can stop. Everyone is fed and
clothed and no one is crying. But if that's all it is then really, at the most
basic point, we have failed—or whoever it is that's supposed to be carrying
things along has failed. And so, because God cares for the people and for
us, a platform is built—a pulpit, if you will—and Ezra the scribe stands up
on it and reads. For many long hours he reads the law and comments on
it. And then all his helpers spread out over the assembly and explain the
meaning of the words so that all the people understand.

This is important, because if you can understand the Bible—which you
can—you can begin to know and love God. But if you don't bother, then all
the other work hasn't been for any lasting purpose.

Seriously

And I confronted them and cursed them and beat some of them and pulled out their hair. And I made them take an oath in the name of God, saying, "You shall not give your daughters to their sons, or take their daughters for your sons or for yourselves."

NEHEMIAH 13:25

I'd love to see *this* as a model of leadership. Why haven't I ever heard this in a seminar or anything? That and the prayer, "Remember them, O my God, because they have desecrated the priesthood and the covenant of the priesthood and the Levites," and the very last line, "Remember me, O my God, for good," which is my life verse.

But seriously, stop taking foreign wives. Why is this so hard to understand? How is it possible that the minute the exiles return they do the very thing (or at least one of them) that they were thrown out of the land for doing? It's not just the repetition that's frustrating—the habitual doing of the thing you were told not to do every single time you were told not to do it; it's the discouragement of the pastor when he has to circle back to the same set of topics over and over and over.

I always used to be mad that the sermon every week was about how to be saved. *Why can't we ever talk about something new,* I would mutter in the back row, drawing designs on the back of the bulletin, not bothering to crack open the Bible in front of me. "Because you're not even listening," the preacher would have shouted at me if he had been able to hear my thoughts.

Dignity

But Queen Vashti refused to come at the king's command delivered by
the eunuchs. At this the king became enraged, and his anger burned
within him.

ESTHER 1:12

There you are in one of those palatial, old kitchens: sweat dripping down
your face and off your arms, stooping over a massive flame, turning the
spit with some large dead animal on it, shouting at the stupid dog that
keeps trying to steal food, everyone going and coming. The fierce heat,
the choking smoke, the chaos, the dishes going to and fro and back and
forth. Will you ever have a moment to get off your aching feet and lean
your head back against the wall?

You may shudder at the thought of catering a feast that goes on and on
and on, for days and days, with tables and rooms full of drunken men.
Happily feasting drunken men, but drunken all the same. It would be
horribly difficult. But catering the feast would be infinitely preferable
to being the queen who is called upon to exhibit herself before them all.
Dignity, in most cases, is better than fame, fortune, and wealth, so I think
Vashti's firm refusal to obey her husband, the king, is gutsy and rational.
Would that I could behave so rationally half the time.

Plus, it sets up the wonderful moment of God's loving, provident care
for his people.

Timing

> *"For if you keep silent at this time, relief and deliverance will rise*
> *for the Jews from another place, but you and your father's house will*
> *perish. And who knows whether you have not come to the kingdom for*
> *such a time as this?"*
>
> ESTHER 4:14

So the king, having unburdened himself of his disobedient but sensible queen, finds himself lonely. And what better course, when you're lonesome, than to gather a large harem of beautiful young women and hold some sort of contest to decide which one should be queen. The Ancient Bachelor: a magnet for every insecure young woman of the realm—except that Esther isn't insecure. But she is beautiful and kind, and all the beauty treatments succeed in making her yet more beautiful.

She wins the contest. The king likes her best. He makes her queen.

All the while the political intrigue of the court unfolds in the streets beneath her window. Suddenly, she finds herself poised to do a hard thing—to ask the king for an audience, to plead for the fate of her people, God's people, who now live under the threat of destruction and brutality. And so of course she hesitates. She is afraid. She is anxious.

Esther's situation is unique. It is not the ordinary type of stand that most of us are called to. It is not the pitiful discomfort of belief in God in a world that hates God, that moment of deciding whether or not to pray publicly at the restaurant or attach a cross to your twitter handle. But if you need courage, if your stomach is turning over, you could try whispering to yourself, "Maybe I was put here for such a time as this."

Honor

So Haman came in, and the king said to him, "What should be done to the man whom the king delights to honor?" And Haman said to himself, "Whom would the king delight to honor more than me?"

ESTHER 6:6

You've probably been so swept up in this incredible story that you've secretly read ahead and smacked into the carnage and woe awaiting this bitter, difficult man. "How can one person be so evil and selfish," I always think. But the answer is right there on the page.

When someone asks, "Hmmm, I really want to honor someone, how should I do it?" I beg you to be practical and always assume that they're not thinking about you.

But you know how it happens. It creeps up on you. You do some small job for someone, but you feel like it's a big one. You wait around, hoping they'll notice. You recount to yourself how much time you spent helping them and how you felt while you were doing it. You gradually inflate the meaning of the task to epic proportions. The suspense builds. You wait. And then, the next time you happen to see the person, they don't mention it at all.

In this way you see that they didn't think it was that big of a deal. They didn't understand that they needed to go out of their way to thank you for whatever small thing it was that you did. With each small, un-thanked job you ask yourself, "Who would anyone delight to honor more than me?"

Avoid the terrible downfall of Haman. Don't ever ask this very bad question.

ESTHER 6, 7, 8

Have You Considered

And the LORD said to Satan, "Have you considered my servant Job, that there is none like him on the earth, a blameless and upright man, who fears God and turns away from evil?"

JOB 1:8

Satan is roaming up and down and to and fro, wrecking everything, blighting the earth, ruining all the nice things, devastating whatever he can. You'd think God would put greater limits on him, lock him up some place where he can't do anything really awful. It's so troubling and upsetting that God—not someone else, but God—drew Satan's attention to Job. Surely there must be some mistake. Maybe a copyist wrote it down wrong.

We know that the Lord can draw the righteous out of temptation, so why doesn't He? And Satan isn't even righteous. Satan is the actual worst. And Job, of all people, is as nice as they come. You couldn't find a more upright, decent guy than Job.

As you've probably heard, things go very badly from here on out. Every possible calamity will befall Job from the hand of Satan. And it's going to be awful. But at the most basic point, God can be held to account, because he allowed it.

Are you in trouble and woe? Do you long to have someone to blame? Blame yourself, of course, and Satan, obviously, but then turn your eyes to the Lord. Job will give you some language for when you can't help but ask, "What!?"

JOB 1:1–19

The Lord Takes Away

Then Job arose and tore his clothes and shaved his head and fell on the
ground and worshiped. And he said, "Naked I came from my mother's
womb, and naked shall I return. The LORD gave, and the LORD has taken
away; blessed be the name of the LORD."

JOB 1:20—21

Everything is gone, except his wife, of course. She remains endlessly. Why isn't she sad about her children and all her stuff? Maybe she is.
Maybe she's so crushed with grief that she is stuck in the accusation and
anger stage.

Anyway, everything is gone. The incredible wealth. The cattle. The
riches. Gone.

And the children are gone. Eldest to youngest, all gone. All that work.
All those years of babies crying. The anxiety of children getting sick. The
stress of adolescence. Gone. All of it for nothing. The loss is so immense.
Catastrophic. Epic. And yet just like other kinds of loss all over the world
every day.

Gather all the losses of all time and pour them into Job's hands, his
aching, broken body, and listen to what he says. "The Lord gives and the
Lord takes away. Blessed be the name of the Lord." Is he insane? Or is he
more sane than any human has ever been?

God holds all things in his hand. When bad things happen, you can lay
them at his feet. But do it with a modicum of praise, a meager thimbleful
of trust, a pinch of worship.

With Friends Like These

Now when Job's three friends heard of all this evil that had come upon him, they came each from his own place, Eliphaz the Temanite, Bildad the Shuhite, and Zophar the Naamathite. They made an appointment together to come to show him sympathy and comfort him.

JOB 2:11

I never know what on earth to say when something terrible has happened to someone I love. I stumble around, feeling the fool, wishing I could sink into the floor, overcome by my own vanity mingling with grief for the person in front of me. I usually mutter, "I'm so terribly sorry. You are constantly in my prayers," and leave it there. Which makes me better than Job's "friends."

Job has three of them—besides his nagging, unpleasant, though probably grief-stricken wife. A fourth friend will come along later. But these three, they made the journey from their own homes, and generations of Bible-readers, toiling through this book, think it might have been better if they hadn't bothered. They sit in silence for seven days, not saying anything—which is an incredible mercy. But then they decide to unstop their mouths and let Job have it.

"You should try to be a better person," they all say. "You should have more faith," they all council. "You should sin less. It's clearly your own fault," they all explain. And so on for a thousand iterations, in a thousand generations. But Job isn't a fool, and neither is God, so eventually Someone will come along and tell them to go jump in a lake.

Bitterness

Therefore I will not restrain my mouth; I will speak in the anguish of my spirit; I will complain in the bitterness of my soul.
JOB 7:11

It's hard enough to lose everything, to sit there in the ash heap of life turning over your loss, contemplating it from every possible angle, just wanting God to take you home. But then to have to cope with the vaguely well-intentioned family and friends who, in their anxiety for your eternal salvation, sit down next to you and won't give up telling you how wrong you are?

Ever notice that with all the bad things that happen in life—the bad things that God himself allows, and in many cases orchestrates—it's the troublesome, ordinary, day-to-day sympathy that's the most impossible to handle.

But God is big enough to handle that too. Though he feels far away, distant, uncaring, feelings don't always reflect reality. If your feelings were always the truth, there wouldn't be any hope for you. Though he feels far away, though he seems uncaring, though you cannot possibly understand what he is doing or why, in reality he is very near. He hears your complaints and responds in the most personal possible way—a way that you will only see a long time from now, in another person whose body was afflicted, who lost everything he had.

Don't restrain your mouth. Pour out the bitterness of your spirit to him. Don't keep it all together. Don't try to pretend everything is okay. Let your soul be the shattered, broken thing that it is. And God will carry on doing whatever incomprehensible-to-you-thing that he is doing.

JOB 6, 7

No Doubt

Then Job answered and said: "No doubt you are the people, and wisdom will die with you."

JOB 12:1–2

People keep asking me if it's really okay for Christians to use sarcasm. When, if ever, they wonder, has God been sarcastic? Isn't sarcasm just very unkind insincerity? Shouldn't we all be sincere and mean what we say?

But Job took up his discourse and said, "Ya'll, I'm in a whole lot of pain and you are persecuting me, and nothing that I'm saying is penetrating your very thick, very sincere skulls."

The problem with "sincerity," with "always saying exactly what you mean," is that very often sincere people are sincerely wrong. They believe with their whole hearts that God doesn't let bad things happen to good people and that they are good people. If something bad has happened, it is because someone else has sinned or because "society" needs to be burnt to the ground. God, if he exists, will totally let *them* into heaven, and so the long day wears on. Some people even believe things like "what goes around comes around," or, "God helps those who help themselves," or the very worst, "God won't give you more than you can handle." It is, I suppose, possible to kindly and calmly try to explain to someone why what they are saying is foolish, but sometimes it's okay to cut through the lies with, "Sure, let me know how that works out for you."

So, yes, sarcasm is okay sometimes. Job uses it pretty effectively here. Keep reading to hear even Jesus being sarcastic.

I Shall See

"Oh that with an iron pen and lead, they were engraved in the rock forever! For I know that my Redeemer lives, and at the last he will stand upon the earth."

JOB 19:24–25

All the "comforting" is taking a dreadful toll on Job, as all these discourses drone on. "Haven't you done enough," Job cries out. "Can't you just leave me alone? I wish I had a pen! An iron pen! So that these words could be written down and last forever." Not that the suffering should last forever, but the words and the memory should be written "in" the rock, "forever."

Rock? What rock?

Attend closely to the words of the whole chapter. The words are Job's, but they hearken a long way off into the future. There will be a moment when the Redeemer stands, when God has put *him* in the wrong, when the net is closed around *him*, when *he* cries violence and there is none to help, when the darkness is close-set, when the net is closed around him, when the glory is stripped away and the crown exchanged for nakedness and shame, when the Lord's wrath is kindled against him and he is counted as an adversary.

But he *will* live. At the last he will stand upon the earth. And Job, and you, and me, will see him for ourselves, in our flesh. Our eyes shall behold him, and not another.

Burning Anger

And when Elihu saw that there was no answer in the mouth of these three men, he burned with anger.

JOB 32:5

Job did not suffer because he had sinned, or because he was evil. Neither, however, was he perfect. In all his discourse back and forth with his "friends," he hasn't been right all the time. Rather than glorifying God, he has justified himself and his complaint.

I hope that none of us would scold Job. The least bit of suffering tempts me to question the very existence of God, let alone the causes of evil in the world. The glory of God and the goodness of God are my least favorite topics when I am in pain.

Job's friends, of course—and this is what we should all aim for in the important work of comfort and consolation—could have sat with Job as he wrestled it through, could have tried to honestly work it out *with* him, rather than *to* him. Unfortunately, it is always easier to see how other people are going wrong than it is to see it in one's own self.

So in the end, everyone is wrong except for the young, prescient Elihu. He "burns with anger" about how wrong everyone is, and sets out on a long discourse of his own to explain, in detail, how God being God is essential, how Job's friends have adopted the least helpful theological worldview imaginable.

I Had No Idea

"I had heard of you by the hearing of the ear, but now my eye sees you; therefore I despise myself, and repent in dust and ashes."
JOB 42:5—6

All the lamenting and blaming and arguing winds down to its exhausting end and everyone finally stops talking—and then God shows up. Not that he wasn't always there. But, you know, sometimes, when you have plenty to say and you keep on saying it, God doesn't bother to have a word in edgewise. He just waits. And then when he does speak, well. He asks Job a lot of questions, a lot of terrible questions that Job can't possibly answer. "Were you there? In the beginning, were you there? Do you really think you know and understand?"

And the great overwhelming impactfulness of God's audible communication effects not only the hearing of Job's ears, but also the seeing of his eyes.

You can hear about God. You can wonder about him and think about who he might be. But if you find yourself face to face, ear to ear, eyeball to eyeball with his words in this book—with the true discovery of who he is—well, then you repent. You crumple into a ball of sorrow amid the crumbs and juice on the kitchen floor and say, "I'm so sorry. I didn't know. I'm so sorry."

And then you try to stand back up and carry on, but from then on everything is slightly different.

A Tree

He is like a tree planted by streams of water that yields its fruit in its
season, and its leaf does not wither. In all that he does, he prospers.
PSALM 1:3

Blessed, or happy, are you when you don't turn around and meander after wickedness and wicked people. When you don't follow the natural progression of first trying to keep up with evil, and then, having finally caught it and recovered your breath, setting your stride to walk along beside it, and then, in the end, sitting down to really revel in and enjoy its presence.

The many imperceptible sins of the heart and mind push you to keep an exhausting pace. You find yourself wasting time keeping track of who you talked to so unkindly about that lady at church. Will it get back to her? Or, in staying one step ahead of your bitterness, you add more fuel to tend the flame. Then you can decide whether to swallow your rage and speak kindly in the face of offense, but why would you. Honesty is so important. Worn out at the end of the day, you wander around one website, and then another, and then another.

Or, you could just stop. You could walk away from the restless striving, the pursuit of so many worthless occupations, and instead plant yourself next to the tree that is also the living water. The stark tree upon which hangs the river of life, just to jumble all the metaphors of the entire Bible. And you be a tree: a tree whose roots go deep, a tree whose branches never wither.

Into Your Hands

But you do see, for you note mischief and vexation, that you may take it into your hands; to you the helpless commits himself; you have been the helper of the fatherless.

PSALM 10:14

The world likes to pretend that God neither exists nor is paying attention. You could, of course, put yourself in the category of the world; you could rightfully lump yourself in with them. You don't do nearly a fraction of the things you're supposed to do, and you do all sorts of things you're not supposed to. And it would be right, some of the time, to say that you live as if God isn't paying attention.

But as you pray through these prayers, written by people like you who are clearly not that good, you may, like them, put yourself in the place of goodness. You may, here and there, plead with God as if you are one of the good ones, and beg him to do something about all the bad ones.

It is a wise and good thing to look around the world and the people both near you and far away from you, and ask God, even to beg him, to do something about them. To reckon with the sins, the evils, the unrepentance of the wicked.

And you may do that because you believe in the good one, the One who hears and sees. He sees not just the great, huge evils of the world—because certainly he sees those—but He notes even small irritating vexation and mischief. Not only so, he takes them all in hand.

Because

My God, my God, why have you forsaken me? Why are you so far from
saving me, from the words of my groaning?
PSALM 22:1

Sometimes, in the routine doldrums of struggling along through life—of
trying to believe, and of trying to beat your way through all the words of
this book—you might wake up to terrible news. Or find yourself sitting on
a pile of receipts and papers that show a balance of nothing. Or lying in a
hospital bed, or standing next to a grave, or just completely alone. And in
those moments, you might look up at the vast expanse of the sky and you
might say these words of the psalmist, or simply put your head down and
weep them. You might be overcome by the experience of groaning for-
sakenness. And as you read the rest of these words here, of the physical
devastation, the mental and emotional pain and grief, you might think,
"Yes, that's where I am. Where is God? Why isn't he listening? Why isn't
he doing anything? It can't get any worse. I cannot any longer bear the
circumstances of my life and the grief of my soul."

But lift your eyes and hear the words again—spoken by another, far-off
from you. Listen to the word cried out by a man naked, broken, bruised,
and hanging there in the vast expanse of a cloudy, darkening sky. A man
forsaken, who, when he cried these words, knew that his Father's back
was turned against him, and he was left alone to die.

Because he was forsaken, you will never be forsaken.

PSALM 22, 23

No Dead Kmart

*Walk about Zion, go around her, number her towers, consider well her
ramparts, go through her citadels, that you may tell the next generation
that this is God, our God forever and ever. He will guide us forever.*
PSALM 48:12—14

I have tried numbering the buildings in my fading American town. Here
there are no citadels, no ramparts. There used to be some lovely, big
houses, but now they are mostly crumbling from neglect. I try sometimes
to lift up my mind's eye away from the gray, sprawling mini mall—whichever one I happen to be stuck inside. There are so many. They squat on the
landscape in utilitarian ugliness. It's not completely awful because you
can find decent food on a lunch hour, and there's a drive-through ATM
in the parking lot. But this is not the vista of loveliness I wish I could
contemplate with my whole soul. And rather than praise God, I complain
and moan, wondering why he couldn't have done something to the people
here to make them want to build something beautiful.

But it won't always be so. Someday, some far-off day, when I have my
gorgeous new body and something decent to wear, the city I survey will
be a feast for the eyes, a balm for the soul. Everything about that city is
light and grace. The streets glow, the lines are stately, measured, perfect.
There aren't any problems. There are no cracks, nothing is broken or shut
down. No dead Kmart obscures anyone's view.

Metaphorically Speaking

Know that the Lord, he is God! It is he who made us, and we are his; we are his people, and the sheep of his pasture.
PSALM 100:3

In my long lost childhood, I sometimes had the job of pushing the sheep and goats and cows out of our yard in Africa. It would have been so useful to have a fence, but there was none. The goats would climb all over and eat everything. The cows would rub against the trees and try to knock them down. The little shepherd children would sit back, eating mangos, and laugh as I whaled around, awkwardly, with a stick, trying to get all the animals to go back to their own houses.

The sheep were not fluffy, or cute, or nice. They were large and mean, and, if provoked, would lower their heads and charge, like some great wild beasts.

Surely God, in likening me to a sheep, in making sheep into some kind of grand metaphor, some elaborately painted picture of himself in relationship to me, surely *he* isn't being unkind. Am I, really, a sheep of his pasture? Am I like this stubborn, stubborn, mean, stubborn creature who is not only stupid enough to die in the wilderness, but mean enough to charge, enraged, into the shins of its caretaker?

And he is the one who made me! Who thought it would be good to have it this way.

Well, I will try to stop arguing; though, as a sheep, there isn't much I can do about it.

Glad

I was glad when they said to me, "Let us go to the house of the LORD!"
PSALM 122:1

I was rushing around in a panic—trying to get all my bundles properly tied and my mental lists completely sorted. I knew I was forgetting something important, so I double-checked again: food for the way, skins of wine, changes of clothes, feed for the mule, money, presents for the relatives—there had to be something else . . .

All over, the bustle of everyone else double-checking their packing—calling out greetings one to another, shouting last-minute instructions for the two people staying home—rose as a clamorous joyful roar. Kind of wished, for a thread of a second, that I could have stayed home—frankly—because this journey is just so much work. And I hadn't slept properly. All night I had been sure I was going to forget something. I'd had three of those lurid, technicolor dreams where the donkey eats all the money and I arrive with nothing.

But finally there was nothing for it but to turn and walk from the dusty courtyard, even though there hadn't been time to clean the way I'd planned. Off we went, all our steps pointing south. Going up.

And then, suddenly, I was glad. I was glad when they said, "Let us go to the house of the Lord." Yes. I want to go. Even if some of the bundles fall open, or something gets lost along the way and I still have to face all the cleaning when I get home.

Praise the Lord

Praise the LORD! Praise God in his sanctuary; praise him in his mighty heavens!

PSALM 150:1

Here we come to the end of the psalms, the songs of the Bible. I hope you are sad, as I always am when I get to the end. But then I'm happy to immediately turn back and begin at the first one again, going round and round for the whole of my life.

The psalms begin with a warning, and a caution, and a promise. But they end with praise. Praise the Lord. All the time, praise the Lord. Praise the Lord when you feel like it and when you don't; when things are going badly and when they are going well; when you are healthy and when you are sick; when life is complicated and when it ticks along smoothly; when you get along with everyone, even yourself, and when you are out of sorts with everyone.

By this point, with all the praise, and the singing, and the crying out for help and salvation and mercy, with all the reminding, all the repetition—by this point you should be well away from the council of the wicked. You should have run away from the scoffers. You should be sitting somewhere quiet, like a calm and planted tree, soaking up the water of life. Praise the Lord.

PSALM 148, 149, 150

129 The Fool

The fear of the LORD is the beginning of knowledge; fools despise wisdom and instruction.

PROVERBS 1:7

There are so many things to be afraid of on an average, unremarkable day. I could be afraid for my children, wanting them to be safe and to do well and to be healthy. I could be terrified of losing my husband. I could be anxious (by reason of experience) about losing my keys. I could certainly be afraid of there not being enough money. I could be afraid of not hold-ing all the things in my life and my head together. I could waste time be-ing afraid of other people not liking me.

Of one thing I am not usually afraid, however. One being in particu-lar does not fill my heart and mind with dread and anxiety. You might be shocked to learn that the one thing I am not afraid of is the Wrath of God. In fact, it is entirely possible for me to carry on a whole day without thinking about him, or his wrath, at all.

In this way I am the preeminent fool. All the fears that I carry around should give way to the one Great True Fear: the fear of God and his perfect holiness. I should look up to the heavens, I should look into the depths of the ocean, I should turn over the pages of Scripture, and tremble. Awe should overcome all my fear. If it did, I would be less and less a fool. I would slowly become wise. Knowledge would creep softly in.

Your Way

Trust in the LORD with all your heart, and do not lean on your own under-
standing. In all your ways acknowledge him, and he will make straight
your paths.

PROVERBS 3:5—6

How does that song go? "I did it my way"? Sometimes families want that played at their dearly departed's funeral—not quite the message, I think, that is helpful, especially with this sharp dictum staring me in the face.

You've got to walk one way or another. You can't stand still in the path, eternally contemplating which way you should go and what you should do. Most people today will admonish you to "follow your heart" or "make your own happiness," or something like that.

The thing is, the choice *is* important. On the one hand, you can try to rely on yourself and your ability to hold it all together—as though, by some miracle, you understand and can rightly judge all the complexities of reality, and your life, and everything. Or, on the other hand, you can incline yourself, your way, and your time toward God. The incline might be shallow or it might be steep. Approaching that slope may make your heart shake with terror and fear. But if the incline, the inclination, the leaning, is toward a person greater than you—a person who holds all knowledge and wisdom and understanding in himself—then the way will be completely straight. You won't fall off or wander away, neither to the right nor to the left.

The Ant

A little sleep, a little slumber, a little folding of the hands to rest, and
poverty will come upon you like a robber, and want like an armed man.
PROVERBS 6:10–11

So many curious and practical lessons can be taken from nature. Consider, for instance, the ant, who runs around like a frantic maniac. From dawn to dusk this tiny creature goes back and forth, back and forth, over the mountains you lay in his way, or out of the wall next to your capacious sink to feast on the contents of your dirty dishes. He is always busy, always moving. Whereas you, you have a hard time dragging yourself out of bed after watching one too many episodes of whatever-it-was. Now you've got to face work and everything, and all you really want is to climb into that wretched hole with that aggravating ant and lie there while he keeps going up and down and back and forth. But nobody in his nest would welcome you. They would chirp silently and wave their front legs at you and complain to each other that You're Letting Everyone Down.

You have to work. You must keep moving. But don't forget: someone else has already accomplished all the benefits of all your striving for you. As you fold your hands in rest, later this afternoon, anxious that poverty is creeping up behind you, remember that you are already poor, that the love of God is pretty rich, and that someone, having finished all his work, did finally sit down and is still sitting there, gathering up all your anxieties as you bring them to him, every single one.

PROVERBS 6, 7, 8

The Stupid

Whoever loves discipline loves knowledge, but he who hates reproof is stupid.

PROVERBS 12:1

I taught my children to say "stupid" in French so that I won't be so offended by their persistent, childish, usually playful insulting of each other. Children are notable both for their truth-telling capabilities, and for their cruelty—at least, mine are. Indeed, though I discourage the use of this word, I cannot escape the harsh truth that we, all of us, including me, are just a little bit stupid. There's no way around it. The human self, turned inward as it is, can't see clearly enough to avoid all stupidity.

However, there is a way to become less stupid over time, and that is to accept correction and rebuke. The thing about rebuke is that it opens the ears of faith. If you can listen to someone tell you that you've done the wrong thing, said something awful, that your instincts were off, that you handled something badly, then you are imperceptibly turning toward God—whose first, basic message is, "You're wrong." If you can hear someone else—and then him—say that, you are on your way to true happiness. A happiness which includes knowledge of all things. And who doesn't want to be happy and smart rather than sad and stupid?

Don't answer that.

The Feast

Better is a dry morsel with quiet than a house full of feasting with strife.
PROVERBS 17:1

Lest you ever feel inclined to pity the poor person sitting alone at McDonald's, slowly working through one of those epically unhealthy burgers, drinking the whole larger option of soda, staring out the window at you as you struggle by with your groceries piled into cumbersome and expensive reusable bags—the fresh herbs, the organic slab of grass-fed beef, the kohlrabi, the quinoa—consider the trial awaiting you before you pity him.

He sits in warmth and comfort, alone, eating something he loves without the trouble of wondering whether or not the shallot has been chopped too roughly. He is not testy because the phone rang just as the roux was coming together, and it was a call that had to be taken, and so now the roux has to be started again from scratch. He will go out into the crisp, chill air to his life, enjoying the beauty of the sky, the pleasure of work he enjoys and has mastered.

You, on the other hand, will continue to sweat in anxiety and frustration over a dish none of your children will eat anyway. You set the rich, locally and ethically sourced, perfectly-presented plate on the table, losing your mind as the thin, cutting whine of a child shatters what was left of your peace—each forkful you manage simply another step further into strife and discontent.

Sometimes it's okay to pick up fast food. That's all I'm saying.

Don't Say It

*The name of the L*ORD *is a strong tower; the righteous man runs into it and is safe.*

PROVERBS 18:10

Your name is overused and sounds hollow and thin on the lips of all the people who shout it all day long. You wish someone would just not use it, just one time. Even "Hey you," would be better. The worst is to hear your name spoken in that way that reinforces to you how low you are on the totem pole. Or in that incessant whining way of the person who wants juice, and won't stop shouting until you pour it. "Just stop," you whisper, "just don't say my name."

But the name of the Lord isn't like your name. Even if you occasionally say it in the wrong way, in anger, or to express your surprise and horror. The name of the Lord isn't just a word. It is a strong tower, round, so that you can go up to it step by step, stopping to survey the lay of the land as you go. If you turn to the Name of the Lord, if you cry it out from the depths of your irritated soul, the Lord himself hears and answers and comes to you and is there with you, in the midst of all the people shouting yours.

135 The Stream

The king's heart is a stream of water in the hand of the LORD; he turns it wherever he will.

PROVERBS 21:1

It's the easiest thing in the world—standing, as I often am, slinging various bits and pieces of onion and garlic into a pan, rummaging around in the fridge trying to figure out how to make something out of nothing, listening to the news of the day—to despair and believe that good will never prosper. Meanwhile, the powers of the world rage and storm over my social media feeds, corrupting first themselves, and then others, laying violence upon violence. "Does God even know?" I sometimes wonder. "Is He paying attention?"

Yes, he is. The heart, mind, and interests of the kings of the earth are well known to God. In fact, their plans and souls are like water that spills out and flows downhill into the great big pool of God's own plans. They can't do anything that He hasn't already seen and known.

And do not be sad. For you also are a regular, though small potatoes, despot. You are the king, or maybe queen, of your domain. Your soul and thoughts and plans are also held in the hand of God, directed by him in the course of his plan for all creation. You cannot surprise Him. But you can trust him with all the evil that flows past you, to you, and, in more tragic moments, out of you.

The Envy

Be not envious of evil men, nor desire to be with them, for their hearts
devise violence, and the lips talk of trouble.
PROVERBS 24:1—2

Envy makes the world go round. I don't know how to get through the day
without mentally moving myself and the few pieces of furniture I really
like into other people's nicer houses. When I sit in someone else's new-
ly-remodeled kitchen, drinking their nice warm, milky drinks, I consider whether or not I would like to be wearing their shoes, or whether I
would like my hair to fall in a similar kind of way. When I look at my own
pinched face in the mirror, I believe the lie that if I looked like that and
had that stuff, I'd probably be happy. Well, happier. Probably.

Every now and then—because envy is for every time of the day—I scroll
through the internet and look at the lives of people who are wickedly pur-
suing their own ends, who are maligning the name and purposes of God,
but who look really gorgeous while they are doing it. And I, toiling away
in obscurity, I think, "Well, that's not fair. Think how much good I could
do with all their money, how much good I could do if my nails were pro-
fessionally painted!"

"No," says God. "You don't want the wickedness that goes with it, you
don't want the trouble. What you have now is perfectly good for you."

The Model Wife

A continual dripping on a rainy day and a quarrelsome wife are alike; to restrain her is to restrain the wind or to grasp oil in one's right hand.
PROVERBS 27:15–16

You and I, of course, are nothing like this. I hardly know what the word "quarrelsome" means, except as I have been able to observe it in other people.

But then, it is always easier to see and understand things in *other* people—those horrible people who pick at their husbands and children and friends and never let anyone get away with anything. I myself, for instance, would never bicker. I would never nag or whine. I would never be totally irritated by the constant sprinkling and redistribution of crumbs by my children on the kitchen floor. I would never say anything to my husband as he stands, swinging a soaking, water-logged teabag back and forth, back and forth, so that when it finally lands in the sink there is no more tea left in it to drip out. I would never say anything about the piles of papers and books all over, under, and around his desk. The way he leaves his shoes flung down as if to purposely insult me never draws a word from my lips.

I am just not that kind of person. I am a model of kindness and restraint. I am a model of modest self-control.

Excellent Women

An excellent wife who can find? She is far more precious than jewels.
PROVERBS 31:10

I expect Lemuel hoped that someone out there would eventually find an excellent wife. When he asks "who can find"—even though it sounds rhetorically like an impossibility—he just means that you should be really happy when you finally do find her, however it happens. She will be the most precious person any man can find, if indeed he can manage it.

And of course, so many women, both now and long ago, enjoy so much being the kind of woman described here. Who among us doesn't love to leap up before the rising of the sun? To gather flax and wool? To dress everybody in scarlet? To make sure everyone is more than fed at every single, tiny, unrelenting meal? To build a lucrative side hustle that is basically a successful real estate venture?

The problem with this strong, precious woman is that she's so concentrated on other people. She wakes up and thinks about, and works for, others *all day long*. Who can even understand such a person? No, I'm pretty sure this description is some sort of spiritual metaphor for the Church and Israel.

Also, my children don't even look that good in red.

Also, I don't have servants, so . . .

¹39 Vanity

Vanity of vanities, says the Preacher, vanity of vanities! All is vanity.

ECCLESIASTES 1:2

What a distressingly broad summation of human existence. Really, King Solomon could have gone in for a touch more nuance.

Isn't there *some* escape from the futility of life? I ask this every morning, turning a stubborn eye against my unmade bed to contemplate my worthless wardrobe. What's the point? If I pull up and smooth the covers, I will only rumple them again at the end of the day. If I put on those trousers, they will only show me the assault of time against my waist. I turn, in despair, to that great ocean into which all the rivers run: my inbox. What would Solomon have to say about how, if you send an email, you get three in reply, how if you clean it all out and file everything into folders, in the morning it is as if you did nothing the day before. What would be his metaphor? Would it be the wind? The dry ground? The impossibly circular nature of a day where each task runs into the one before it, and nothing is ever finished?

Or perhaps the Preacher is wrong. Perhaps the trouble of the work—of making the bed in the morning, of walking into the bright sunshine at the noon hour, of finding some pair of trousers that clothes the aging body, of spreading a thin ruby-red layer of raspberry jam over a slice of real bread—can arrest and even halt despair. Perhaps another preacher will step onto the dry ground and finish some new, perfect, eternally satisfying work.

Burnout

All things are full of weariness; a man cannot utter it; the eye is not satis-
fied with seeing, nor the ear filled with hearing.
ECCLESIASTES 1:8

I'm not a millennial, but every time I find a millennial burnout quiz, I
take it with a vigor that belies the fact that I always come out with a high
burnout score. Self-diagnosed burnout, no matter your age or situation,
is the best and quickest way to feel better about how bad everything is.

Truth is, when you are totally centered in on yourself—when your own
ego is the measure of all things, as it is with each and every one of us,
when vanity is the force that drives the world and the world's economy,
and the world's values—well, then you're going to end up weary. Tired.
Worn-out. Also dissatisfied and ticked off about everything.

I can pretend all day long that I intend another's good, that I am phil-
anthropic, that I have another person in mind. But at the root, deep down
in the center of the world, is the self: myself, yourself, himself, herself.
All of us orbiting around ourselves, measuring everything by what our
eyes can see. The self is so deep, so essential, that we needn't speak of it or
acknowledge its existence. It is the foundational element of the universe.

With each passing day the weariness of humanity, struggling along,
driven by the self toward the self, gets a little more tired, burnt-out,
worn-out.

Do I Have Too Much Stuff?

. . . a time to keep, and a time to cast away . . .

ECCLESIASTES 3:6

My mother gave me a little card, a long time ago, that says, "You can't have everything, where would you put it?" I have it propped up on my dresser so that when I'm folding my clothes in the manner prescribed by Marie Kondo—which is actually a very useful way for jamming twice the number of items in a drawer and never getting rid of any of them—I can ponder that strange maxim. If I can't have everything, can I at least have more?

Eventually, of course, it is time to "cast away," to bag up all the stuff and shove it in the back of my car and take it to a big warehouse where nice people take it out of the back of my car and fling it into these sort of metal cages and wheel it away. I didn't bother to sort it very well, which is fine, because they will do it for me.

All my wretched stuff then gets shipped off to other places already overwhelmed with the cast-offs of our corporate dissatisfaction. Maybe someone will wear that horrible shirt I couldn't fit into for a few weeks before throwing it into a trash heap. The garbage of the world piles up and I, still miserable about the stuff I do own, go out and buy a little more to make myself feel better.

Is Ecclesiastes over yet? This book is such a downer.

142 Nailed It

The words of the wise are like goads, and like nails firmly fixed are the
collected sayings; they are given by one Shepherd.
ECCLESIASTES 12:11

Is there no remedy for the vain emptiness of all human existence? Is this really the end of the matter? Work really hard and then die? Or, could there be something more?

I mean, that's why you're toiling through all the pages of the Bible, isn't it? Because you've seen a glimpse of something that doesn't fade away? Because you have hope? Because though you are tired, and weary, and have heard and seen everything, maybe there's something you missed in all your searching? Solomon didn't ever seem to put his finger on it. He gathered all the wisdom in the world into one place, catalogued it, memorialized it, and then finally had to say—help.

But something greater than Solomon is here. Some deeper wisdom is nailed in place to a hard piece of wood, fixed violently, malevolently by the "wisdom" of the senseless wanderer. That's you and me, both of us kicking sharply against the One who would have cared for us, who would have gathered us into the fold to feed, to anoint, to love forever.

This Wisdom doesn't grow tired, doesn't give up, doesn't accumulate knowledge and understanding to no purpose. His wise words fix you, when you hear them, to Himself.

143 She Sounds Great

I compare you, my love, to a mare among Pharaoh's chariots.

SONG OF SOLOMON 1:9

My husband is always trying to get me to feel better about myself because when I feel better about myself I'm nicer to him. Somehow, self-loathing is an impediment to a comfortable frame of mind which in turn effects how I treat other people. I tend to say, "Today I look like some sort of diminutive hippo with skin issues," and he will say, "No, you're beautiful." "If you dare compare me to a mare among Pharaoh's chariots, so help me, I don't know what I'll do," I respond. "I wasn't going to," he promises. Calling a woman "horsey" just isn't that nice anymore. I, for one, feel like this is a good thing—not to question the Bible or anything.

Though "self-esteem" has had its day and should disappear into the netherworld of forgotten and useless history, feeling awful about what you look like or even what you are like *inside* doesn't really make a person nicer or better. Some kind of positivity is good for a body, mostly because God made it, and it's a nice thing to have.

One of the mercies of having nice friends or a kind husband is that you don't have to do this for yourself. Other people can say stuff to cut through the garbage you are saying. When it's a man in love with a woman as she is, instead of what she wished she could be, it's even nicer. Of course, the nicest thing of all is when you discover that God doesn't think of you as a horse, but loves you more than all of Pharaoh's chariots.

SONG OF SOLOMON 1, 2, 3

First Comes Love

*Your teeth are like a flock of shorn ewes that have come up from the wash-
ing, all of which bear twins, and not one among them has lost its young.*
SONG OF SOLOMON 4:2

This just means that you have all your teeth—thank goodness—and that
they are even and pearly white. I'm grateful that when my husband fell
in love with me, he didn't examine my teeth in this way, because mine
are crooked and stained with tea. I have had an awful lot of work done on
them, including a root canal, to little or no effect.

This love, between Solomon and his beloved, doesn't end happily. It
is the vain shadow, the kind of broken desire that we each suffer on this
side of the grave. Even so, the longing, the intense passion, the pain, the
hope—these are all on God's side for us.

The point being that it's such a good thing to fall in love—even unhappily—if you can manage it. But the reason that it's good to be in love—and
more than that, to love someone actively with your whole self—is because it gives you an *amuse-bouche* of the fact that God loves you. He left
everything in the dead of night, his house, his home, to come after you.
He came a great distance to look for you. He was willing to risk everything.
And, he also knows the number of your teeth.

Be Reasonable

"Come now, let us reason together, says the LORD: though your sins are like scarlet, they shall be as white as snow; though they are red like crimson, they shall become like wool."

ISAIAH 1:18

Is reason even possible? Will it be that I look at God and have a conversation or an argument? Will it be like a long, contentious Twitter thread? Where he and I lob accusations across space?

What about the fact that I can't even reason with myself, or with my children, or with all the people in my life whose minds I can't see any better than my own? Reason requires knowledge and understanding. If I were going to be reasonable, I would have to know myself. I would have to be able to discern, in the early morning, whence derives my bad mood, and why I didn't remember to shut the cupboard before I bashed my head on the corner of the door.

Anyway, this sounds more like a declaration, some kind of judgment mixed up with a strangely personal proclamation about the future. Come, now? Right this minute? Is that an order?

"Yes," says God. "I'm going to deal with all the stuff that makes it impossible for you to know who I am."

I mean, I wouldn't mind being more reasonable. It might be nice to be able to use my mind to make sound judgments, to converse reasonably with other people, especially my husband. I hate sitting back in my chair, groping around in the dark for language to explain myself, and then looking up to see the ubiquitous expression of uncomprehending in the face of my beloved. Fortunately, God doesn't ever misunderstand Israel—or me for that matter.

ISAIAH 1, 2

146 Where'd You Get Those Shoes?

The Lord said: Because the daughters of Zion are haughty and walk with outstretched necks, glancing wantonly with their eyes, mincing along as they go, tinkling with their feet . . .

ISAIAH 3:16

Some of the daughters of Zion, the rich ones, lived in elegant palaces sloping down the hill of the City of David, the temple up at the top, and their houses nestled right into the rock, looking out over the Kidron Valley. The houses were luxurious, far removed from the rabble and rubble on the other side of the town. They could relax on the roofs of their houses in the cool of the day and feel complacently satisfied with how things were working out for them.

And here I am sitting in my own house far away. I couldn't possibly be thought of as haughty or even rich. My neck is short. I can barely get the angle for a decent selfie. My shoes are ugly and don't make any noise. If I sit on my cool, shaded porch in the summer and look out over the town sloping away from me—not having to bother, just at the moment, with all the muck down below—it doesn't make me a bad person. Obviously, this verse is about somebody else—maybe you.

I am the very picture of humility: putting everyone before myself, thinking of everyone and trying to make them more comfortable. I don't defraud the poor. All the feasts that I keep are with a true heart. I never just go through the motions.

The Vineyard

He dug it and cleared it of stones, and planted it with choice vines; he
built a watchtower in the midst of it, and hewed out a wine vat in it; and
he looked for it to yield grapes, but it yielded wild grapes.
ISAIAH 5:2

The hill slopes away into an idyllic, green valley. As you round up and over and stop, surveying the land before you, you catch your breath at the stunning view, the rays of the sun glinting over neatly planted rows of gnarly, ancient vines. A low stone wall at the base of the hill circles up, and you turn and catch sight of a snug stone house protected by a tall tower, brooding over that sublime scene. It is serene, tranquil, perfect.

You couldn't possibly afford this land, this vineyard, this view, the wine yielded from all those grapes. Whoever owns it must be so fortunate, so happy.

But you blink. As twilight falls you strain your eyes to that someone has come along and spoiled everything. The grapes have gone sour, rotten. The wall is crumbling and has been torn down in some places. The house and the tower are actually in ruins. Their beauty is marred, scarred, spoiled, wrecked.

It's you. You are the vineyard. Your heart, your mind, your soul. You have yielded only wild, spoiled grapes. And the tragedy of your fall is great. If only something, or someone, could come and restore this once exquisite landscape.

ISAIAH 5

Ouch

And he touched my mouth and said: "Behold, this has touched your lips;
your guilt is taken away, and your sin atoned for."
ISAIAH 6:7

Just like he is love—which is a lot easier for me to be excited about—God
is definitely holy. But what is "holy" anyway? Aren't all the things that we
like and do already holy?

Isaiah might have had this lackadaisical attitude before he went to the
temple on that dreadful day. He wasn't unused to being there, since he
was someone allowed to go in past the barrier meant to keep out all the
congregation of the people. There was the lampstand, and the table for
the bread, the place to burn incense. No chairs, of course, because the
work of atonement wasn't ever finished. It's not like Isaiah was invited in
to sit down and put his feet up.

It didn't seem to be an unusual moment. Except that once he got in,
the familiar sense of stillness melted away and Isaiah found himself truly
in the presence of God—a God who is so holy that Isaiah felt himself coming apart at the seams. "Holy, Holy, Holy," a complete amount of holiness,
resounded from the rafters. Isaiah was desperate for a cure, for some alien help to stop him from being swept away. Which turned out to be a fiery
coal, burning hot from the altar, to touch his lips and cleanse his mouth.

God is perfectly holy and you are not. But in his great love he always
provides a remedy—a way for you to know him—if you can bear it.

The Great Light

The people who walked in darkness have seen a great light; those who dwelt in a land of deep darkness, on them has light shone.
ISAIAH 9:2

I like to surf around the internet, judging badly-lit houses and the people who don't arrange and layer their lighting the way I would. "Humph," I sniff, "I wouldn't put that sconce there. I would recess that. That corner is too dark." But then, and this is so upsetting, people visit my house and I can tell they are annoyed by the lighting. They come into my kitchen and, when I turn my back, surreptitiously, as if I won't notice, flip on the overhead light. And then I have to wait until they wander into another room before I flip it off again. For heaven's sake, I have carefully arranged my kitchen lamps so that the counters are only illuminated enough to see what I am doing, but not so much that you can see all the dirt.

Isaiah says "the people" who walked in darkness have seen a great light. And you might be tempted to think that "they" are other people, the ones who have bad kitchen lighting, or are in some other way wicked. But don't kid yourself—"the people" are you. You walk around in the dark. Your eyes are accustomed to the dim, dirt-hiding illumination. There's just enough light that you can carry on, but not enough to see what is actually wrong. The Light, because you are in darkness, is for you. It's going to be such fun, all that light that can't be switched off, no matter how hard you try.

The Violence

The wolf shall dwell with the lamb, and the leopard shall lie down with the young goat, and the calf and the lion and the fattened calf together; and a little child shall lead them.

ISAIAH 11:6

Show me a little boy, and I will show you a child who longs to be *this* child. Though I constantly preached a gospel of peace and kindness, my two sons were always ready to stick their hands down any kind of hole "to see what would happen" or to rejoice over one animal devouring another. What is more wonderful than a lion eating another creature, especially a goat or a lamb? It would be so disappointing if all the animals lay down together without any blood or gore.

But this child—not any child, but *the* child, the Promised One, the hope of the world—did not have an ordinary thirst for blood. This child would be one who was willing, once grown, to absorb our violence into himself, in his own flesh. He came peacefully, stretching out his hands to a devouring, angry world, and offering himself as the kind of lasting peace that doesn't just stop brutality but remakes the inclination of every creature, man or beast.

It is the only way, this perfect atonement for the world, that true peace— between lion and lamb, between man and God—can be accomplished.

In the meantime, the lust for blood, and the lust for war, lives on even in the most tender-hearted child.

ISAIAH 11, 12

151   Babylon

Therefore all hands will be feeble, and every human heart will melt.
ISAIAH 13:7

It is always important, when reading the Bible, to consider the context of the passage. When you're flying along and read "go and do thou likewise," you should stop and see what's going on. Is it a story about someone? Is it a universal command? Is it a description of something? Who is talking and to whom? Also, you should factor in your own confirmation bias, where you only see the bits that make you feel happy about who you already are. Even when you have answered all these questions and done all this work, a lot of it will fly right over your head. You should still try though.

So anyway, this chapter is great because it's about the destruction of Babylon—wicked, terrible Babylon. Babylon who snatches the babies from their mothers and dashes them against the rocks, who rapes the women, who slaughters the men, who roams over the whole earth destroying everything. God will judge these wicked people. Everything they did to the nations that surrounded them God will do to them. The people of Israel sit up and cheer. This is the kind of prophecy they can get on board with. It is just and right for him so to do.

Of course, Isaiah also prophesied that, much later, someone would come not only to show Israel *her* own wickedness, her own evil, but to take her place in the gruesome judgment of death that should have been hers.

But if that thought makes you unhappy, just read this chapter several times and don't bother with any of the others.

The Trusting

"You keep him in perfect peace whose mind is stayed on you, because he trusts in you."

ISAIAH 26:3

I know this is quoted by people trying to be comforting, but every time I hear it, I shudder. It feels like a taunting accusation. Hey you! If you only trusted God more, he would give you His awesome, perfect peace! Too bad you're such an untrusting wretch! No peace for you!

Curiously, though, this single verse is stuck inside two long chapters about the resurrection of the dead, about how God will not only swallow up death for those he loves, but about what it will be like for them and him while they wait for him to do it. It's not an "if-then." It's not a challenge. It's not God throwing back in my face how little I trust him.

I'd actually sort of like it to be "if-then." If I do this thing for God, then he will be obligated to do for me what I want, or think I need. Whereas trust ruins the whole plan. Trust means sitting around, be it with cheerful peace of mind or nail-biting anxiety, waiting long past the moment you thought you could endure anything, saying over and over, "God hasn't forgotten," and then standing up and carrying on as if everything is really fine. The "perfect peace" in which he keeps you might feel tumultuous and awful or like being blown along by the wind past all your troubles, or sometimes both at the same time. It's only afterward, when everything *is* fine, that you discover you needn't have chewed off your nails.

Here a Little, There a Little

And yet the word of the LORD will be to them precept upon precept, line upon line, line upon line, here a little, there a little, that they may go, and fall backward, and be broken, and snared, and taken.

ISAIAH 28:13

Sometimes the stupidity of other people is almost unbearable. This is the case when you are trying to explain something to someone who has already made up his mind, or made her plans, and refuses to see why those plans are impossible. But it is more usual when you are trying to say anything to a child.

I've gone through the same pile of books with six children, and there comes a moment in every school day when the children look at me blankly and forget everything they previously knew. In which case I set my jaw and begin to speak louder, slower, and with a heap of anger. This is also the case when I tell them to clean their rooms, or anything really. Almost everything I say is met with blank unknowing.

Yet the word of the Lord is even worse, mostly because he is God, but also because, as God, he is eminently understandable. And yet we persist, generation after generation, in not understanding, in looking away from the page altogether. Alright then, says God, I'll say it really slow and loud, with my jaw clenched, because for real, if you don't listen, you will fall backward and smack your head and not recover.

ISAIAH 28, 29

154 Going Home

And the ransomed of the Lᴏʀᴅ shall return and come to Zion with singing;
everlasting joy shall be upon their heads; they shall obtain gladness and
joy, and sorrow and sighing shall flee away.
ISAIAH 35:10

I used to sing this in boarding school. It was one of the many songs we sang that I can't find online or anywhere because they were peculiar to that institution. I would sit in the sea of other children, pretty miserable about being there, wanting desperately to go home, missing my parents, wishing I were dead, but also curious about what would be for supper and itching to get out of church and go run around. The words of these lines would waft over and cut through my own misery and loneliness.

That "sorrow and sighing"—those uninvited guests insinuating themselves unbidden, tormenting me in the middle of some pleasure or distraction—would some far off day "flee away" never to return was an astonishing thought.

What is "everlasting joy?" I would wonder as we sang, my head drooping as I contemplated the everlasting Sunday hours stretching out before me. Lunch on Sunday meant sitting in family groups rather than all mixed in, but I had no family—no brothers or sisters. I had to fill in other people's tables, sitting with my legs dangling, locked in helpless grief, wishing I could be with my own parents.

But eventually, inevitably really, because God owns time and the souls of those he buys back, you are let go, you run home, all the way back, singing boisterously as the scenery flies by.

ISAIAH 34, 35

Going Forward

A voice cries: "In the wilderness prepare the way of the LORD; make straight in the desert a highway for our God."

ISAIAH 40:3

The wilderness has always been a tetchy subject for the people of Israel, tragically under the impression as they were that once they left the land of Egypt—and with it the succulent leeks, onions, garlic, and even melons— they would go straight into the Promised Land. They thought this because God *told* them they were going to the Promised Land. But, like children, they couldn't imagine how much time it would take to get there. And they didn't think that God would demand anything from them on the way.

But God did want something from them. He wanted them to love, honor, and worship him; even just a little bit of affection would have been a start. But the farther they went from Egypt, the more irritated and grumbly they became. And so, God led them around in a circle—not the circle of life, but the circle of death—to die, one by one.

But now, now the wilderness will not be a circle. It will no longer be a winding road leading far away from the longed-for destination. No, the wilderness will be a straight shot. You start out, and you walk in a straight line, and you arrive. There's a voice calling you. Listen to it, go straight toward it. Don't get distracted and do a lot of terrible things on your way there.

I Know

> *"For I am the LORD your God, the Holy One of Israel, your Savior. I give*
> *Egypt as your ransom, Cush and Seba in exchange for you. Because you*
> *are precious in my eyes, and honored, and I love you, I give men in return*
> *for you, peoples in exchange for your life."*
>
> ISAIAH 43:3—4

God is talking to Israel here. He has gone, and will go, to the depths and heights and ends of the earth to be with Israel. It's so awkward, embarrassing really, because Israel, all this time, has stretched out the distance between herself and God. She has formalized it, made it more of an arranged affair than an intimate one. She is not in love with God. She doesn't mind if he hangs around, but on the whole his attention is intrusive, bothersome. His incredible declaration here, "I love you," is met with, "Thank you," and sometimes, "I know."

The trouble is, do you really want to be up close against such an intense, such an open, such a boldly declared love? You don't get to have a lot of say about its terms. If you try to formalize and distance the relationship, you will yet be persuaded, hounded even, by a jealous lover.

Or so Israel thought. There wasn't a lot to be gained by letting God come close—close enough to hear, close enough to see, close enough to brush by in a crowd. And, let's not fuss around, so also with you and me.

Nothing to Look At

For he grew up before him like a young plant, and like a root out of dry ground; he had no form or majesty that we should look at him, and no beauty that we should desire him.

ISAIAH 53:2

How like him. If it's not something fancy to look at, why would I bother? I am so easily enticed by striking, shiny, pretty things. I've spent more time thinking about the paint color of my living room, and the arrangement of my furniture than, tragically, wondering about the beauty and majesty of God. How like him to come in such a form that I would not be visually or aesthetically compelled by him. How like him to come in such a way that I would have to work to understand.

You might say his rough, unappealing form is like Scripture itself. There isn't anything about it that initially compels you to take another look. You gaze at the jumble of words, you try to untangle the line of David, you try to sort through the many occasions of violence and disaster . . . it is a great puzzle. And most of the time, it just isn't that captivating. You, like so many on the average Galilean hillside—listening to a plain-faced, plain-talking, plain-dressed man—keep wondering why you're still there, why you're still listening.

It's not because of you, obviously. It's somebody else, some greater thing, holding you in place, giving you persistence when you have never persisted before.

ISAIAH 52, 53

Not My Idea

"For my thoughts are not your thoughts, neither are your ways my ways, declares the LORD."

ISAIAH 55:8

You could not have made a more understated declaration of something so basic and true in the whole history of the world. You wouldn't do *anything* the way God would do it. You probably wouldn't create anything. You certainly wouldn't let Satan in to wreck it. You would make sure that Adam and Eve didn't completely blow it for the rest of their offspring. You wouldn't let babies die or oceans rise. You wouldn't let there be war. You would make sure that everyone, particularly the lowliest, had clean water. Let's be honest, there wouldn't *be* any lowly, least of all you. No, that's right, the thoughts of God, nor also his ways, are not even a little bit like yours.

Having acknowledged this unremarkable, though heartbreaking fact, move forward ever so slightly and consider that maybe, since God isn't like you, you could wait and discover why it is that he is doing things the way he is.

I mean, to make another disappointing observation, you didn't make yourself. You don't control the rain. You don't make the seeds grow. You didn't put anything in the sky. How should you know what a being so much greater than you is going about? You can't know, but you can try to learn, by continuing to toil through that book, the Bible.

How Bright, Exactly?

The sun shall be no more your light by day, nor for brightness shall the
moon give you light; but the Lord will be your everlasting light, and your
God will be your glory.
ISAIAH 60:19

Every so often I try to imagine that heavenly realm, where, with all the angels and hosts of heaven, I will sit. I mean, hopefully I will sit. I'm hoping at least in eternity to have a few moments to sit down, to not always be running around picking up Legos and wiping off the kitchen table. As I'm doing all that, I try to imagine what it will be like not to need any light, either bright or dim, because the Lord himself will be my light, and God will be my glory.

It sounds nice, of course, and I'm definitely looking forward to it, but, well, what will it be like? Because part of the pleasure of the light is the darkness that it pushes back—the way the light glows against the shadow. A room without any darkness, what kind of room is that? The only rooms I know of without any darkness are big-box stores. Believe me, wandering around a massive warehouse with florescent lighting doesn't really sound like heaven.

In this matter, I am going to have to go with trust. I am going to just hope, and even pray, that though I cannot see it yet with my own eyes, it will be wonderful to be in the light of the Lord all the time. Not just spiritually, but physically also.

ISAIAH 58, 59, 60

The Wedding Clothes

I will greatly rejoice in the LORD; my soul shall exult in my God, for he has
clothed me with the garments of salvation; he has crowned me with the
robe of righteousness, as a bridegroom decks himself like a priest with a
beautiful headdress, and as a bride adorns herself with her jewels.
ISAIAH 61:10

God understands the terrible stress you endure, trying to figure out what on earth to wear. It's not like it doesn't matter. You can't go around with nothing on. Some try, of course, but it puts everybody else in such an awkward position, having to be with someone not wearing enough.

No, clothes do matter. Because not only is your soul broken by sin, but your body also. God's first action, when Adam and Eve rebelled, was to clothe them—taking on to himself, though much later, their nakedness. Every time you put something on you are getting to participate in Adam and Eve's futile, anxious quest to cover their own nakedness and shame. Of course, you struggle. Likewise, you should be pleased when some article of clothing works out perfectly and your dress has pockets—that part is about God's provident mercy.

And, of course, if you happen to be in the way of getting married, you should spend a large portion of your anxiety on What You—and everybody else—Will Wear. If you have to go to a wedding, you might as well make the best of it and put on something nice.

It's not just vanity, it is yet another glimpse of that most gorgeous garment, the Lord's own righteousness.

The Basket of Broken Things

"For behold, I create new heavens and a new earth, and the former things shall not be remembered or come into mind."

ISAIAH 65:17

We moved house a few years ago. We packed up not just the things we liked, but the stuff we hated as well. In the new house we slowly sorted through it all and began to throw away the garbage. Not that I would accumulate garbage . . . Oh whatever, that's totally what I did. Anyway, a bunch of pretty things that I did love were broken in the move. A pair of Luxembourg espresso cups, some wedding china, the little glass Delft souvenir clogs. I gathered all the remains into a basket and found that I was often carrying it around, trying to figure out what to do with it. Eventually I shoved it in the cupboard in the pantry. It remains there still, though rearranged into a new bigger basket as I have continued to add every nice piece of glass we have ever broken.

I know it's all going up in a ball of fire. I know I can't keep it forever. I know that there's something better, and I would probably be fine if I let it all go. What gets me, as I periodically sort through it, feeling sad about all the loss, is the idea that I won't even remember the former things, they won't even come to my mind. But so great will be the glory of the new things, so lovely will be the new earth and the new heavens, that it will utterly absorb my attention. I won't have time to wander around with my basket of broken things.

Dismay

"But you, dress yourself for work; arise, and say to them everything that I commanded you. Do not be dismayed by them, lest I dismay you before them."
JEREMIAH 1:17

Obedience isn't easy—just to say on the page something that you knew already. But imagine, for a sad, terrible minute, that you are Jeremiah. He discovers, by the mouth of the Lord, that he has been formed, chosen from before the foundation of the world, to do an epically unpleasant job. He's going to have to go around saying the very words of God to a lot of people who are not even a little bit interested in hearing them. He is going to speak, and everybody is going to want him to be quiet. He is going to do God's will, and everyone is going to want him to stop it.

It won't be without some consolation. God assures Jeremiah that he loves him. That everything, eventually, is going to be okay. And that consolation shouldn't be overlooked. The only way that anyone does anything that God wants is because he, or she, knows that God is there, that it really is his voice, that God really does have a plan for the future.

Still, the call, for Jeremiah at least, comes with a terrible warning. "Do not be dismayed, lest I dismay you before them." Although it does seem, from Jeremiah's great moaning through the whole book, that maybe God relaxed this strict imperative. Dismay, indeed, is written in every line.

163 Worth a Shot

"And I will give you shepherds after my own heart, who will feed you with knowledge and understanding."

JEREMIAH 3:15

I knew a man once who wanted to be a policeman because it was the quickest way *he* knew of to become rich. Everyone who heard his desire was not the least bit surprised because bribery was how the job of policing got done. That was long ago and far away, but we all know that some people exploit the people in their care and profit at their expense.

Sometimes that corruption becomes part of the established order, and there's nothing that anyone can do to get rid of it, short of breaking the institution or society apart and trying to start over. Except that when you do that, the new invention is still populated by all the people who made such a mess of the last one. Then all the people in whatever kind of organization it is start blaming the leaders—call them "shepherds" on a whim—trying to divorce themselves from any culpability they had as a participant. Shepherd and people—oh lets go all in and call them "sheep"—together can't reform or mend anything and so they blame each other, and make hash of everything. The sheep bite the shepherd, and the shepherd slaughters and devours the sheep. There's no way out.

Or rather, there is a way out. The person in charge could be, what's that called? . . . transformed. The shepherd could have a "heart," a will, a mind, a whole person reoriented so entirely that, rather than blaming and then eating the sheep, he taught, instructed, and fed the sheep with the pleasant and kindly hope of the actual truth.

JEREMIAH 3, 4

When He Called

"And now, because you have done all these things, declares the LORD, and when I spoke to you persistently you did not listen, and when I called you, you did not answer . . ."
JEREMIAH 7:13

I don't know if I've mentioned it before, but if something goes wrong—if you are unhappy, if circumstances arrange themselves badly, if you are filled with grief, if you have done the wrong thing and need to turn around—the absolute best thing to do is fall down on the floor and cry out from the depths of yourself to God. If you cry to him, he will always come and help you, one way or another.

But what of the moment when *he* calls to *you*? What happens when God, not out of need, but out of desire, calls to you? What if you hear his voice? What will you say?

Israel heard God calling her over and over and she wearied of the call. She wished he would stop it. She didn't listen to what she heard. She scrupulously ignored him.

It's true, the call of God comes with conditions. It means the abandonment of yourself and your plans for him and his. It means giving him your whole attention. Like Israel, you might be inclined to stop up your ears, to beg him to be quiet. You might pretend he is talking to other people. Unfortunately, when God calls, he is not satisfied with no answer. He doesn't go away quietly. He only gets louder, and then finally the persistent call becomes downright unpleasant.

Delicious

Your words were found, and I ate them, and your words became to me
a joy and the delight of my heart, for I am called by your name, O LORD,
God of hosts.
JEREMIAH 15:16

Imagine for a moment that you're God and you've prepared a most glorious feast. Everything is cooked to perfection. The flavors, the colors, the symmetry—all delight and refresh every sense. The feel of the linen tablecloth under your hand, the crystal under your fingertips, the aroma of food and wine, all of it transport you by their splendor.

You set this beautiful gift, because you are insane, in front of several unruly, obnoxious children and they do not notice the care, the attention, the work. Indeed, *they* do not care. The tastes are too complicated for them to understand, the china too delicate for their immature touch.

But then, that poor prophet—your beleaguered and obedient servant—stumbles in and you make him sit down and take a little wine and taste everything. He leans back in his chair and you look in his face, anxious to see what he will say. And then, by grace alone, his eyes light up and he heaves a happy sigh.

It might be the way you, not being God in this case, feel when you walk the long road down the church aisle to stand, or kneel, and put your hands out, to be given a bit of bread, to take a sip of wine, to take the Word of Life into your own self. As you walk, and then stand, and swallow something clicks into place. You taste some delicate delight, some rich consolation you had never imagined possible.

For You

O Lord, you have deceived me, and I was deceived; you are stronger than I, and you have prevailed. I have become a laughingstock all the day; everyone mocks me.
JEREMIAH 20:7

Far off from the day of Jeremiah, another man falls heavily to the ground. His face is contorted with spiritual and mental pain. Blood runs down from his brow. His hands twist in anguish as he grips the rock, steadying himself. He lies fallen, desperate, crying out for help. He prays. He implores God. He cannot look into the future with any solace or hope or desire or understanding. He would like to run away. He would like never to have been born. He, in the sweating, bleeding temple of his forehead, is carrying the entire weight of the world's rebellion, humanity's universal rejection of God. His body and spirit threaten to crack and break under the weight.

But this single man is stronger than any other, stronger than I, stronger than you. As he staggers under his burden, he becomes a laughingstock—the person who gathers all your embarrassment, all your shame, all the moments that could be used against you to make you small and bring you down.

The crowds jeer. What weakness. How foolish.

Are you also deceived? Have you not yet put the burden of yourself onto this man? He is passing by, but it is not yet too late.

Don't Push Your Luck

"When one of this people, or a prophet or a priest asks you, 'What is the burden of the LORD?' you shall say to them, 'You are the burden, and I will cast you off, declares the LORD."

JEREMIAH 23:33

It is a hassle to carry around someone who thinks she has it all together. It is an enormous chore to lug around someone who thinks he is operating under his own steam. "Why are you so tired?" the person might ask wonderingly as you struggle along under the heavy weight of her blind, misguided, imagined self-sufficiency.

Or, try dragging along a child who thinks he is walking, and making the flailing movements of someone walking, but is not actually walking. You struggle and wrestle and the child looks around at you, smiling happily, and asks you why you're panting and sweaty.

On the other hand, there's the child that leans in, that holds on. While she might be heavy, while it might be difficult to carry her, she is not the same kind of burden. To the one who says, "Please carry me," you can hardly deny such a request. But to the one who says, "What's your problem," to that one God says, "I'm done. I'm putting you down. I'm not carrying you anymore."

Except God, yea, even God, even when he says going to put you down, that he's done with you, when you turn around and run back to him, he will pick you up, however heavy and wretched you are, and carry you.

In that same year, in the seventh month, the prophet Hananiah died.
JEREMIAH 28:17

I don't know if you've given it any thought, but you could die at any moment. Mercifully, God is unlikely to let you know in advance. When you suffer from a terrible dream where you are running slowly from danger, as though through sand, and just as you are dying, you startle awake all panicked and unhappy—that's not God letting you know ahead of time of your own imminent demise.

Except if you do something terrible, like incite an actual rebellion against God, and then hear from Jeremiah, God's actual prophet, that God is going to kill you. In that case, fear might be a rational response. Because fear might (although it didn't here) produce a change of heart: a desire not to die, a desire to repent and throw yourself on the mercy of God.

In other words, you can trust what God says. He always does what he says he's going to do. He doesn't change, he is only very, very, very patient. So if you were, for example, to read this book—not *this* book, but the Bible—and discover that you are a sinner in need of a savior, the first thing you should do is stop rebelling against that Savior and instead call out to Him him to save you. And when he calls your name, when you read that you are to repent and turn to him, it's an excellent idea to do that, because you never know, you might get another chance.

Awesome Miracles

"And no longer shall each one teach his neighbor and each his brother, saying, 'Know the LORD,' for they shall all know me, from the least of them to the greatest, declares the LORD. For I will forgive their iniquity, and I will remember their sin no more."

JEREMIAH 31:34

If I've said a thing once, I've said it at least seven times. *Everything* I say I have to say too many times to even count. Nobody can remember anything I say. And not just everybody else, I can't even remember what I just said myself. I ask a question and forget that I asked it, and forget to listen for the answer, and ask again as if I hadn't just. Nor can I remember what I am planning to do, even when I've written it down—even when I've kept it in mind all day. When it comes to the point of doing it, it slips from my mind.

God is always having to send prophets and preachers to remind his people to give a fig about him. Even then they don't listen.

The greatest possible miracle in all of creation, in all of the universe, is the moment when a person listens and knows and remembers God. It isn't the healing of the body. It isn't the sudden stopping of a car that was destined to hit someone. It isn't when you are about to drown in the ocean, and someone throws you a float. It isn't when the cancer drugs kick in and it turns out that you get to live a little bit longer. The biggest miracle of all was when you heard God and discovered that you wanted to go on hearing him.

What a Deal

"And I bought the field at Anathoth from Hanamel my cousin, and weighed out the money to him, seventeen shekels of silver."
JEREMIAH 32:9

God promised to destroy the land of Judah by the might of Nebuchadnezzar. Now it was finally time for it to happen. So of course, as the Babylonian army marched into town, God commanded Jeremiah to buy a field. What could be more practical than acquiring a piece of property in the most financially worthless nation in the whole world? But God isn't practical. He doesn't mind putting his servants and friends out and making their lives more difficult.

The fact is, the land isn't worthless. Its ruin is only temporary. It will be, for a little while, laid very low, hurt, and broken. It will lie fallow for a while. It will rest. It won't produce anything worth having.

But then, when everyone has gone on to other, more prosperous ventures, like a slow resurrection from the dead, what looked like a terrible business deal will turn out to be something beautiful and useful. Buying the land as the storm of destruction grows and darkens, while temporally foolish, nevertheless eternally illustrates the hope of God's promise.

Rather like how God, you know, purchases you in the midst of ruin and despair. Looks like a bad deal on his part, but it will turn out pretty well in the end. Something like that.

No Wonder No One Signs Up

Yet neither the king nor any of his servants who heard all these words was afraid, nor did they tear their garments.

JEREMIAH 36:24

I feel like, if God wants people to like him, he should make things lots easier for the people actually doing what he told them. Obedience, in other words, should produce actual physical safety and enough food to eat and relief from anxiety. It's the least he could offer if he wanted me on Team God. This is one reason why the whole book of Jeremiah is such a drag. Jeremiah is obedient. He does and says all that God tells him to. He doesn't even prevaricate or cower in the corner.

In this case, he dictates everything that God tells him to Baruch, who writes it out in columns and then takes it to the temple and reads it aloud (because Jeremiah has been banned from the temple). And then he, Baruch, is hauled off to read it for the palace and court, all of whom are horrified and feel they should tell the king—which they do, after sending Baruch off to get Jeremiah and go, the two of them, into hiding. When they take the scroll in to the king, the king hacks off the columns one by one as they are read out to him and burns them in his little firepot.

So, from his hiding place, Jeremiah has to write the scroll all over again, with additions about how bad it was to burn the first one, which was probably a real pain. I hate having to do something over again, after someone ruins it. Anyway, I feel like God could just be a lot nicer to Jeremiah.

Yuck

So they took Jeremiah and cast him into the cistern of Malchiah, the
king's son, which was in the court of the guard, letting Jeremiah down by
ropes. And there was no water in the cistern, but only mud, and Jeremiah
sank into the mud.

JEREMIAH 38:6

It's not at all unusual for leaders of countries and businesses and church-es to prefer to surround themselves with "yes-men." It can be tricky to announce bad news when everyone around the conference table wants to hear good news. How are the third quarter numbers? How is the minis-try doing? How are those negotiations going with that big international diplomatic effort? What's that? No one signed up to teach Sunday school? Are you serious? There's no money left? What do you mean that other country just developed a nuclear weapon? Come on, guys! We need to pull together as a team. Now whose fault is this? "Yours," the team whispers, but no one says it out loud.

Poor Jeremiah, he doesn't get to be the yes-guy. All he is allowed to say is no to the headstrong person bent on driving his tiny country into the very dust. But power is power, and Jeremiah, in consequence of his bad news, gets lowered into an abandoned cistern, a pit if you will. "And Jeremiah sank into the mud" has to be the most disappointing verse ever. Funny how no one remembers this verse when they are adopting the "hope and a future" one as a talisman for life.

Anyway, I feel like speaking truth to power is overrated. I hate being uncomfortable, and cold, and covered in muck.

It's Not Fair

. . . Ishmael the son of Nethaniah and the ten men with him rose up
and struck down Gedaliah the son of Ahikam, son of Shaphan, with
the sword, and killed him, whom the king of Babylon had appointed
governor in the land.

JEREMIAH 41:2

One of the most impossible ideas to penetrate the dim individual and collective minds of humankind is that the evil that befalls them might be
fair and right. I am so inclined to believe myself good that, when disaster
falls, I undertake the critical work of self-justification. It isn't right that
I should be injured in this way. Whoever has sinned (not me) should re-
mediate this terrible circumstance. This is not fair.

So thought Ishmael, royal son of Nethaniah. He could not imagine
that it could be right and fair for God to allow disaster to overtake Judah.
The king of Babylon had no business appointing a governor of his own
choosing. The king of Babylon was wicked to tear down the temple and
haul away Judah's aristocracy to his own court. All of Jeremiah's admo-
nitions that the people should obey this foreign power, that they should
honor Nebuchadnezzar, that those that stayed should settle down and
plant their vines seemed to Ishmael a great evil. Therefore he, incited
by the king of the Ammonites no less, took matters into his own hands
and murdered Gedaliah.

Those remaining fled to Egypt in fear, dragging Jeremiah along with
them. Jeremiah, who never ceased to call the people with the grating
voice of God's merciful judgment. Ah, well, it's too bad, especially since
everyone falls into this traitorous fault in one way or another.

It's Not Over Yet

*"You said, 'Woe is me! For the L*ORD *has added sorrow to my pain. I am weary with my groaning, and I find no rest.'"*

JEREMIAH 45:3

This *should* be where the book ends. Jeremiah warned Judah. The people—the king in particular—did not heed his warning. They were all either killed or carried off into captivity. The king of Judah watched his sons die and then had his eyes put out. That gruesome scene was the last thing he saw. Jeremiah elected to stay in Judah to support the appointed governor, Gedaliah. But Gedaliah was murdered and all the people again disregarded Jeremiah's word that they should submit to the king of Babylon. The few remaining people fled to Egypt, taking Jeremiah who warned them with each passing mile that they were doing the wrong thing. And so there he remained, in Egypt, awaiting the inevitable destruction of that country also by Babylon. Amen.

Unhappily for the beleaguered reader of the Bible, there are yet seven long chapters more, of the usual kind of prophecies that God breathes out: the repetitive, intimate poetry of a God who persists in talking, though no one listens.

You might think God is persecuting you, is making everything harder and more complicated than it needs to be. You might be discouraged by how, whenever you do something, something else unravels so that you never make any progress. Or worse, you might look at some exhausted Christian who goes from one misfortune to another and imagine that she is just bad and God is judging her. Whichever, it's fine to be depressed. This is seriously depressing.

JEREMIAH 43, 44, 45

Drink Up

"Babylon was a golden cup in the Lord's *hand, making all the earth drunken; the nations drank of her wine; therefore the nations went mad."*

JEREMIAH 51:7

Babylon, as you probably already know, isn't just an ancient place with gorgeous hanging gardens and a powerful king, who for one brief moment conquered the known world, whose history is intricately woven together with that of Judah. Though she is that, throughout Scripture she sprawls on her opulent couch as a type, a picture of a world in violent, drunken rebellion against God.

Babylon is opposed to Zion, the city of God. Zion, the beautiful woman whom the Bridegroom takes as a bride, but then finds that she is always running away to commit adultery with other lovers. Zion should abhor the wickedness of Babylon, and, indeed, in some moments, she does. But here, in desolation, Zion, the city of God, staggers and falls drunk, full of Babylon's rich, sickening wine.

And not just Zion—all the nations of the world adore and search after that golden cup. They will drink down, gasping for breath, never satisfied, their mouths full of the wickedness that she pours out.

I like to think of myself, sometimes, as living in Babylon, exiled, against my will. I try to make the best of it. I try to walk the line between contentment and conflict, between hating the world and loving the world, between temptation to drink of the cup of God's wrath, to stagger and fall, turning instead to grab the cup that God . . . well, I don't want to ruin the story. Suffice it to say that even Babylon as a place is not outside of God's grace.

JEREMIAH 51

Cancelled

And the king of Babylon struck them down and put them to death at Riblah
in the land of Hamath. So Judah was taken into exile out of its land.
JEREMIAH 52:27

One of my favorite TV programs features a foodie writer who traipses around the world tasting exotic foods. He often points out that one nation or civilization invading another is a boon for culinary development. Sure, a whole civilization was destroyed when explorers landed on the shores of South America, but look at the wonder and delight of the potato. And, of course, so many people still loath the French, but does anybody really hate their food? Not many. It's a delicious way to consider the manner in which humanity jostles across national lines precisely because it doesn't take into account the inevitable brutality of conqueror over vanquished.

Any student of ancient history might say, "Well, Israel pushed out the Philistines and the Moabites and all the people living there. It's their turn now." Except that God provides a different explanation for the destruction of one people by another people—at least in this ancient time. Now, of course, we should not be so sure.

If Israel had obeyed God when he put her in that narrow strip of land, pushing out the people before her, she would have been allowed to stay. God would have blessed her and given her all that she longed for. But she did not. She went searching for those other gods, those ideas, those delicious, exotic, forbidden dishes. And seriously, Jeremiah's commentary was not scintillating. No one tuned in. The ratings were terrible.

How lonely sits the city that was full of people! How like a widow she has become, she who was great among the nations! She who was a princess among the provinces has become a slave.

LAMENTATIONS 1:1

I live in a place where whole neighborhoods lie blighted, desolate, emptied of all the people who once enlivened the parks and houses and shops. This vibrant city succumbed to the vagaries of economic shifts beyond the control of all the people now gone. This is the place where people are "from." None of those people would ever choose to live here now. Worst of all, the leaving was slow. It happened over decades. The shadows of all the departed stalk the streets, dragging people like me down into a Sheol-like despair.

I, however, have nothing on Jeremiah's wrenching cry of desolation over the destruction of Jerusalem. Her imposing walls are crushed. The lovely narrow roads and alleys are full of rubble and blood. The trees have been hacked down and rooted up. So many people lie dead, with no one to bury or honor them. Everyone who was worth anything, who had any money or status, was carried off. There are only a few poor people left to pick up the pieces. Except that the devastation is so complete there aren't many pieces left to pick up.

Jerusalem was like a lovely woman who had everything she could ever need or want—husband, money, children, lavish house—and in a few minutes all she had is gone. Worst of all, it was through her own folly that ruin struck her down. Looking at her, prone, despoiled, unable to get up, you feel both pity and a sickening sense of justice.

The Steadfast Love

The steadfast love of the LORD never ceases; his mercies never come to an end; they are new every morning; great is your faithfulness. "The LORD is my portion," says my soul, "therefore I will hope in him."
LAMENTATIONS 3:22–24

In the midst of such ruin, such immeasurable loss, Jeremiah—probably because he has some practice—does not despair. He, though not Israel, knows God is faithful and kind. He loves God still.

That's the catch—if God takes everything away from you, can you love him? Most people don't love God even when he has given them everything. Though not "them" out there: even I often examine what God is holding out to me—himself—and recoil.

The "mercy" part, then, is a great stripping away, a having everything that you thought you needed and everything you wanted—including your own sense of yourself and what you are like and who you are—removed, sometimes gently, sometimes rather forcefully, and in its place God's own self established. The "great faithfulness," the "mercies" are being returned again and again into the hands of God who takes everything and replaces it with himself.

This is a hard love that never ceases. These mercies that go on every morning are intimately ruinous. The hope that you discover is devastating enough to set you outside the tempting reach of any paltry, worldly, idolatrous love.

The Lament

The hands of compassionate women have boiled their own children; they became their food during the destruction of the daughter of my people.
LAMENTATIONS 4:10

I hear a lot from Christians about the importance of "lament" as a spiritual discipline when terrible trials befall a community. After generations of thinking that the Church was on an upward trajectory toward glory, toward bringing about the kingdom of God on the earth, to look around and see only a handful of ash is, to put it mildly, disheartening. "How could this happen?" ask previously unengaged churchgoers. "We had such a great pastor!" or "We just built a multimillion-dollar building!" They look around and find hatred and animosity and idolatry entwined around the very soul of the community and recoil in horror. Then they embrace "lament" as a first step to fixing whatever has gone wrong.

And it's not for nothing that this book is called "Lamentations." Jeremiah stands back from his decades of work and catalogues the wrongs done by his people. He looks over his beloved city. He considers the immense sin that toppled walls once so strong, so virtuous, so gracious.

Of course, the first step to anything getting better is to feel bad about what has gone wrong. But that is only a rather small step, a slim volume wedged in between the record of all God's words to his people about what *he* thinks they should feel and do—which could be boiled down to actual repentance (saying sorry for real) and actual trust in the only one who can do anything to make it better (God).

The Burden

Like the appearance of the bow that is in the cloud on the day of rain, so was the appearance of the brightness all around. Such was the appearance of the likeness of the glory of the LORD. And when I saw it, I fell on my face, and I heard the voice of one speaking.
EZEKIEL 1:28

The prophets in the Bible did not just speak words into the sky, or to themselves, divorced from other people hearing and then reading what they said. They had to say these words to real people, to write them down in books that would be read right then. The double burden of seeing visions and hearing words and then having to deliver and translate those visions and words to others had to have been exhausting.

The glory of God is so immense, so bright, so overpowering that Ezekiel falls on his face. He can't stand up. And then he hears the voice. Not the kind of voice he would mistake for hunger, or the whispering of his own imagination. For everyone who endured God's voice, it was such an overwhelming communication that no mistake could be made. If it could have been mistaken, the prophets wouldn't have carried on for so many chapters and years. They would have quit and gone into the coffee bean roasting business.

Ezekiel has to begin walking the difficult way of the others, of Isaiah and Jeremiah, who were similarly undone in the presence of God. Be grateful you don't have to be a prophet. Be grateful you can read the words instead of hearing them.

Then I Ate

And he said to me, "Son of man, feed your belly with this scroll that I give
you and fill your stomach with it." Then I ate it, and it was in my mouth
as sweet as honey.

EZEKIEL 3:3

"Do you want a gummy bear?" I ask the little kids muscling their way
through the door into my Sunday school room. They always do. Who can
resist a little sugar so early in the morning? "The word of God is sweet,
like honey," I say, as they reach out their grubby hands. They look bemused, as well they should.

What happens when you eat anything—sweet or bitter, pleasant or
repulsive? Whatever it is, once you've swallowed it, will go all the way
down. It's very hard to get it back out on your own terms. Whatever you
eat has an exacting kind of power over you. It will make you well, or increase the sickness of your body. Never mind what it does to your mind
or emotional state.

"I love gummy bears," one fluffy little girl announces when I place a
golden bear in the palm of her hand. "Can I have more?"

"Come back next week," I say, "and have another."

Because, though you bite down on the word of God, though you im-
bibe the scroll, though you anxiously examine your insides to see what it
is doing to you, yet you cannot ever really be full. As long as it is there to
eat, your hunger for its sweetness will increase, until you finally look that
same Word in the face and have your fill.

EZEKIAL 2, 3, 4

Rooms of Pictures

> *Then he said to me, "Son of man, have you seen what the elders of the*
> *house of Israel are doing in the dark, each in his room of pictures? For*
> *they say, 'The LORD does not see us, the LORD has forsaken the land.'"*
>
> EZEKIEL 8:12

God drags Ezekiel around the countryside in a series of hideous and disturbing visions. He is made to see past the veil, past the appearance of the thing to its true reality.

A lot of people think that they would like to have this sort of experience. They want to "drill down" to the "essence" of something, to dispense with all the pretense and really get to the truth. I've even heard Christians say this, with all due sincerity.

That only works if you think God can be fooled, which most of us actually do think. *We* know. It is God who doesn't know and who will believe whatever we tell him.

All the people in this vision are carrying on the outward and visible worship of the temple, but, when the sacrifice is all burned up, they scuttle back into their private rooms where they have drawn up the pictures of what they really believe, the gods whom they really worship. Like going to church and singing and praying and smiling brightly, but all the while being eaten up with unconfessed, bitter anxiety for yourself, with a deep preoccupation of what you are owed and how you are going to get it. As if God can't see into that dark, supposedly hidden realm—as if he doesn't "look on the heart."

Who Even Knows

And as for their appearance, the four had the same likeness, as if a wheel were within a wheel.

EZEKIEL 10:10

Wheels within wheels, don't you know.

Try sketching a picture in the margin of what this amazing creature might have looked like. What in heaven is Ezekiel seeing? It seems like the power of English, I mean Hebrew, is failing him. For those who like to say that God is beyond our knowing, that he is a mystery, this little bit of imagery might be a support to them.

We can't really know what in the cosmos he's describing here—although, who's with me in hoping that there will be some kind of fantastical (to us) mythological being spinning around in heaven? But here's the thing: even though this chapter boggles the mind, in a literal way, all the words in all the other chapters of this book are pretty clear.

Stop worshiping yourself. Turn to the Lord that you might be saved. Before terrible events befall you. God is bigger than you. He has the power not only to bind up, but also to destroy. He has everything in his hand. His eyes—which seem to be sort of in the shape of wheels, which are also within wheels—are everywhere. Nothing is going to escape his notice.

Turn to him before it is too late.

184 An Anxiety Diagnosis

And say to the people of the land, Thus says the Lord GOD concerning the inhabitants of Jerusalem in the land of Israel: They shall eat their bread with anxiety, and drink water in dismay. In this way her land will be stripped of all it contains, on account of the violence of all who dwell in it.
EZEKIEL 12:19

One way you can know you are a sinner in need of a savior is to count up the number of times God commands you not to be anxious, and then time the intervals between rising tides of anxiety. Anxious when I awake, anxious when I fall asleep, and anxious when I cook dinner, I am not even diagnosably anxious. My anxiety is within the normal range.

The people of Israel had plenty to be anxious about. They didn't want to worship God, though they wanted to look like they did. While they were busy sacrificing in the temple, bringing their offerings as they had been commanded to do, they were also building lots of shrines to idols all over the place and worshiping at them. And idolatry is the most terrible kind of disobedience. And disobedience is the seedbed of anxiety. Don't ask me how I know.

Violence builds and threatens as the people try to find some way to avoid their impending judgment. But there was no way to avoid it. God always does what he's going to do. Which, if you think about it, is the ultimate remedy for all human anxiety.

War and Peace

*"Precisely because they have misled my people, saying, 'Peace,' when
there is no peace, and because, when the people build a wall, these
prophets smear it with whitewash . . ."*
EZEKIEL 13:10

Peace, it should come as no surprise, is better than war. It is better *not* to
fight with anyone than to have a problem with every single person who
happens by. If you think that's a crazy thing to say, well, you might think
about getting some help.

Trouble is, my idea of "peace" is comprised of two dubious requirements. First, everyone should leave me alone and let me do whatever I
like all the time without interfering with me and my plans. Second, it
would be great if we—you and I—could just not have any conflict. If I've
offended you, I wish you'd just pretend that I hadn't. If I build a big wall in
front of my house to keep you out, go ahead and paint a nice mural on it to
make yourself feel better. In this way, we can be "peaceful."

The actual name for this is not "peace" but "passive-aggression" with a
hefty dose, sometimes, of pure aggression. It's especially winsome when
leaders of countries, or pastors of churches adopt my two requirements
for world peace—leave me alone and stay away from conflict. For that to
work, you must constantly write sermons and deliver press releases about
how peaceful everything is. Because, you know, if you say something, especially on the internet, then it *is* true. You don't even have to look it up or
ask someone who might have more information or something.

EZEKIAL 13, 14

> *"And when I passed by you and saw you wallowing in your blood, I said to you in your blood, 'Live!' I said to you in your blood, 'Live!'"*
> EZEKIEL 16:6

There was once a baby, only a few minutes old, who was mutilated by whoever delivered her into the world, and then was placed, perhaps even by her mother, by the side of the road where she might be found, covered in her own blood. The writhing pains of birth ended, the mother returned to whatever kind of life she had before. Someone else chanced by within that very hour, and gathered the baby up, saving her life. Many people who came to know and love this child as she grew wondered at this strange happening. Why would someone do that? Was it some kind of superstitious act? Some kind of offering?

The child not only lived but grew strong and beautiful, astonishing everyone who had the good fortune to know her.

You might think this is just some retelling of the Scripture, but no, it really happened to that real child that I know. As you struggle along through the Scripture, wondering at God's anguished command to his people to "Live! Live!" you might think he is just being metaphorical, or even hysterical.

Except that, in some wretched sense, we are each that baby, cast by the road, covered in our own blood. The person who picks me up, and picks you up, and picks up your neighbor uses own blood—not like the blood of Abel crying murder from the ground, but his own—as the very cry to Live!

The Likeness

"Behold, everyone who uses proverbs will use this proverb about you: 'Like mother, like daughter.' You are the daughter of your mother, who loathed her husband and her children; and you are the sister of your sisters, who loathed their husbands and their children. Your mother was a Hittite and your father an Amorite."

EZEKIEL 16:44–45

Everyone thinks my daughter looks like me, even though really she doesn't. She looks like my husband. Her face is his, and her nose, and even her eyes. But because we often walk next to each other, matching our pace through the grocery store, or down the long aisle at church during communion, everyone thinks she looks like me. And acts like me. In some unfathomable way, she is an outward manifestation of who I am— my sins, my decisions, my humor, my sensibilities.

How ironic of the Father, who will perfectly reflect himself in the Son, to liken Israel (and by extension us) to our mother. And not a good mother. Not a comforting, faithful mother. This is the mother who tarts her daughter up and puts her on reality television. Her husband shuffles along behind, too weak to do anything.

The Father, after some hundred number of years, is going to send the Son to win a Bride. Yes, even a bride who is the daughter of such a mother. There, at the end of a long aisle, the bride's countenance will be transformed to reflect the glory of the groom. The "loathing" will be supplanted by joy.

The Branch

> *On the mountain height of Israel will I plant it, that it may bear branches*
> *and produce fruit and become a noble cedar. And under it will dwell*
> *every kind of bird; in the shade of its branches birds of every sort will nest.*
> EZEKIEL 17:23

A branch is broken off a tree and planted far away by itself. Its boughs stretch and strengthen. Each leaf unfurls in perfection and beauty. The tree itself produces fruit. It is so attractive that birds come, many different kinds of birds, to nest.

Long after Ezekiel sees this branch, this tree, this shade, these birds, a man will hold up a mustard seed and liken it to a kingdom. "The Kingdom of God is like this tiny seed," he will say. "It grows into the biggest and most beautiful of all trees. Birds will come from a far off and nest in its branches." The people around him will stare at him uncomprehendingly.

Later still, I will wander around my garden pulling up weeds, wondering why everything takes so long to grow, about the smallness of the seeds, about the glory of a tree that sways and bows in the wind, and yet is safe enough for a nesting bird to shelter her young.

Then I will go inside and wish that God would organize the trees and birds into neat categories instead of jumbling them all together, my mind inevitably straying to those haunting lines, "The tree of life my soul hath seen, laden with fruit and always green: the trees of nature fruitless be, compared with Christ the Apple Tree"—that single man hanging on a rough, bare tree gathering all the bright images in himself.

At Evening

"Sigh, but not aloud; make no mourning for the dead. Bind on your
turban, and put your shoes on your feet; do not cover your lips, nor eat the
bread of men." So I spoke to the people in the morning, and at evening my
wife died. And on the next morning I did as I was commanded.
EZEKIEL 24:17

Ezekiel's wife dies. God tells him that she's going to die, and then she
does die according to his word, and then Ezekiel is not to visibly mourn
or take any of the comfort associated with public grief. He is to go on as if
nothing significant happened.

"What on earth?" you say. "Can't he be sad?"

Ezekiel called her the delight of his eyes. She was precious to him. To
lose her would be death for himself. But no, he's not to show any external
signs of grief. And Ezekiel bends himself, painfully, to the will of God, to
the hand of the One who made him.

In this, Ezekiel is a sign, a picture of the coming judgment. Jerusalem
will be shattered. The idolatry of the people will be weighed. They will be
cast down into the pit. God will let the judgment fall without preventing
it. God will turn away his head and not mourn.

How could he? How could this possibly be good?

Only because much later, the Father, when his own child dies, will
again turn away. He will forsake his beloved for you, because he loves you.

Who Said Anything About Dying?

*Say to them, As I live, declares the Lord G*OD*, I have no pleasure in the death of wicked, but that the wicked turn from his way and live; turn back, turn back from your evil ways, for why will you die, O house of Israel?*
EZEKIEL 33:11

How on earth should I know? This must be a rhetorical question.

But also, if anyone bothered to answer, which they won't because why would they, the answer would be, "What are you talking about? We are not going to die. We are fine. There is no problem here. Furthermore, who are these 'wicked' of whom you speak?" That's a loose summation of the Scriptures to this point: "I don't want you to die," says God, and all the people answer, "Who said anything about dying?" Round and round in a circle for long stretches of human history.

The first step in recovery, as everyone knows, is admitting that you have a problem. If the doctor tells you that you are dying, and you argue with ti-tanic measures of hysteria that you are not, in fact, dying, then of the two of you, you are the crazy one, not the doctor. Your anger with the healer, your rushing around trying to convince people that he is "super negative" and "mean" are not only not impressive but will also not heal you.

Until the ill and perishing person can see the kindness of the physician, can glimpse his willingness and ability to do whatever it takes to heal and to save, can see the sudden threatening horror of death, there isn't any hope. The doctor—in this case God—tears his hair out in maddened frustration. Seriously, you would too if you had to deal with someone that obtuse.

The Shepherd

"And I will set up over them one shepherd, my servant David, and he shall feed them: he shall feed them and be their shepherd."

EZEKIEL 34:23

David is long dead. David has disintegrated into the dust and his bones and flesh are no more. David is but a nostalgic memory to anybody beating his sheep, trying to get them to go into the safety of the pen at night, exhausted and annoyed by how hard it is to find decent pasture.

So, who is David here? What is God talking about? Who is this shepherd who feeds the sheep and cares for them? Is David going to rise from the dead? Or reincarnate? And if so, that is weird.

Or could this be the Good Shepherd, the perfect Shepherd, coming in the lineage and household of David? Is this the One who will lay down his life for the sheep? Will he call them each by name, and lead them out in safety to find pasture? Will he bring them to clear, calm water? Will the sheep actually listen to him instead of to the voice of a stranger? Will he guard and keep the sheep so that none of them perish?

It could be, I guess. I mean, I seriously hope so. There are so many fake, lying shepherds trying to steal and devour the sheep. So many declare that the Bible is so hard to understand that this could be any random person.

Don't listen to them, little sheep. Don't follow them. Listen for the voice of the true Shepherd, and when he calls, obey him.

The Streams of Living Water

Then he brought me to the back door of the temple, and behold, water was issuing from below the threshold of the temple toward the east (for the temple faced east). The water was flowing down from below the south end of the threshold of the temple, south of the altar.

EZEKIEL 47:1

It's so strange how Moses all those years ago had to strike the rock. When he struck it, water gushed out to quench the desperate thirst of the people in the wilderness. Later on, Moses was supposed to speak to the rock, but he got angry and struck it, and struck it again, and so wasn't allowed to go into the Promised Land.

Now, all this time later, water is "issuing" forth, flowing right out of the temple.

Far off from this moment, a man will stand up at the very moment a chalice of clear water is being carried up from the pool of Siloam below, to be poured out over the altar, and he will cry loudly so that everyone can hear him, "If anyone thirsts, let him come to me and drink. Whoever believes in me, out of his heart will flow rivers of living water."

It's strange how the human heart is like a rock that must be struck open. It's perplexing that a man could be likened both to a rock *and* to the living water. It will be so astonishing that when he gives up his spirit and is stabbed in the side with a spear, that water will flow from his side.

EZEKIAL 39:25–40:4, 47:1–48:35

Text of Terror

So the steward took away their food and the wine they were to drink, and
gave them vegetables.
DANIEL 1:16

He did this, horrifyingly, because they *asked* him to. They made an actual
request to have all the rich, luxurious delicacies of the court, including
the wine and the meat, be taken away and in their place be given plain
water and vegetables—hopefully *at least* with a sprinkle of salt and a drizzle of olive oil.

Here's the trouble about food, though, and why these young men are so
remarkable. Whenever anything bad happens to me, I'm inclined to eval-
uate my food opportunities as a way of emotionally coping with whatever
bad thing I feel is happening. It is a quick step into the hidden belief that
I am "owed" whatever it is that I am consuming.

These young men didn't want to eat anything that would defile them.
They didn't want to drink wine, a portion of which had been poured out
on the ground before some Babylonian god. They didn't want to eat the
richly spiced meat delivered directly from some shrine. They wanted
their inward hearts, the calories flowing in their blood, the very contents
of their stomachs to be true to the God they knew had come with them
all this way, to the very table prepared for them in the presence of their
enemies. I mean, grass and water are biblical I guess—the food of helpless
sheep. Blech.

You Could Try to Pray

. . . and [Daniel] told them to seek mercy from the God of heaven con-
cerning this mystery, so that Daniel and his companions might not be
destroyed with the rest of the wise men of Babylon.

DANIEL 2:18

God didn't send the people away from Judah into captivity without a plan to bring them back. Nor did he send them away alone. God goes with the people as they are spewed out of their true home. When they arrive in a far-off country where they don't know the language or the people or the food, he provides for them. They build houses and plant gardens and vines and attempt to be content.

And God raises up a prophet, and leaders who will listen to his voice. But this prophet, Daniel, isn't going to speak the words of God just to the people of Judah. His words will also be for his captors, for the strangers who have torn him out of his homeland.

Daniel finds himself facing certain death along with all the other "wise" people of Babylon. He has to fling himself on the mercy of God to be saved. And also, he asks his friends to pray for him.

Sometime, if you are in a tight spot, you might ask some of the people who love you to pray for you, that God will provide a way out of your trouble. It's one idea anyway.

DANIEL 2

Small Gods

*King Nebuchadnezzar made an image of gold, whose height was sixty
cubits and its breadth six cubits. He set it up on the plain of Dura, in the
province of Babylon.*

DANIEL 3:1

So, here's a little tip. As much as you love yourself—taking the tempera-
ture of your feelings every morning, pondering your mood as you lie upon
your bed at night, arranging the feelings and plans of everyone within
your realm so that they daren't hassle you—one way you can still be better
than this guy by not actually making a golden statue of yourself, setting
it up in the corner, and then compelling your subjects to bow down and
worship it.

Granted, this poor idolater is the king of the known world. He is
stuck in one of those whatchamacallums, echo chambers, where only his
own voice resounds back at him. He probably didn't start out trying to
be an egomaniac. It's the sort of thing that can—and often does—happen
to anyone. You slowly drown out anyone who has the power to contradict
you, and then even the people who see things only slightly differently
become intolerable.

The trouble is, the only difference between you and Nebuchadnezzar
is the extent of your realm. Maybe your kingdom is comprised only of you.
But maybe you have a husband, or a wife, or a child, or a dog. If you are
ruling over them—in golden, blind comfort—it might be wise to stop and
see if you can hear some other voices, perhaps even the voice of God, saying, "Stop it."

DANIEL 3:1–7

The Fire

He answered and said, "But I see four men unbound, walking in the
midst of the fire, and they are not hurt; and the appearance of the fourth
is like a son of the gods."
DANIEL 3:25

It is the fashion nowadays to promise good things to people who decide to
"accept Jesus." Having trouble in your marriage? Poor? Sick? All you need
is to have enough of the right kind of faith and all that bad stuff will disappear. Too bad this little story completely destroys that kind of promise.

These young men were the only people in the room not committing
idolatry. Everyone else was bowing down to the big golden statue as if it
were God. Of course, bowing down before this statue was a small way of
bowing down to the self. You worship something that's not God because
you see a reflection in it, some spark of yourself you want to keep alive.
But three young men said, "No." And look at their reward. They were
bundled up and flung into the fire.

Now, I know a miracle occurred and their lives were spared, but—and
it is a big one—they didn't know that there was a miracle coming to spare
them a horrible death. The miracle of belief had already happened, and it
was enough; they were satisfied, they were willing to die.

A fourth man comes and walks around in the fire with them. That same
man, when you are in a hot place because of how much you love God—
when the whole world is determined to kill and destroy you—he will come
and be with you. He will be so close that you will have courage to endure.

DANIEL 3:8–4:37

We Might as Well All Be Changed

*Then they came near and said before the king, concerning the injunc-
tion, "O king! Did you not sign an injunction, that anyone who makes
petition to any god or man within thirty days except to you, O king,
shall be cast into the den of lions?" The king answered and said, "The
thing stands fast, according to the law of the Medes and Persians,
which cannot be revoked."*

DANIEL 6:12

If you ever get to be in charge of a whole country, be sure to make it possible for laws and edicts to be revoked. Making a law against changing your
mind is, to put it mildly, insane. What are you, you human king? Are you
God that you don't need to change your mind?

That's right, God doesn't need to change his mind. All the people who
are waiting for God to get better, to change and become nicer, to evolve
into something more like them are wasting their precious time. Which is
more sensible? For you, a human king, or queen, or grocery store clerk,
or mother, or anybody really, to dig in and decide you can't change—but
that God must?

If you answer wrongly, you might go ahead and build that statue after
all. God doesn't change. We are the ones who are commanded to change.
If you love God, who doesn't change, and he tells you to do something, go
ahead and do it, even if it means being thrown to lions. Because another
thing that can change is your body—from one that can be torn apart to one
that can't. Change: it's practically always a good thing.

DANIEL 5, 6

He Was Always There

"As I looked, thrones were placed, and the Ancient of Days took his seat; his clothing was white as snow, and the hair of his head like pure wool; his throne was fiery flames; its wheels were burning fire."

DANIEL 7:9

When Daniel wasn't busy helping the rulers and kings of Babylon to not be so awful, when he wasn't praying and getting in trouble for praying, when he wasn't instructing the magi about God and his plans and his Scriptures, he was sometimes troubled out of a well-deserved rest by disturbing and terrifying visions.

Some of those terrifying visions included the numbering of days until God himself would walk into the word to save it. Beasts with horns and wings and teeth crowded into his mind, leaving him spent and exhausted. A saga of a male goat with a horn that had to be broken shattered his peace. And then there came a vision of one like a Son of Man, who was and is and is to come. This luminous person came and was presented before the Ancient of Days and was given everlasting dominion and glory and a kingdom, that everyone should serve him.

Here is no dumb idol, no statue, no marbleized figure, no malleable lump of clay to reflect something inside of the human person. Here is the glory of God, from before the foundation of the world.

If you feel like bowing down and worshiping someone, this would be the One.

199 What Wondrous Love is This?

*At the beginning of your pleas for mercy a word went out, and I have
come to tell it to you, for you are greatly loved. Therefore consider the
word and understand the vision.*

DANIEL 9:23

It can be too easy—mostly because of the exciting stories and heroic acts
of God in the first half of this book—to miss the peculiar life of prayer that
sustained but also troubled Daniel.

I won't lie. Prayer is usually my last resort. It's the thing I try after
I've gone through a hidden, internal journey of despair. I get some bad
news or an email I don't know how to answer, or am inconvenienced or
something, and this occasion is the launch pad into first horror, second
panic, third anger, fourth more horror, and finally, if I ever get around to
it, prayer. Thank heaven I'm not Daniel and never will be.

God weighed Daniel down in prayer. And the visions he endured were
disturbing, sickening even. But then Daniel carried the further burden of
the desolation of his people. Though he lived in a foreign land, he never
for a moment ceased to feel, to long for, to grieve over the iniquities and
sins of Judah. And rather than being angry about them, or trying to justify
them, he gave this great unbearable burden to God. And God, in return,
showed Daniel his glory and his salvation. In the verses following this
one, the very timeline of the Lord's redemption is laid out, because, said
the angel Gabriel, "You are greatly loved."

DANIEL 9, 10

And I Feel Fine

And I heard a man clothed in linen, who was above the waters of the
stream; he raised his right hand and his left hand toward heaven and
swore by him who lives forever that it would be for a time, times, and
half a time, and that when the shattering of the power of the holy people
comes to an end all these things would be finished.
DANIEL 12:7

I do rather like looking around for signs of the apocalypse. It's fun to read
the news on Twitter and think, "Well, if that doesn't trigger it, I don't
know what will," and then sit back, waiting. After a few minutes I become
bored and wander off to go pull weeds in my garden. It seems like things
can always get worse, and do, and yet we go on as we always have done.
Tumult, plague, wars, rumors of wars—one by one they come, and we fer-
vently pray for them to go.

The man clothed in linen holds up both of his hands, as if doubling
or intensifying his oath. There's going to be a moment, after a perfect
amount of time has gone by, not really known to any of us, when suddenly
"all these things would be finished."

Is it the return of the people to the Promised Land from their exile?
Probably not, because whatever this is, it involves "the shattering of the
power of the holy people" which sounds like a serious drag. Assuming I or
you are "one of the holy people," which is a dubious assumption, I do not
in the least look forward to the "shattering" of any power. I really hope
this is completely metaphorical or has even already happened.

Then Comes Marriage

When the LORD first spoke through Hosea, the LORD said to Hosea, "Go,
take to yourself a wife of whoredom and have children of whoredom, for
the land commits great whoredom by forsaking the LORD."

HOSEA 1:2

The hardest thing about the Bible, I think, is that it's not about me. It's not an instruction book for how to live my life or make decisions. The Bible is about God and what he is doing to save sinners. So, why on earth would God say such a thing to Hosea? It would be impossible for Hosea to understand this command if he thinks the words are about him and not God.

Hosea girds up his loins, fastens his belt, straps on his sandals, slicks back his hair, takes one last bite of his breakfast, and goes out to do the Lord's bidding. Where do you find such a wife? He goes and finds a woman who's been around all the blocks. And because God always gets his way, she agrees to marry him. She has some children and Hosea names them—according to the word of the Lord—Jezreel, because judgment is coming to Israel, No Mercy, and Not My People.

Every time Israel went after another god—Baal, Molech, Asherah—from God's point of view it was as if she was selling herself for sex. Those gods, she figured, could give her something that God maybe could but wasn't going to. It's not really suitable conversation for a family situation, or a Bible study, or church. But that's how God sees humanity's rejection of him, and the love humans have for themselves. Like I said, it's not about me . . . or is it?

HOSEA 1

Who Does That?

And she did not know that it was I who gave her the grain, the wine, and
the oil, and who lavished on her silver and gold, which they used for Baal.
HOSEA 2:8

Being so wholeheartedly incurious about God and what he could possibly be saying or thinking, Israel took the rich things God gave her—food, wine, silver, and gold—and used them not only to worship other gods, but as the base materials to actually make those other gods. She took the sustaining provision of God and perverted it for the worship of others. It would be like me sitting down at the lovely desk my husband gave me on the occasion of our marriage and writing a lot of love letters to some other guy—and then moving the desk into that other man's house and living with him. And then forgetting that I was even married and who the desk even came from.

Israel twisted the proper worship of God so often that she was no longer able to see the source of her own life. She took the very creation of God and used it to worship herself rather than him. Thank goodness no one does anything like that anymore.

The internet, for example, is a source of good, neutral, helpful information. Every time I pause for a selfie, or flutter a little tweet, or record a substantive and useful podcast, or Instagram my devotions, I'm just raising awareness, enlightening the world, as it were, to the glory of . . . oh, never mind.

Who Can Understand

"Therefore, behold, I will allure her, and bring her into the wilderness, and speak tenderly to her."

HOSEA 2:14

If we worship ourselves, as Israel did, it is perfectly reasonable for God to chuck the whole thing. He could say, "Look, I tried. I gave you this beautiful earth and these beautiful gifts and you continue to hate me. I'm done. I'm not doing this anymore." That's what *we* do. That's what we say to each other in the face of betrayal and deceit. Nobody expects someone to stay married to a spouse who every other weekend is going out looking for someone else, and when they can't find anyone, descending into prostitution, and then when that doesn't work, paying her own money to convince anyone at all to be with her. What's that called? Desperation. Or more likely a clenched-jaw, gut-level desire to hurt God. But God is perfect, and good. So when Israel only and always cheats on him, what does he do?

He courts her again. He tries to make her fall in love with him, even a little bit. The Bible isn't about us. It's about God, who isn't like us, who does the opposite of what we would. He allures her? He speaks tenderly to her? After she totally and completely rejected him?

It doesn't make any sense.

It's Not Forever

After two days he will revive us; on the third day he will raise us up, that
we may live before him.

HOSEA 6:2

Did I say this already? Death destroys everything eventually. Whether old
or young, rich or poor, male or female, slave or free, it doesn't matter—
every single person dies. It's amazing how we carry on so cheerfully, ig-
noring this great tragedy awaiting each of us.

I, for instance, don't go around terrified of death. I go around thinking I'm going to live a good long time, practically forever, long enough to
eat this cold piece of pizza out of the back of the fridge, long enough to
waste an hour online, long enough to wander aimlessly around a big-box
store waiting for something to catch my fancy, long enough to be irritated
with my children for wanting dinner again when they just had it yesterday. There's no way for me to order my life as if I might soon take my last
breath and still be sane by bedtime. Sure, when someone else dies, death
looms up and I have to look at it and acknowledge, respectfully, that it
reigns supreme over the cosmos and me. But then I wander back to the
fridge by way of the donut aisle, and by morning life is back to normal.

But death does not reign over God. Though every head goes in sorrow down to the grave, yet the power of death, in three short days, was
utterly crushed and destroyed. Two dark, still, terrible days—anxious
days, grief-stricken days. But on the third day, the power and dominion
of death was shattered.

I Called My Son

When Israel was a child, I loved him, and out of Egypt I called my son.
HOSEA 11:1

It's unnerving how God keeps bringing up this Egypt business. Every few books, there it is again. Israel always wanted to go back there for safety and nice stuff, and God was always dragging them back to live in the land he had given them. Still, why bring it up all the time? It's a little weird.

More weird, though, would be to try to explain to the Israelites them-selves, picking their way over the dry ground of the Red Sea, that they had to be in Egypt for four hundred years—to be persecuted and afflicted, to be rescued miraculously in the most inconvenient and terrifying way possible—not because of them, not because of who they were, but because of God wanting to be able to say, several thousand years later, "out of Egypt I have called my son." It's possible some Israelites trundling along with all their stuff and cattle might have been underwhelmed. "What? Do you mean," anyone reasonable would ask, "that this whole ordeal is for *God* to show something to the world? *I* am the one suffering through it!"

But the whole of Scripture is about this child, this son. All of the events, however difficult and irritating they were to endure, point toward him. Because he is the salvation we're all looking for. How can someone from so long ago have anything to do with where we are now? Well, he does. He has everything to do with everything.

HOSEA 9:1–12:1

It's Not the Economy, Stupid

Though he may flourish among his brothers, the east wind, the wind of the LORD, shall come, rising from the wilderness, and his fountain shall dry up; his spring shall be parched; it shall strip his treasury of every precious thing.

HOSEA 13:15

Hosea had an extraordinarily long career as a prophet—something like sixty or more years. He lived through a whole slew of kings in Judah, and the longest rule in Israel, that of Jeroboam. It was a time of unprecedented economic prosperity, of almost everybody having plenty of money to do whatever they liked.

The question of financial well-being is rather a tricky one. When everyone's grapes and wheat are doing well, and there's plenty of trade going along, and the rich aren't suffering, it's pretty easy to assume that God is happy with the way things are, that the economic prosperity is a sign that humanity is awesome. The "flourishing" is interpreted as a good thing.

So when "the east wind," or Tiglath-Pileser, or Shalmaneser, or whoever, starts building up military strength, it never occurs to anyone that it could be "the wind of the Lord."

I hate to say it, but Christians today are often similarly confused. Reclining comfortably in plush seats in church auditoriums, it is easy to look around at the plenty, the grace, the ease of life and take it as a sign that God is happy with the way things are going. Economic prosperity is mistaken as a sign of God's favor. When really, it often goes the other way.

Brokenhearted

". . . rend your hearts and not your garments." Return to the Lord your God, for he is gracious and merciful, slow to anger, and abounding in steadfast love; and he relents over disaster.

JOEL 2:13

We don't have the custom of tearing our robes, for those of us who even possess them—and that wouldn't be me—when we feel really sorry and want God to forgive us. Are there any dramatic visual means of signaling repentance these days? I suppose a person can tweet his apology. In the ancient past, if you were famous, you could go on *Oprah*, or *Dancing with the Stars*. Me, when I'm horrible to other people, which hardly ever happens, I don't look around for public ways to display my grief.

But I suppose I could, perhaps, break open my hard heart, as I would rip a piece of cloth, as a sign of real grief over real sin. I could weep, perhaps, with regret and remorse. I could sit in a heap of despair and beg God, very quietly, for mercy. I could fling myself upon my bed, when no one is around, and admit that the things I have done, and the things I have left undone are evil. I could stop making excuses for myself. I could agree that I am the problem, not everyone else.

Do I want to? No. I want God to congratulate me for being wonderful. But who am I kidding? Not God. I might as well repent. And, of course, the second I do, He relents over any disaster He may have promised me.

The Locusts

I will restore to you the years that the swarming locust has eaten, the hopper, the destroyer, and the cutter, my great army, which I sent among you.
JOEL 2:25

Life is a catalogue of loss. I'm glad I never did, but if I'd ever tried to keep copies of all the things and people and moments I'd lost over the years I wouldn't be able to buy enough floral-embossed, faux-leather journals to contain them. And there are categories of loss: the things that are taken away from me, the things I destroy myself through negligence and sin, and the things that are wrong, and spoiled, though I cannot find anyone in particular to blame, even if I had the energy, time, or inclination to do so.

In Israel's case, she spoiled her own future through idolatry and rebellion. She ruined everything that God made. And so, because she didn't even see the problem, God promised disaster, like locusts going through a field in a few minutes—eating everything the farmer had labored for so anxiously. Like a pack of children sprinkling dirt all over my freshly mopped floor. All that time, all that energy, gone, in a second. Let the disaster come, says God.

And then he relents. He does not go on being angry forever. Indeed, he gives back whatever it is that the locusts have eaten. He will give back the thing, and the time it took to get the thing. How can he do this? I don't know. I feel like it might have something to do with a single man who let go of everything he had to buy back all that I lost.

JOEL 2:18–3:21

The Disaster

Is a trumpet blown in a city, and the people are not afraid? Does disaster come to a city, unless the LORD has done it?

AMOS 3:6

Yes, of course. The answer is yes to the first question. If a trumpet is blown, people cower in fear. But the next question, asked with the breezy nonchalance of the first, as if the answer is just as obvious, makes some of us sputter, shrinking at the very thought. If a disaster falls upon a city, is God to blame?

I, the modern reader, back uneasily away. God knowing the exact moment the bad thing was going to happen means he could have prevented it. It is not, therefore, at all irrational or crazy, when a bad thing happens, to straightway cry, "Why would God let this happen?" Everybody asks this. And they should, whether they believe in God or not. Clearly God can handle the insinuation.

But, having asked the question, do not be too quick to settle on an answer. Indeed, what matters most is *how* a person asks this question. When there's an earthquake, or a war, or rising flood waters, or a pandemic, you can cry out "Why God!" either in anger and rage—or you can fall on your face and ask it in humility, repentance, and sorrow. Because everything that happens, both good and bad, is meant to turn you back to God, to make you walk closer to him. It is under his realm, and you should go to him and ask him about it. But make it a real ask, not an angry accusation.

AMOS 1:1–3:11

Real Housewives of Bashan

> *"Hear this word, you cows of Bashan, who are on the mountain of*
> *Samaria, who oppress the poor, who crush the needy, who say to your*
> *husbands, 'Bring, that we may drink!'"*
>
> AMOS 4:1

The Lord is not a flatterer. He isn't going to say something nice about you if there isn't anything nice to say.

It's not very nice for him to call these rich, fancy women cows. If He weren't God, a tweet like this would rightly cause a tweetstorm. These women are the upper crust, the elite, flawless in their makeup and hair and social position. They rule over the land through their husbands—their weak, cowed husbands. Defrauding and oppressing the poor, indulging themselves, throwing parties and joking about how much they can drink, making their husbands serve them yet more wine, they are The Real Housewives of Bashan.

Don't be too sad if you're too poor to indulge yourself. Don't be sad if you can't afford to live like the rich and famous. So what if your shoes are last season, or you can't get your hair frosted, or you've never had your eyebrows threaded and don't even know what that is. Better a bag of secondhand sweaters and a mediocre box of wine than the opportunity to ruin other people's lives. By the same token, no matter your economic and social status, if you are throwing your weight around and taking advantage of anyone, don't be surprised when God turns out to be angry with you.

AMOS 3:12–4:13

The Deluge

But let justice roll down like waters, and righteousness like an ever-flowing stream.

AMOS 5:24

I do occasionally fall into the effortless longing "for Jesus to come back." It is always when I am suffering some inconvenience or humiliation. "How can I go on like this?" I cry, shaking my fist at the cosmos, and then I wish, usually aloud, for the return of our Lord. As if, when he comes, I will be congratulated for all the good things I've done and for my purity of heart, and all my enemies will be told how wrong they are.

That's pretty shortsighted, apparently, or so sayeth God through the mouth of Amos. Don't long for the day of the Lord. It's not going to be great. Especially if God is justifiably angry with you, as he is here with the people of Israel and Judah. He "hates" their feasts. He feels sick about them. Instead they should "let justice roll down like waters," as if some dam has been maliciously constructed that holds back that powerful, scouring current.

Scouring does imply a certain cleansing property. Justice, when it rolls down, sweeps away wickedness and evil. It counts out to each what they are owed. It is the sort of thing one wishes would happen to other people.

What a marvelous thing that God himself goes and stands in the way of this mighty, ever-flowing stream so that I am never swept away in its eternal, purifying torrent.

The Rest of the World

Saviors shall go up to Mount Zion to rule Mount Esau, and the kingdom shall be the LORD's.

OBADIAH 21

Israel was already in exile when Judah was carried away to Babylon. The land lay devastated. Nearby, Edom, the ancient cousin of Israel, sat around twiddling his thumbs, watching the dismantlement of his neighbor's land and stuff and aspirations and dignity. While he was twiddling, he aligned himself with Israel's enemies, hoping for a good and profitable return.

But God is the God of the whole world. This comes as a surprise to so many. The kings and presidents and principalities of the world do not reckon that they have to answer to anybody but themselves. It is discourteous and provoking that God, if indeed he exists, would pick out only one group of people to display his temperament and character. And why Israel? Israel is such a small nation, and pretty easy to loathe. It makes all the sense in the world to Edom that God would get fed up and sweep Zion away.

But whatever the world and the nations and kings of the world think about it, God is keeping careful track of every single thing that happens at every level of power. He doesn't just see the poor, he also sees the hidden thoughts of the mighty. But I don't want to sound like a religious fanatic, so I'll just stop there, before hinting at what he might do about all that he sees.

Because He Told Them

Then the men were exceedingly afraid and said to him, "What is this that you have done!" For the men knew that he was fleeing from the presence of the LORD, because he had told them.

JONAH 1:10

Jonah is my kindred spirit. If you are angry, or worn-out, and don't suffer any fools—either gladly or otherwise—Jonah might be your dearest friend too. I'm not trying to be weird. I know he is long dead. Still.

The key line, in case you missed it, is "because he had told them." One of the worst things about being a "creature," about being a wimpy, created being is that even when I do not mean to, in fact, *especially* when I do not mean to, I am always "telling them." I am always saying far more about myself than I intend. I give myself away by the expression in my bitter, beady eyes. I tell the whole story by the way I stand. I let it all out in the manner of my walking from one place to another. Then I open my mouth, and the full measure of my wretchedness, pressed down, shaken together, spills out of the boat and into the sea.

Of course, there is always the possibility that Jonah "tells them" because he is proud and excited about what he is doing. But honestly, he doesn't seem like that together of a person, which is why I love him so much. He's the kind of stubborn, self-focused person who would let slip something like, "I'm running away from God because I hate the people of Nineveh. They are the absolute worst."

JONAH I

Look Before You Leap

*And the L*ORD *spoke to the fish, and it vomited Jonah out upon the dry land.*
JONAH 2:10

It is a kindness to warn people ahead of time if they are thinking seriously about becoming a Christian. They should consider carefully before leaping in (that's just a terrible joke). Or if you were encouraged to put your faith in God so that life would get easier—all your problems would be solved, all your dreams would come true, all the money would roll down into your lap—you may have thence discovered that the experience of the believer is often painful and disappointing. At least it was for Jonah, if not for you.

Poor Jonah, dispatched to do something he felt was morally reprehensible, hounded unto death until he did as he was told, rescued miraculously, and yet in a disquieting way that markedly resembled the grave, sent once more to the original task, enduring the patient mercy of God when he accomplished that task badly.

This is the trajectory of the Christian. To have your life knocked out from under you. To rejoice over your own salvation but then still have to face the ugliness of yourself, over and over and over. To discover that it is really about God all the time. To find that God has taken a liberty with the intimate circumstances of your own life to paint a picture of himself. Seriously, try Buddhism or something.

The Heart of the Matter

*And the L*ORD *said, "Do you do well to be angry?"*

JONAH 4:4

There you are, sweltering in 120-degree heat—no water, no cooling breeze, nothing. God has basically come through for you, you might admit—grudgingly—if you let yourself think about it for a minute. Sure, you were completely disobedient. Sure, you care nothing for the salvation of the world. Sure, you have a terrible attitude. And sure, you are still alive when you should have perished at the bottom of the sea. But honestly, it is so hot! God must not care for you at all.

And there you have it in a nutshell. Are you angry? Do you think God owes you something? Did you pick up this book because it had the word "angry" in the title, and thought, "Yeah, I'm angry. I'm fed up. I've had enough. I can't deal. Things are too awful and I'm just too tired to go on with any of them anymore. Where is God anyway?"

And to you, and me, and Jonah, God says, "Do you do well to be angry?" I mean, I think the clear answer is, *Yes.*

But the answer is really no. You do not do well to be angry. You aren't God. You don't know. You don't care enough, or at all, about what he is doing or who he is. On what basis are you angry? Ought you not rather be grateful to know a God who doesn't kill you even though most of the time you are acting like you hate him?

So there the matter sits. You struggling away in the heat. God loving you. You being sure that he hates you.

216 Don't Speak

"Do not preach"—thus they preach—"one should not preach of such
things; disgrace will not overtake us."
MICAH 2:6

The most irritating thing in the world is sitting in church, flipping again
through the bulletin, stifling a yawn, waiting for the preacher to just hurry up and end already. Everyone knows the average person can only pay
attention to one thing for ten minutes. That's how long it is between com-
mercials . . . or maybe it's only five minutes? I don't even know. I only
have time for YouTube.

And then there's the "content." I don't like to go to church and be made
to feel discouraged and sad about myself. I need something uplifting to
get me through the week. Life is bad enough without the preacher going
on and on about how awful I am, even if he does use the word "we."

Disgrace will not overtake us . . . except that it already has. The disgrace of death, the ruin of pride, the vainglory of self-sufficiency—it's all
there if anyone wants to see it.

The message needs to be heard, desperately. Sinners need to turn to
the Lord and beg for mercy, not tune out because it's not an interesting
message. God is calling you—shouting for your attention. Listen to him
while there is still time.

MICHAH I, 2

The Declaration of War

Thus says the LORD concerning the prophets who lead my people astray,
who cry "Peace" when they have something to eat, but declare war
against him who puts nothing into their mouths.

MICAH 3:5

Perhaps in your journeys around the world and social media, you have come across "prophets" and televangelists who like to say that all *is* well and will be well—if you send them a donation. "Blessings to you and peace," they say when they have cashed your check. Well-fed, traveling in private jets, they lead people astray.

"I would never be like that," I say to myself when I scroll past their YouTube channels. I'm above being controlled by the baser needs of the body. I am more spiritually-minded and don't melt down when I'm hungry or thirsty. I would never blame others or manipulate them if things weren't working out for me.

But in truth, it takes just a little lack of this or that to make me look around for someone to blame—the people around me, and God of course, who promised, didn't he, to take care of all my needs. But God desires righteousness, justice, obedience, and mercy. When I or anyone else use other people to satisfy my own needs, the peace that I proclaim will turn into war—and God will be the one waging it.

No One Wants Him

*"O my people, what have I done to you? How have I wearied you?
Answer me!"*

MICAH 6:3

Human history is the long story of everybody being really fed up with God. He doesn't do anything that anybody wants. When the weather is fine, I complain about the need for rain. When it is raining, I fret about it never being sunny. When I am sick I can't believe how badly my life is turning out. When I am well, I am bored, and it is probably God's fault for not letting me live in a more interesting city or providing me with a bigger income so I can buy whatever strikes my fancy this moment. He can't do anything right.

But how has the Lord wearied you, really? Is it his providence? His care for you in all the realms of your life? Is it that he hasn't perfectly sorted everything out, so that you have to constantly throw yourself on his mercy? Or that you can't see the next step and feel like you are always wandering around in the dark? What is it? Why are you so tired? Maybe it's the law. Maybe God has given too many rules. You can't follow them all, and he should have made the number smaller. Maybe you are just tired because you feel like you will never come to the end of this book.

It is God's fault? Maybe you are making yourself tired. Maybe you should stop blaming God for everything.

He Has Told You

*"He has told you, O man, what is good; and what does the L*ORD *require of you but to do justice, and to love kindness, and to walk humbly with your God?"*

MICAH 6.8

"What does God want from me?" You always said you wanted to know. But by that you meant, "What very special job does God have in mind for me that only I can do? What fulfilling occupation awaits me that will enable me to move somewhere cool?"

Consider then these three things that the Lord requires of you and how impossible they are. He wants you to "do justice," he wants you to "love kindness," and he wants you to "walk humbly" with him. What would this take?

Well, first of all, it wouldn't matter where you lived or what kind of awful job you had or whether you were married or unmarried. It would mean that you constantly had to assess the truth of whatever was in front of you, and then unerringly follow in the way of that truth. It would mean being impartial. It would mean not bowing to the trend of the day, but to always let God assign the categories of Good and Bad to whatever you had under consideration. Then it would also mean not running over everybody with your newfound vision, but properly esteeming yourself as the mostly bad person that you are, so that the "justice" might occasionally go against you, as you are very often wrong.

He told you, you wretched man, or woman, or whoever. Why aren't you doing it? Why are you crying? Seriously, join me for a pie, because there's no way we can accomplish this without help.

MICAH 6:6–7:20

All People Everywhere

An oracle concerning Nineveh. The book of the vision of Nahum of Elkosh.

NAHUM 1:1

Well, it's too bad that Jonah didn't live to be a hundred and fifty years old or so, because the thing he wanted most in life—the total destruction of Nineveh—is finally on the divine to-do list.

When the Ninevites repented all those years ago, as a result of Jonah's half-hearted preaching, they didn't, as expected, remain particularly curious about the God who spared them, nor did they attempt to pass on the story of that remarkable moment to their children and their children's children. Indeed, if they were anything like all people, when disaster didn't fall, they probably wrote the whole incident off as a fluke and went back to their wicked ways.

Which included, as I'm sure you know, some of the worst atrocities in the ancient world, not to mention human history. The Assyrians were famous for their cruelty. That's why everyone was so terrified of them, and why Jonah would have felt physically ill about God's decision *not* to destroy them.

Nahum's name means "comfort," and surely the people of Israel and Judah felt comfort about the thought of Assyria finally getting what they knew they deserved. And yet, it is so strange of God to address the people of Nineveh again, in person, both speaking about them and to them. As though he would be their God if they would only turn to him and live.

God is Not Bad, No Really

There is no easing your hurt; your wound is grievous. All who hear the news about you clap their hands over you. For upon whom has not come your unceasing evil?

NAHUM 3:19

It is tedious, this divine litany of the evil of all people everywhere. And more than tedious, for it is considered a wicked thing to say, in the year that I am writing this, that I am not—nor are you—inherently good. Your most important task is to discover who you are and then "live into" whatever that is. Self-discovery is a salvific act, the only way to be okay. If anyone comes along to tell any of us that we are *not* okay, that you are suffering a "grievous" wound, that my "unceasing evil" is spoiling everything, that person would be considered wrong and bad.

Which essentially makes the Christian God, revealed here in these ancient Scriptures, wrong and bad. So that's awkward.

But here's why walking away from the pursuit of self-discovery and personal goodness is a relief. First of all, you can't really "discover" or "know" yourself. Try for a bit. Try getting fully in touch with yourself even for a few moments. You won't be able to do it. Something will elude you. Your hormonal makeup, for example, or the reasons why you prefer one kind of food over another. You cannot know yourself.

But God does. He knows how wounded and evil you are. And yet, when you turn to him, though the world "claps their hands," which is not a good thing in this case, yet God will take you in the palm of his own hand and cure you of yourself.

That's Not What I Meant

"Look among the nations and see; wonder and be astounded. For I am doing a work in your days that you would not believe if told."
HABAKKUK 1:5

It's rather dangerous, or at least a bit risky, to look around at all the wickedness, as Habakkuk does, and ask God what he is going to do about it. It's so bad, Habakkuk says, how can you possibly tolerate it anymore? And God answers and says, "Oh, don't worry, I am going to judge the wicked. You're absolutely right. I shouldn't put up with it anymore. Only, here's the thing, I'm going to judge wicked Judah by the might and terror of the much more wicked Babylon, and then, when Babylon's cup of wickedness is full up, I'm going to judge them. Don't you worry, Habakkuk, no one will be getting away with anything!"

Habakkuk, as you can imagine, is not excited about this.

I mean, it's so easy to see the awful things going on in, say, the "Church" in its biggest grandest sense. Bad shepherds, bad sheep, bad everything. It shouldn't be like this, we cry. We can do better and God should do something. But then, when you find out what exactly God is willing to do, because none of us are more just than God, and his justice can reach far into the darkest crevasses of every human heart, it gets too personal. But then it is too late to say never mind.

Pick Your Idol

"But the LORD is in his holy temple; let all the earth keep silence before him."
HABAKKUK 2:20

So the thing about idolatry is that it's not really about the idol, it's about you. Just as the Bible is about God, is a reflection of God and who he is and what he is like, so an idol is about you, is a reflection of who you are and what you are like. That's why it doesn't really matter what it is that you idolize. At the root of it, you are worshiping yourself.

Me, because I'll go ahead and tell you how evil I am, I love my cell phone. Not only is it smooth and shiny, not only does it "connect me to the world," it responds to me and my every whim instantly, as if I am a short, middle-aged, pot-bellied god. My phone is a lot more sophisticated and lovely than whatever gold-plated god the Chaldeans crafted for themselves. It stood there all smooth and shiny and they came and prayed to it. It didn't say anything back. It didn't even hear them praying. But they felt restful after they had talked to it, mainly because they had really been talking to themselves. The silence of the god comforted and reassured them.

Trouble is, there is a real, true God who has His own thoughts and words and feelings. And you can't customize him to make him more interesting or acceptable to you. He is not silent. On the contrary, when you come into his presence, you should be silent. You should be the one to listen, mute and still.

That Sounds Weird

*. . . yet I will rejoice in the L*ORD*; I will take joy in the God of my salvation.*
HABAKKUK 3:18

Some people say that joy is something you can choose—like ice cream or a good attitude. Joy is better than happiness, they say, and you can work on the joy part because it "doesn't depend on your feelings." You can be "joyful," just like you can "be content" no matter what is going on.

It's a bold claim, especially as God, in this tiny book, has just explained how he is going to let fall his sweeping judgment first over his own people, and then over the people he made use of to judge his own people. Judgment is what's for dinner and it's not going to taste good and nobody is going to like it.

And yet Habakkuk "will" rejoice in the Lord, he will "take joy" in the God of his salvation. As if somehow seeing God in his holiness, in his perfection, in His justice will settle things for Habakkuk in a way that answers all his questions. It will be "joyful" to see God deal it out to all the people who deserve the bad things coming to them, even if those are his own people.

Just like, I suppose, when God finally and completely judges the world he has made, on the last day, and everyone gets to see how it really was, without being able to hide or anything, and it turns out that God really was good all along. Seeing that and having it settled will be good, who knows.

Maybe You Don't Really Get It

"I will utterly sweep away everything from the face of the earth," declares the Lord.

ZEPHANIAH 1:2

In a destructive reverse of creation, in the order that he made everything, God will sweep it all away, beginning with humanity.

I can feel you staring over the edge of the book, maybe even rolling your eyes. I get it, God is going to judge Israel, and Judah, and Babylon, and Nineveh, and everyone. You keep saying that. Seriously, you don't need to say it anymore.

The trouble is, you probably don't really get it. You may get it in one sense, that God is unhappy with wickedness and has the power to do something about it. But when scrolling around the internet or driving in your car, you really don't get it, you feel like things are just always going to go on the way they always have, and so you are both afraid and not afraid, afraid of the world, but not very afraid of God. Besides, it is fashionable right now to play down the apocalypse, as if meditating for any length of time on how and why God might destroy the creation he has made is a waste of time, as if it will make you a useless person to society as it trucks along down the broad, wide, road of destruction. Now is what matters.

Which is true, now does matter. But it matters because of what God will do later.

Exultation

The Lord your God is in your midst, a mighty one who will save; he will rejoice over you with gladness; he will quiet you by his love; he will exult over you with loud singing.
ZEPHANIAH 3:17

How extraordinary, you being the beleaguered idolatrous sinner that you are, that God should not only think about you, should care to know about who you are and what you are doing, but should be ready to come and save you. He doesn't have to. You don't deserve it. But don't you want to be saved? Don't you *want* him to pull you out of the pit that you have dug for yourself?

But he doesn't stop with just saving you. He's really happy about you. He rejoices. His exultant joy breaks forth in song.

It's as though you had fallen into a dark hole, having wandered away to do something you wanted to do even though you had been expressly forbidden to do it. Then God counted up all the ones that belonged to him and realized that one was missing. You were missing. And so, he left all the others and went looking, and kept looking, never stopping until he heard you there, crying. (That's why crying out is so important. It's easier to be heard if you're screaming in panic.) He comes and pulls you out of the hole and carries you home, and gradually you stop crying. He calms you down. And once he has got you back home there's this great rush of relief and joy from everyone, and you yourself are so relieved and happy. It's like that.

Simply Glorious

"The latter glory of this house shall be greater than the former, says the LORD of hosts. And in this place I will give peace, declares the LORD of hosts."
HAGGAI 2:9

It's unusual for something to become nicer as time goes by. Everything mostly decays with age, including buildings. They start out bright and clean and then the plumbing goes, and a crack appears along the ceiling, and after a bunch of years someone descends into the deep recesses of the structure and discovers that the foundation has cracked. Then the Babylonians sweep in and knock the whole thing down.

Haggai was probably an old man when he traveled back to his homeland—upwards of seventy at least—and tried to spur on everyone who returned from exile to the discouraging work of picking up the scattered stones and putting them back together again. To describe the post-exilic temple as being of "modest" construction is a kind way of saying that it looked insignificant and depressing. Also, the exhausted builders were constantly attacked and mocked.

This, then, could sound like hollow encouragement—"Hey guys! Don't give up! It's going to be glorious, and peaceful, seriously, it'll be great!" Which is exactly the sort of "comfort" I resent. Leave me alone, I always want to say, this is terrible.

But *God* is saying it. And it will be very grand once Herod gets in there to build himself a legacy. But it won't be peaceful. That will take the peculiar glory of that strange sounding, unremarkable man who makes cataclysmic peace by reconciling you to God by the blood of his cross.

Where is She Going and Why is She in That Basket?

And he said, "This is Wickedness." And he thrust her back into the bas-
ket, and thrust down the leaden weight on its opening.
ZECHARIAH 5:8

Unless you've been living under a rock (not the rock in the verse, just
any big rock) for the last long while, you'll know that this is not politi-
cally correct—this idea of a woman shoved into a basket. Not only that,
but calling the woman "Wickedness" is unseemly. Is it acceptable for God
to exploit the image of a woman to talk about "the iniquity of the people
throughout the land?"

If you read through the whole of Zechariah (which you should do),
you will be in good company. Zechariah himself keeps saying, "What are
these, my Lord?" or "Where are you going?" and "What is it?"

It seems like the woman, whoever she is, is pictured inside of one of
those trading receptacles so preferred in the ancient world. Grain would
be measured out into some basket or something, and a heavy rock used
to weigh it. The woman called Wickedness is measured against her own
deceitful and false weights and sent away to be set up as the idol in the
temple of the god she worships. Metaphorically, of course. Zechariah is
seeing one of those fantastical visions God likes to use to tell us all something peculiar about himself and his feelings about us.

As I've said before, the Bible is really hard to understand, incomprehensible even. Especially as we all know that all people are good all the
time—especially women—and God is the one who is suspect.

Why Did I Come in Here Again?

"And when you eat and when you drink, do you not eat for yourselves
and drink for yourselves?"
ZECHARIAH 7:6

You'd think that losing everything and going into exile for seventy years would cure Israel of unfaithfulness forever. But then, you'd think that being rescued out of Egypt and walking across the Red Sea as if it were dry land would keep you from whining when you get thirsty and moaning when you feel like you're going to starve to death.

You can tell yourself, "I'm totally never going to forget the mercy of God," all the live-long day. "Wow, this experience has been so awful," you can remind yourself, "that I'm never going to sin again!" But then you turn around in your kitchen and forget what you came in for, and remember that you're out of milk and must drop everything and run to the store, and while you're at the store you remember a few other things, and then by the time you get home you're tired and so you scream at one of the many people who seem to be making so many demands on you. Eventually you crawl into bed, and a few hours later you wake in the grey dawn and try to think what you're supposed to do that day. Yesterday is, for all practical purposes, gone forever. The point is, you can't remember. You can't.

So yes, you eat and drink for yourself and not for God because you can't figure out how to do anything else. It would be so great if God would take the burden of remembering off you.

ZECHARIAH 5, 6, 7

The Price of a Slave

Then I said to them, "If it seems good to you, give me my wages; but if not, keep them." And they weighed out as my wages thirty pieces of silver.
ZECHARIAH 11:12

That's the price of a slave—thirty pieces of silver. Silver sounds expensive now, even in little bits, but it was such an inadequate amount that when they weighed it out to him, Zechariah took it and threw it down in the house of the Lord. He flung it down. The wages of a slave—paid for tending sheep.

Sometime, much later, a man would stand in the house of the Lord—his own house, actually. He would have taken on the very form and nature of a slave, not grasping at his rights as owner of the house. The money, thirty pieces of silver—a pittance—would have bought his betrayal. He would be stricken, beaten, afflicted, marred beyond any human recognition. His sheep, seeing him thus besieged, would scatter. The one who sold his life away would take the money and throw it down and then go away himself to die. You might stand far off and wonder about this man—wonder at this plain, ugly, disfigured slave. What had he done that he should be so struck? That his life should be thrown away for so little? Look at him. Lift up your eyes and see the salvation of the world.

ZECHARIAH 9, 10, 11

I Didn't Mean Like That

*"I have loved you," says the L*ORD*. But you say, "How have you loved us?"*
*"Is not Esau Jacob's brother?" declares the L*ORD*. "Yet I have loved Jacob*
but Esau I have hated. I have laid waste to his hill country and left his
heritage to jackals of the desert."

MALACHI 1:2–3

Many people who are unhappy in marriage suffer because they aren't able to talk clearly to each other. One person will say something, and the other person will hear the opposite of what the speaker intended. "I love you," says the one, but the other one hears, "I hate you." Then the hearer shouts, "Why do you hate me?" and the original speaker shouts back, "You jerk!" And they give up and get divorced. Seems ridiculous, especially if the two just took the trouble to repeat back what was actually said, instead of what they thought they heard.

"I have loved you," says God, and before he can even go on to say why and how, his partner in the conversation mutters, "Oh no, you haven't. Not even a little."

"Haven't I loved you? I have totally loved you."

Israel stares back though hard eyes. The way he loves her isn't what she wanted. She doesn't want to deal with his jealousy, with his judgment either of her or of the people she is so anxious to cozy up to. If only he would go away and leave her alone.

MALACHI 1:1–2:16

He is Coming

> *"Behold, I send my messenger, and he will prepare the way before me.*
> *And the Lord whom you seek will suddenly come to his temple; and the*
> *messenger of the covenant in whom you delight, behold, he is coming,*
> *says the LORD of hosts."*
>
> MALACHI 3:1

First the messenger comes to prepare the way. A young man wearing camel hair, sounding exactly like all these prophets you've forborne with. He will stand out stark against the spiritual landscape of his people—against the world—calling to all, to you, to listen, to prepare yourself because of the one who is coming after him. This one will come suddenly, drawing everyone—even you—to himself.

All the words of all these books have been pointing singly to him. They have painted pictures of him, they have hinted broadly, they have even come right out and said it—Someone is coming.

Who? Take a deep breath before you answer, because it is right there in the line. Indeed, if you race by, you are likely to miss it because it seems so unlikely.

The Lord—the Lord whom you seek—this is the person who will come. When you see him, what will you do? When you hear his voice, what will you say? When he calls your name, will you go with him? Even if he isn't what you thought? Even if he overturns everything?

Don't lose heart. You have come so far. But he has come even further.

Finally

> *. . . and Jacob the father of Joseph the husband of Mary, of whom Jesus*
> *was born, who is called Christ.*
>
> MATTHEW 1:16

Four hundred years or so pass quietly by, and Israel waits and waits for her salvation, wondering if God will ever bother to speak to her again. Some of the people of Judea move up north past Samaria, to Galilee, to resettle and reclaim the land of Israel, to try to live holy lives as the law requires. They aren't rich. They aren't elite. They don't appear to be consequential at all. They are eking out a living on the land, trying to make the best of it. If you walked through town you wouldn't notice anything interesting.

But that the line from David has been perfectly kept, though not by any human care. One single carpenter is there in Nazareth building whatever it is that people need, for however much they are willing to pay. And there's a young teenage girl whose uncle happens to be a Levitical priest somewhere down in Judea. She has the most common possible name, and if you saw her filling her water jars at the well, you wouldn't think anything about her.

Except that the moment is right. God is ready to save the world. This man, and this young woman: from before time, they were always going to be the ones God knew and chose to care for his own child.

Senseless

Then Herod, when he saw that he had been tricked by the wise men, be-
came furious, and he sent and killed all the male children in Bethlehem
and in all that region who were two years old or under, according to the
time that he had ascertained from the wise men.

MATTHEW 2:16

Is this senseless violence? Is this one of those times everyone stands around in stunned horror, surveying the horror and wreckage, grief radiating in waves of desperate anger? What is it about the killing of children, in every generation, in every age? All these little ones pulled from their mothers—who can bear to look?

And yet, it was the usual thing to do if you were a potentate with any amount of power in the ancient world. You would kill all your rivals, all the children of your siblings, all the children of the person you had murdered in your successful, bloody bid for power. Herod was not above killing his own sons and wife, and his wife's parents. Why wouldn't he kill a town of babies if it meant he could eliminate any threat, however remote, to his rule—such as it was.

But it is for these that the Savior comes breaking into the world; his own way and life is marred by the violence and grief that characterizes every human community. For those of us so committed to death as a solution, as the obvious thing, he is threatening. In other words, it makes all the sense in the world—the hostility we will all feel toward this infant king.

Thanks So Much for Coming

But when he saw many of the Pharisees and Sadducees coming to his baptism, he said to them, "You brood of vipers! Who warned you to flee from the wrath to come?"

MATTHEW 3:7

Here is John, preaching in his warm, friendly, inoffensive, seeker-sensitive way. He totally has the modern, skinny-jeaned pastor look down, touching his fingertips together in sincere, impassioned oratory. His tattoos are perfectly curated, his hipster glasses epic. He perches his coffee on his stool and uptalks his opening joke and his welcoming congratulations about how he knows you have a lot of places to go in the desert on a weekday morning, but he's glad you decided to join him today. Don't forget to pick up your gift of a free Bible on the way out. Oh, shoot—I probably have the wrong guy.

How crude of John to go out to the wilderness at all—far away from where any of us want to go—to stand in a muddy river. How unkind of him to insult those who show up to see and hear him. Is that even a thing? To call a segment of the population snakes? Snakes in the grass. A group of snakes in the grass.

So far, we have had the death of a lot of children, and now a crazy man flinging insults at the assembled congregation. This is ridiculous. So you might think, but you are not God. You are the one who needs rescuing. Look a little deeper. You might need the warning about the snakes. Make sure to accept the free Bible.

But he answered, "It is written, 'Man shall not live by bread alone, but by every word that comes from the mouth of God.'"
MATTHEW 4:4

Believe me, I know you can't live by bread alone. In this modern age, you can't live by bread at all. Are any of us even allowed to eat bread? I, myself, long to eat bread. I think about it all the time. The piles of glorious, golden bread in a bakery . . . the packaged rows of bread in the store that by themselves taste like ashes, but that, when toasted and lathered with real butter, turn out to be delicious . . . almost as delectable as my own loaves mixed first in my industrial grade mixer, and then delivered into the warmth of my gas oven.

How clever of the devil to offer the Son of Man some bread. It must have been the most aromatic and tempting loaf of all. If I were standing there, knowing that eating it would be the wrong thing—because every time I eat bread now, it is the wrong thing—I would have grabbed it. Just taken it like Eve, averting my gaze and eating it all before I could reconsider.

But I am not the Son of Man. I wasn't there but he was. He said no without hesitation. The way I would have grabbed, he said no. And he himself is the Bread who gives life, who keeps me alive. How clever and vindictive of Satan, 2000 years later, to make it so that most of us can't eat bread at all without sickness or guilt. Well played, Satan, well played.

Immediately

Immediately they left their nets and followed him.

MATTHEW 4:20

"Immediately" is such a troubling word.

I would like other people to attend to me immediately. I frequently point out to my children that they need to immediately obey. They stand there and look at me in shock, like they can't even understand what I am saying. Of course, when they want *me* to do something, not a minute of my time may be spent not attending to their urgent cries.

I confess, I am always exasperated when anyone else wants me to do something for them on their own timetable. What I like to do then—and this is because I'm more holy than a lot of other people—I like to say quietly to myself that I can't be controlled by the tyranny of the urgent, I need to wait and pray and see if it's something God really wants me to do. And usually I'm pretty sure God probably doesn't want me to do it, because deep down I don't want to anyway. Whatever it is.

How extraordinary that these men just stood up and walked away from their whole lives because of what Jesus said. Just like that. Immediately. It's not the demands of a child, or the tyranny of the urgent, it is the necessity of being rescued out of a burning house, out of a perishing flood. Just go with him. Don't try to take anything with you. Quickly now, just go to him.

Immediately.

MATTHEW 4:12–25

238 Go On, Be Perfect

> *Seeing the crowds, he went up on the mountain, and when he sat*
> *down, his disciples came to him. And he opened his mouth and taught*
> *them, saying . . .*
> MATTHEW 5:1–2

You know, because he is a great teacher, like Gandhi or the Buddha . . .
except that in the course of these many chapters, the weight of what he's
going to say will make the whole crowd despair.

Go on, read the whole sermon. Grit your teeth and go out and do all
that he says. No? Maybe just pick one thing. Like, work really hard and
don't envy anyone for a whole week. And when you've mastered that, pick
another one. I know, go with the not being anxious about what you eat or
drink or what you wear. Don't worry about it. Jesus told you, he said not to
be anxious. What's the matter with you?

When we teach, all of us who are not Jesus—including Gandhi—we
teach so that the person being taught can do something, can gain knowledge and understanding that will lead to action. So when Jesus winds up
with Be Perfect, and he's teaching, it must mean that you can eventually
be perfect if you work at it.

Or maybe someone greater than Gandhi and Buddha is here. Maybe
the command to be perfect is about you seeing that no matter what you do,
you will never be perfect.

Go ahead though, collapse back on the grass, and shed bitter tears. You
can't do it. You can't be perfect. Admit it and then read the sermon again.

Astonishment

And when Jesus finished these sayings, the crowds were astonished at
his teaching . . .
MATTHEW 7:28

Astonishment is what you feel when you see something you weren't expecting. It's when you're going along in your car, mile after mile in the gray
depression of modern life, from one frustrating errand to another, and
then you go around the bend and see the heavy clouds lightened by a shaft
of pink, dying light. Astonishment comes when you are facing something
you really, really don't want to do, but you were going to grit your teeth and
do it anyway, and then suddenly you discover that someone else did it for
you—that you don't have to face it. Beauty, relief, joy, astonishment.

It's not another scroll through Facebook and then, in a moment of en-
nui, clicking on the Two-Cats-Were-Sleeping-And-You'll-Never-Guess-
What-Happened-Next video. You totally knew what they were going to
do, and you were disappointed with yourself for bothering to click. It's
not another wander through Target to see what kind of faux candles are
available this year. Are you kidding? Roughly the same ones as last year,
except that none of them will fit in the little holder thing you bought for
forty bucks.

Jesus said all he had to say. He did not hide any of it, did not try to lure
you in, did not try to manipulate you or get some kind of fake surprise
out of you. He spoke calmly and completely, and yet what he had to say
was astonishing.

Worthy

But the centurion replied, "Lord, I am not worthy to have you come under my roof, but only say the word, and my servant will be healed."
MATTHEW 8:8

"I'm not good enough to come to church," someone said to me once, "so I'm going to make some adjustments, try to get things in order, and then I'll probably come." I nodded and smiled a big fake smile and said I hoped I'd be seeing her there. But she's never come. Because, surprise, she doesn't feel worthy. She feels that she's not good enough. But maybe she could try a little harder and then God would probably be happy with her progress and she'd be able to come to church and feel God's pleasure at her work of scraping her own life into some kind of order all by herself.

And, oh, how much do I know how she feels! I long, I wish, I constantly desire to be able to go to church and feel a sense of warm well-being—a feeling of God's pleased congratulations to me for being so good, working so hard, getting rid of all the stupidity and sin in my life. The last thing I ever want to have to say is that I'm Not Worthy, that there isn't anything I can do to make my own self better. And this feeling, this desire, is so pervasive—not just to me and my acquaintance, but to the world—that Jesus takes his turn being surprised by the words "I'm Not Worthy" coming out of an actual human being's mouth.

The Healthiest Place on Earth

This was to fulfill what was spoken by the prophet Isaiah, "He took our illnesses and bore our diseases."

MATTHEW 8:17

It's not like, way back then, you could go to a doctor and get a quick antibiotic if you had a fever or an infection. No one could send you through a CT scan to see what the outcome of your illness might be. Doctors did the best they could with what they had. And you were going to die of something anyway, some day. Illness: it is the property of being human.

Jesus comes and teaches so differently, and the crowds gather. And then he heals Peter's mother-in-law. She's laid low, and given the time and circumstances, who's to say if she will survive? Lying there, achy, sick, everybody around her anxious because there isn't anything they can do. And Jesus comes in and heals her, just like that. She doesn't even have a recovery time where she has to take it slow to regain her strength. She goes from being sick to well in an instant, full of all the energy that accompanies true health.

She gets up and bustles around, taking back her realm, making sure everyone has what they need to be comfortable. And so, of course, the whole world rushes over to Peter's house to rid themselves of the burden and trial of ill health. Capernaum is disease-free, the healthiest place in the world. Until it means listening to the words Jesus is saying. And then, meh, maybe being sick isn't so bad after all.

MATTHEW 8:14–34

Be the Sinner

"Go and learn what this means, 'I desire mercy and not sacrifice.' For I came not to call the righteous, but sinners."
MATTHEW 9:13

You might like to exclude yourself, as so many have, from the category of sinner. Oh, I see, he came for the *sinners*. Well, that lets me out then, because I'm a good, decent person, and always very kind. I'd better make sure and tell my neighbor about Jesus. He, being a terrible sinner—and not righteous at all—will be interested to hear this important news about this wonderful person who has come to save him.

Whereas, if you can't be included in the category of sinner, you can't be part of the group that gets the mercy of God.

Mercy is such a glory. Mercy is the means by which God hears you when you cry out to him in hopeless desolation. Mercy is the gift he gives you by listening to you when you are at your lowest. If you haven't received mercy, you can't understand who God is and what he is like. Go and learn what it means. Go, and in the ordering of your life, try to look at yourself as the person who is sitting by the side of the road, holding a sign, begging for something you should have provided for yourself but didn't. You *are* asking for a free handout. Don't be the person in the car, trying to calculate how much change you have in the bottom of your glove compartment. Be the person by the side of the road. Be the beggar. Then you can begin to understand what this means.

What Would Jesus Do?

At that time Jesus declared, "I thank you, Father, Lord of heaven and earth, that you have hidden these things from the wise and understanding and revealed them to little children . . ."

MATTHEW 11:25

It's these little occasional prayers of Jesus that cause me never to ask myself, "What would Jesus do?" Or worse yet, "What would Jesus pray?" When you ask yourself what Jesus would do—especially if you have been terribly busy and haven't had a moment to crack open the pages of The Bible, or been able to get to a decent church service in a long time, and have only heard snatches of mediocre sermons on the radio, listening as long as you can before you become so irritated you quickly change over to anything else, anything else in the world is more bearable than meandering, second-rate preaching—you will only end up with an answer that hazily reflects you.

Certainly, it's not very nice of Jesus to hide stuff from anyone. Why would he do that? Wouldn't he want everyone to know whatever it was he was saying? And yet here He publicly thanks his Father for concealing something essential. Imagine if any Christian—either good or bad—stood up and prayed such a prayer. But the wisdom of God is foolishness to the world. What seems best to us is not at all the way that God goes about doing his work.

MATTHEW 11

Greater than Jonah

"The men of Nineveh will rise up at the judgment with this generation and condemn it, for they repented at the preaching of Jonah, and behold, something greater than Jonah is here."

MATTHEW 12:41

Some pictures of Jesus in the Old Testament are hard to find and hard to understand. Others are easy to find because Jesus himself tells us where they are. You trot off to have a look, squinting your eyes to try to make out the likeness, and then backing away in horror.

Which part of the life of Jonah, exactly, makes him a useful picture for understanding Jesus? The disobedience? The hardness of heart? The anger?

But that's not how these little signs work. Don't look at the person, per se. Look at the circumstances, the unusual things that happened, the odd objects lying around.

Look at how powerful the word was that went out from Jonah's mouth. Though he passionately hoped that nothing would happen when he spoke, the word did not return empty. It accomplished the purpose for which God sent it. It struck the hearts of all those who hated God, and they turned to him and lived.

Of course, there was also the stuff about Jonah being chucked in the ocean, about being inside the fish for three days (get it?)—one man by his own life saving the lives of everyone in the ship, all the sailors also believing, the perfect prayer that Jonah prays—all that.

Fairness

"For to the one who has, more will be given, and he will have an abundance, but from the one who has not, even what he has will be taken away."

MATTHEW 13:12

Too often, I am sorry to say, Jesus deliberately undermines the preferences and values of the age. In this instance, the thing that most occupies the 21st century imagination—fairness—is the last thing Jesus happens to be worried about. He didn't come to even things out. He didn't come to make sure everyone got a little something—the way I carefully portion out a golden, fluffy cobbler so that no child has even one piece of fruit or fleck of cream more than any other child. In the end, some people will have everything, and other people will have nothing at all.

Is Jesus talking about possessions, do you think? If he is talking about humanity's stuff, then everyone will be happy or angry as circumstances dictate. Sadly, it is not the stuff. He is talking about *himself*. In the end, the little bit of knowledge that some people have, the little bit of understanding of who God is and what he is going on about, in the end, if they say no to Jesus, even that little bit will be taken away. Whereas to the one who looks to Jesus and says yes to everything that he is, to everything that he says, that person will possess everything.

It isn't fair, I guess, but if you don't want him around during your whole life, you'd be disappointed to be stuck with him forever.

Herod

And the king was sorry, but because of his oaths and his guests he commanded it to be given.

MATTHEW 14:9

The heat and noise of the celebration, of so many men drinking and eating, wafts up over the walls into the night air. If you're going to celebrate your birthday you might as well do a good job of it, or so you told yourself earlier in the day when you were trying to shove yourself into the special clothes ordered just for this occasion. All your friends, some of your enemies—everyone together for the celebration.

Therefore, abounding in beneficence, you don't stop to question yourself as you launch into the main entertainments of the evening. You keep drinking. You keep eating. And then your stepdaughter, or whatever she is in relationship to you—who even knows—dances in all dressed up in . . . well, what exactly *is* she wearing? Whatever. All your friends and enemies are enthralled. If you were a better sort of person you would call for a shawl, or something, to cover her up.

You lift your glass amidst the thumping and cheering, you shout over the din, "That was amazing, you can have anything you like in the whole world!" She narrows her eyes and asks for the head of a man on a platter—a man who scares and torments and fascinates you. The head of John. What was the name of that other guy who took a foolish oath so many years ago? Who sacrificed someone innocent? Never mind, you can't remember. Surely your word matters more than anything, especially with this clamoring audience. You give the order.

But oh, oh the headache in the morning.

So Many Choices

"For what will it profit a man if he gains the whole world and forfeits his soul? Or what shall a man give in return for his soul?"

MATTHEW 16:26

It might be better if you just try to get through the day without thinking about this too much. There are so many pressing tasks to attend to that the consideration of your own soul might be something you can worry about later. Just shove it down, and don't think about it. Go shopping. Turn up the volume on the TV. Pull out your phone and have another scroll through Twitter.

Or you could work harder. You could try to amass money and power and influence. If you're in a church, you could work really hard so that other people will feel guilty and begin to defer to you. You could even visit the sick and give money to the poor so that other people will notice you and feel envious. You could tick other people off by getting really skinny, or buying a new car, or solving the worldwide water crisis.

The main thing is to not look at Jesus, and especially to not look at the wide expanse of eternity behind him. Keep your eyes on the present, on the stuff that's got your attention right now. Maybe your soul will go on forever. Maybe God will pass over you in the great judgment at the end. Maybe you can slip through unnoticed.

On the other hand, if that scares you, you can look at Jesus this moment and beg him to rescue you—to take your own soul into his hands and take care of it forever. That might work too. So many choices . . .

The Unforgiving

"But when that same servant went out, he found one of his fellow servants who owed him a hundred denarii, and seizing him, he began to choke him, saying, 'Pay what you owe.'"

MATTHEW 18:28

There you are, slumped in a gray office chair, sobbing before your creditor. You've managed to spend something like a billion dollars, or all the money that America owes China. You can't even figure out how it got to be so much. You weren't trying to be bad. In fact, you set out to do the right thing, but everything kept going sideways. Every time you tried to get back on your feet, something would go wrong. You would try to make a payment, and the money would slip out of your grasp. You are in worse shape than you, or anyone you know, could have ever imagined. You're hunched there, sobbing, and you hear the guy say, "Don't worry about it, I'll suck it up. You just go on. You don't owe me anything anymore." Is this even for real?

You spring up out of the chair. You thank him, from the bottom of your heart, if that is even possible. You wander out into the sun. And there, as you stumble down the steps, you smack into a guy who owes you a hundred bucks. "Hey, hey!" you shout. "Hey. You owe me one hundred dollars!" You grab him and shake him.

And that, well, that is what every single one of us does. Jesus pays the immeasurable debt of the soul, he buys it back, and then we turn around and hold grudges against other people who barely owe anything in comparison.

That's Disappointing

"Am I not allowed to do what I choose with what belongs to me? Or do you begrudge me my generosity?"

MATTHEW 20:15

Except that we do—we constantly begrudge God and are offended when he doesn't do for us what we think he ought to do. We take our understanding of fair and good and apply it to God, and then we're angry when he doesn't come through for us.

In other words, I can work really hard all day, for my whole life, doing all the things God tells me to do, obediently doing good and not evil, forgiving my enemies, caring for other people first before I obsess about myself (supposing any of this is really possible, and even if it were, would I actually do it?) and, at the hour of my death, I get the exact same reward as the person who, in her dying breaths, clings onto the hope of salvation, onto Jesus himself.

We both die, me being Christian all my life, and she rescued at the last minute. And we get the same reward, and the reward is . . . and try not to be disappointed about this . . . Jesus. Jesus himself is the reward. Not a pile of money, not a mansion, not endless happiness: Jesus. Jesus is what you get at the end. And everyone gets the same, no matter when they come in, because there's enough of him to go around.

But he denied it before them all, saying, "I do not know what you mean."
MATTHEW 26:70

Don't look down your nose at Peter. He's not the only one who has done this—this total denial of Jesus at the critical moment. Sure, it was really public, and he had just made speeches about how he would never be the kind of person to stoop so low. He had gone well out of his way to elevate his own character. "I'm not that kind of person," he had said, waving bread and lamb in the air and frothing at the corners of his mouth, eyes blazing.

If there is any cautionary tale for you—and I guess also for me—it's not to go around making speeches about your own excellent character. "I would never do something like that," or, "Can you believe what he said? I would never have said that." Maybe you haven't—but give it time.

Wait for the stress and pressure to mount. Wait for the critical moment when fear and pride join themselves diabolically together. And then you might be able to see and feel how far Peter fell, and how gracious Jesus was to pick him up and restore him. The same for you. When you discover yourself to be the kind of person you hate, to be a low, slimy, betraying creature, Jesus can pick you up and make you stand, if only you will look at him.

It's All Over

And Joseph took the body and wrapped it in a clean linen shroud and
laid it in his own new tomb, which he had cut in the rock. And he rolled a
great stone to the entrance of the tomb and went away.

MATTHEW 27:59—60

This is a remarkable act of heroism, though perhaps just a teeny bit lack-
ing in faith. Joseph hadn't been publicly associated with Jesus. He and
Nicodemus, both members of the Sanhedrin, had been going along quietly, supporting Jesus in spirit, though not in body, until his trial and
judgment. When it came time to care for his body, they stepped forward
and did it.

And the women who had been with him all along, feeding him and
traveling with him and worrying about him—they had to stand back and
watch two strange men handle his body, his broken, bloody, destroyed
body, packing it in spice and wrapping it in linen. So, of course, the wom-
en followed to see the tomb, and of course they hurried back, as soon as
the Sabbath was over, to care for him properly.

And death and despair covered the land and filled the heart. Everyone
sat in grief and agony, though none of them needed to. If they had listened
to his words, they would have understood what was happening. Same for
you. Take Jesus at his words. They aren't difficult to understand. They are
true. Everything happened as he said it would.

The Guards

While they were going, behold, some of the guard went into the city and told the chief priests all that had taken place.
MATTHEW 28:11

You'd spent the whole day having to crucify the man. His trial had been irregular, part of it taking place at night. You'd marched him back and forth across the city, from the Mount of Olives, back across to the High Priest, then back to Pilate, with stops in between. Then the scourging, of course; then getting the now-weakened victim out of the city to the place of crucifixion. You'd nailed him to the cross in front of the entire city, who'd had nothing else to do but watch, even though it was one of their major holidays. And then the earthquake and the darkness. Everything about the whole twenty-four hours had been surreal.

You were finally asleep in your grimy cot, too tired to bathe, too tired even to eat. Lurid, mocking dreams woke you three or four times. And now there's an uproar outside—the sun is barely even up. You stagger out into the courtyard. What on earth?

Can this really be? That the incompetent relief guards left in front of the tomb *fell asleep*?

But now they swear they didn't fall asleep. There was another earthquake, and some massive, shining man threw the stone over, sat on it, and stared at them, and when they checked the tomb was empty, because of course it was. Honestly, a fitting end to a bizarre couple of days. You have got to get out of this place and go back to Rome where it's safer.

The True Beginning

The beginning of the gospel of Jesus Christ, the Son of God.

MARK 1:1

The word "gospel," as practically everybody knows, means "good news." It's the good thing that happened to the world after all the terrible things that happened from the moment of the Fall all the way on down. Thing is, it doesn't look very good from the outside. It doesn't look spectacular.

A man comes—Jesus—and he holds all power and authority and dominion and glory in his baby finger. One word from him and the stars would alter their course. One word from him and the waves of the sea calm themselves. He holds the created order together in his own being. And what does he decide to do first? Before anything else?

What would you do? Probably not put on a pair of dusty sandals and wander out into a muddy river to be baptized by your cousin who looks like a crazy man. No, you would take on the ruler of the known world, the one who calls himself the son of the gods, Caesar. You would right all the wrongs. You would use all that energy force to do something spectacular.

The thing is, the greatest purveyor of evil deeds in the whole universe is the human heart—yours and mine—and it takes moving the heaven and earth the restore it. And so Jesus came in sandals, with words and maybe a beard, and he did the miracle one person at a time, and most people didn't even see what was going on.

No Contest

And they were all amazed, so that they questioned among themselves,
saying, "What is this? A new teaching with authority! He commands
even the unclean spirits, and they obey him."
MARK 1:27

The arrival of Jesus on the scene brought all the ugliness of Satan out of
the woodwork. Most of the time, it's not very useful to go around looking
for demons here and there, in the hole of a tree or the mind of your best
friend. I like to blame everything on Satan, rather than myself, because
it's easier and more interesting. But not everything can be the devil's fault.

I am far removed from that moment when Jesus began to walk up and
down the tiny length of Palestine, to preach and teach and heal and do
the work he had come to do. At that moment when he first stepped onto
that minuscule world stage, the powers of hell went into overdrive. There
were demons everywhere. Every time Jesus turned around it seems He he
was bumping into someone possessed or oppressed or troubled. And, because two opposing forces can't live together harmoniously, he cast them
all out. It wasn't even close. Gone, banished. And everyone was amazed,
because when we fight against evil—when we bother to, that is—it's sus-
penseful. Good only wins out a fraction of the time. But there wasn't any
contest with Jesus. He had only to say the word, and they melted away.

255 Alone Again

But he went out and began to talk freely about it, and to spread the news,
so that Jesus could no longer openly enter a town, but was out in desolate
places, and people were coming to him from every quarter.

MARK 1:45

There you are. You have the most horrible disease imaginable. Your skin is ruined, and your body disfigured. You haven't touched any other person for as long as you can remember, nor spoken to anyone. You live outside, away from everybody else, in a hovel. And that's it. That's the way it's going to be forever. The loneliness presses in and down on you sometimes; but most of the time you just deal. Because that's the way it is.

Then one day you hear of someone who, it has been said, can heal and restore the totality of the human body. With just a word, he can transform a person from sick to well in an instant. And so you, even though you're not sure you really think it can work, break all the rules and go to find this man. And he does what you hope he will: he completely heals you, and then he tells you not to say anything about it. To anyone. But how can you not? How can you not go and tell everyone?

And so, in all ways, he takes your place. He goes out into the desolate places alone, where you once were, and takes your disease onto himself, and your sin, and carries it all the many long miles to Jerusalem.

That Sounds Exhausting

And he said to them, "The Sabbath was made for man, not man for the Sabbath."

MARK 2:27

This pithy saying does not make sense to the people who hear it for the first time. If they had their wits about them, they might respond that the Sabbath is for God, buddy—but they aren't quick enough.

But to you it might make sense, if you can look Jesus in his biblical eye and try to consider all the pages you've read thus far. The fact is, it is a very comforting thing to be able to know what the rules are and be able to do them. It's a nice thing to know what kind of work to do and then feel happy about doing it.

If you're not supposed to do any work on the Sabbath, because God commanded you not to—never mind thinking about why he commanded it—then you can "work" very hard at resting. You can exhaust yourself not doing lots of things. But the point of the Sabbath is not for you to not work, it's for you to see that you can't do anything without God and that you are nothing without him and that when you stop working he goes on holding everything together.

The Sabbath was made for you to see God and listen to him. It wasn't another box you could check off so that God would approve of you.

MARK 2:18–3:12

Starting Over

And when his family heard it, they went out to seize him, for they were
saying, "He is out of his mind."
MARK 3:21

Jesus is such a disappointment—not just now, but then also. The thing we most want Jesus to do now is congratulate us on who we are. Way back then, he was supposed to come and confirm everyone's righteous rage against the Romans. It was, and is, upsetting for Jesus to come and pick out twelve backward, contentious, morally questionable men to stand in the place of Israel. Instead of saying, "Good job, Israel," by the choice of these men He says, "You have so utterly failed that I am starting over again, and this group of disreputables is better than the lot of you."

His family, understandably, thinks he's insane and comes to take him home. It would be hard to do something more provocative than what he's just done. Frustration, disappointment, and now a little fear taint the mixture of emotions—both ancient and modern—swirling around.

In other words, you're in good company when you run into the brick wall of Jesus' disapproval, and your disappointment in him when he doesn't give you a congratulatory gold star. Don't try to take him by force to do your will. Let him be who he is—God—the judge of you, and not the other way around.

MARK 3:13-4:34

258 Who Did His Hair Though?

And they were filled with great fear and said to one another, "Who then is this, that even the wind and the sea obey him?"

MARK 4:41

I love to watch movie adaptations of Jesus, hair blowing Byronically, his intense soulful expression the means by which he commands the wind and waves. He stretches out his hand toward the screen and calls you to change the world. You look in his eyes and know in your heart that it's his passion, his ocean of love that makes all the cool stuff happen. He's just so awesome, and his hair is so wavy.

Who knows, though, he may have had bad hair in real life. The actual reason the wind and the waves obey him is that he's God. Lots of people looked at him in real life and their hearts did not flutter. Everyone in his hometown thought he was offensive and annoying.

The astonishment and fear of those in the boat, then, is not because of his hair, his great camera presence, his soulful eyes. It is because no one else is able to stop a storm by speaking. No one else is able to make the blind see or the lame walk without modern technology. No one else is able to bring about the resurrection of the long dead by a word.

If the wind and the waves obey Jesus, what business is it of yours to disobey? Why would you constantly do the opposite of what he says? But you do, however captivated you may be by his charming smile and that heartstopping camera angle.

MARK 4:35–6:6

Corban

"But you say, 'If a man tells his father or his mother, "Whatever you would have gained from me is Corban" (that is, given to God) . . .'"

MARK 7:11

This is the perfect scam. What you do is you go in procession up to the temple with your retinue. You have the trumpet blown and arrange yourself so that you look imposing. Then you solemnly declare to the priests, and anybody hanging around to see and hear you, that all your stuff is Corban. It all belongs to God. Every last bit. It's all God's. And so, cleverly on your part, you can't any longer give any of it away, not even to your parents. It all has to be used by you "for the upbuilding of God's people."

You get to go out to expensive lunches and weekends away in the countryside, comfortable in your conscience, because you "gave it all to God," and you're just "using it in trust." Meanwhile your parents and family and those in need around you perish in poverty when you could have been helping and caring for them. And so, in keeping the law—to the letter— you have broken the law to respect and honor your parents.

Be careful when you're trying to justify your conscience through some acrobatic trick. God isn't stupid. Jesus isn't airbrushed and gullible. You may fool everyone around you, but you haven't fooled the one person who matters.

MARK 6:7–7:37

Better Than That

And Peter said to Jesus, "Rabbi, it is good that we are here. Let us make
three tents, one for you and one for Moses and one for Elijah."
MARK 9:5

There wasn't anything about him that anyone would notice or think hon-
orable or glorious. He was plain, acquainted with grief and struggle, born
into poverty, nourished on the bread of affliction, acquainted with sorrow
and strife. He amazed the crowds not with his charisma, but by healing
every disease, and by the substance of his preaching. So it was quite a
shock for Peter and James and John to climb up this mountain, or at least
a very big hill, and have a cloud descend and envelope them in the presence of Moses and Elijah. And then to see Jesus in the blazing light of his
true glory. They didn't expect it. They were totally shocked. Though they
had started to have an inkling as to who Jesus was, they didn't really get it.
Seeing Jesus in this way was a transformative moment for everyone, hem.

And yet, many years later, Peter would say that the book you have
in your hands, the Bible itself, is more transforming, more sure, more
trustworthy. It is plain. It doesn't compel or amaze you. But when you read
it, your wounds are bound up, your life is transformed. You begin to see
the full weight of God's own glory. Don't give up!

Not a Fig

And he said to it, "May no one ever eat fruit from you again." And his disciples heard it.

MARK 11:14

Jesus, as everyone knows, hates fig trees.

Just kidding. Jesus doesn't hate fig trees. The fig tree, as you are probably more than well aware, stands for Israel. It's like a lovely little parable. Every time you see a fig tree (assuming that running into fig trees is a regular occurrence for you), you're meant to think of Israel and remember God's promise of love and mercy and everything.

Except, most embarrassingly, Jesus has just cursed this little tree and literally killed it with the word that comes forth from his mouth. He says, "May no one ever eat of you again," and then goes and cleanses the temple, throwing everybody out of the main court, turning over tables and pouring out the money so that no one will be able to get back all that they had collected. On the way back out of the city the disciples look at the tree and discover that it is withered up, dead.

The strange action of clearing out the temple is a way of saying, "God isn't here anymore." The cursing of the fig tree is a way of saying that Israel is no longer alive. The two things together, God in the temple and Israel as a lovely fig tree, he declares over and done with.

So, of course, they had to kill him.

MARK 10:17–11:33

Willing and Unable

And again he came and found them sleeping, for their eyes were very heavy, and they did not know what to answer him.

MARK 14:40

It's not as if you don't know what you should do. Unless you've destroyed your conscience through neglect and the gradual hardening of deliberate sin, of never going back and saying you're sorry, for the most part you know what you should do. Even if no one ever made you read or memorize the Ten Commandments, you wouldn't have to be a genius to know it is bad to lie, and that perfection is much to be desired over wickedness and incompetence. Of course, if you've actually been reading the Bible all this time, you know also that you are supposed to trust God and worship him alone.

Adding to all that, in these last hours, Jesus gave to his disciples a specific instruction: "Watch and pray." It wasn't hard to understand what he wanted them to do. They understood. They didn't need more information, or a longer instructional video. It was that they were *unable* to do it. They couldn't. Though they tried valiantly, they failed.

And so, even in the Passion of our Lord Jesus, moment by sorrowful moment, the gospel is proclaimed: you need someone to rescue you. And Jesus came on purpose to do just that. Every moment that you don't cry out to him, every moment that you try to muscle through using the broken, tired stuff inside of you, you are telling a tiny lie about the work that Jesus is this moment doing. Rise up from your sleep and cling on to the One whose death is for you.

MARK 12:1–44, 14:1–42

The Mocking

And some began to spit on him and to cover his face and to strike him,
saying to him, "Prophesy!" And the guards received him with blows.
MARK 14:65

While the disciples were physically, mentally, emotionally, and spiritually unable to obey, the guards mocked Jesus. They took it upon themselves
to humiliate and shame Jesus though they had never encountered him before, nor did they know anything of his power and mercy.

Disobedience and weakness, or hatred and mocking: these are the
universal human responses to God. They have been there all the way
along, and they are here in the last moments also. Jesus is received by us,
by his own creation, with apathy, with spitting, hating, mocking blows.

Don't exclude yourself from the crowd. How often are you, while perhaps feeling an emotion of love or affection for Jesus, still left with the
empty, ash-filled hand of disobedience? You felt like you wanted to do
what he told you to. You thought it might theoretically be nice to leave
aside your bitterness, or anger, or weariness. But you couldn't. You don't
feel mockery, perhaps, but your actions say otherwise. Or maybe it's just
your mental and emotional exhaustion that keeps you from doing anything. You can't obey. You don't even care.

You need help. The guards needed help. The crowds need help. You
need help. Look at him. Bow before him. Worship him. Be helped.

And they compelled a passerby, Simon of Cyrene, who was coming in
from the country, the father of Alexander and Rufus, to carry his cross.
MARK 15:21

And everyone turns around and nods at Alexander and Rufus, sitting there
in that early church gathering (which is why Mark so cleverly mentions
them) as the book is read out. The people who are hearing about it for the
first time, who are trying to understand the meaning of this incredibly
strange story, turn their eyes back up front and carry on listening.

This is what they hear: The trial is over, and Jesus is condemned to
die. He's been beaten, mocked, and now, as he carries this most shameful
piece of wood, going forward to be nailed to it, stumbling and falling under its weight, an out-of-town pilgrim, there for the feast, is pulled out of
the crowd and compelled to carry the cross.

The listening congregation lean forward, struggling together to understand. What sort of feast is this? It is the Passover of the Lord. At the
very moment the lambs are being slaughtered, their blood gushing down,
turning the stream running under the temple red, Jesus climbs the hill of
Golgotha to give his life for the world. One man's death would accomplish
what generations of sacrifices never had.

The reading ends and the bread and the cup are laid on the table. The
congregation bows in prayer. They bite down on the bread. They drink
out of the cup. They, like Simon, grasp hold of that cross.

The Unexpected

And they went out and fled from the tomb, for trembling and astonishment
had seized them, and they said nothing to anyone, for they were afraid.
MARK 16:8

There isn't any grand, sweeping, major-keyed, uplifting music to let the
women know that something cosmos-shattering has happened. They
carry their awkward burden of spice and grief without expecting anything
but death to greet them when they arrive. They have no hope that at the
last moment maybe everything is going to be okay. It isn't okay. The special lighting and sound effects, markedly absent because God, who forgot to consult the Christian film industry, do not clue them in. It's the
same road they walked over in the twilight of Friday, the regular stone
and dirt under their feet, the usual clothes, the same hassle of shoulder-
ing everything that has to be carried, the same loss that comes with every
single death. Everyone is broken. Everyone is eventually torn out of the
world—the body shoved in the ground, the stone rolled into place to contain the stench of death.

So of course they run away from the empty tomb in fear and terror. Of
course—when confronted by the stone lying on the ground and the young
man in dazzling white, telling them that Jesus isn't dead—of course they
just run away in confusion. Death always wins. Except not anymore. Now
death is around for only a limited time. It has been broken, ruined.

> *. . . it seemed good to me also, having followed all things closely for some time past, to write an orderly account for you, most excellent Theophilus, that you may have certainty concerning the things you have been taught.*
>
> LUKE 1:3—4

I always like to imagine Luke settled back on a pile of cushions in Mary's well-appointed living room, drinking something or other, I guess probably not coffee, though that would complete the picture, firing off every single imaginable question, absorbing the massive earful he was hoping for, and then staggering away under the weight of such a life, to distill it down into a coherent narrative, something short enough for us to cope with on Sunday morning.

When Luke wasn't ferreting out the people who knew and saw Jesus firsthand, he was one step behind Paul, fretting about that great apostle's health and the insanity of his pace back and forth across the known world. Luke was probably the person who double-checked all their lodgings, attending to all the packing along the way. Or, once forcibly thrown out of town, he would miraculously produce every important document and remedy so thoughtfully secreted about his person. Whereas everyone else, halfway down the road, would begin asking if the money bag had been left behind, Luke would calmly reply, "I have it here."

God uses every sort of person. He uses the scatterbrain. He uses the orderly and organized. But I think, whatever kind of person you are, it's such a good idea to have your eyes and ears open, to be awfully curious about everything, so that when something important happens, you're not the one to miss it.

Hold Your Tongue

"And behold, you will be silent and unable to speak until the day that these things take place, because you did not believe my words, which will be fulfilled in their time."
LUKE 1:20

Poor Zechariah. I always like to joke that it was a mercy for Elizabeth that Zechariah couldn't speak for nine months. Imagine the peace and quiet reaching into every corner of the house and garden. How heavenly. All terribly sexist joking aside, the real mercy was probably for Zechariah himself. Because if he felt like doubting, if he felt like second-guessing everything—the vision, the angel, the message—he had only to try to open his mouth and speak. And then nothing would come out. And so he would know that it wasn't just his mind playing tricks.

So often our minds do play tricks. Our emotions reinterpret events as we go farther away from them. Our sense of what happened fades over time. It's hard to find some objective thing outside of the self to anchor the memory, to establish the truth weeks later. But God's words to the prophets and through his angels weren't nebulous feelings that the hearer could doubt. They were audible words, spoken out loud, or visions, emblazoned in the sky or on the mind. And they always came true, so you could always trust them. In this case, Zechariah needed only to try to speak, and then he could know that every word of God proves true.

LUKE 1:5–25

Mary

And Mary said, "Behold, I am the servant of the Lord; let it be to me
according to your word." And the angel departed from her.
LUKE 1:38

Not very old. Not famous at all. No dexterity puckering up for a selfie.
Not trying to be something she's not. Not wandering around in a mall,
or wherever it is that teenagers go these days, cell phone in hand, jeans
too tight, hair dyed green at the tips, a look of rebellion blazing out of her
angry eyes. That's not Mary. She is quietly at home, doing some kind of
work, being a help and comfort to her parents. And then her whole world
is shattered.

Angelic visitations don't happen to too many people. Maybe none at all.
A few prophets in the Old Testament—Isaiah, Jeremiah, Ezekiel—suffer an
unraveling vision of God, hearing his word so mightily that they, in response, write furiously, trying to unstop their mouths however painfully.

Mary, on the other hand, what does she say? She could say so many
things: What's in it for me? How will it turn out? Why should I?

But no, none of that. She says simply, Yes. Yes. Let it be.

Sometimes if you are struggling to do what you know God wants you to
do, or trying not do what you know he doesn't want you to do, and you are
wrestling in a mire of angst and confusion and unhappiness, you could
stop, and sit down, and take your eyes of the screen, and just say Yes.

Use Words

> *"And you, child, will be called the prophet of the Most High; for you will*
> *go before the Lord to prepare his ways, to give knowledge of salvation to*
> *his people in the forgiveness of their sins . . ."*
> LUKE 1:76–77

Elizabeth, at her old, worn-out age, gives birth. The neighbors are amazed. Kept at arm's length all these many months, knowing that something was going on but not able to gossip about it with any real knowledge, they finally get a chance to know and hear and see the baby. And that's when Zechariah's mouth is opened.

He announces that the baby's name will be John, and he sings a long song about it. This baby is going to grow up and go out to prepare the way, to call out thunderously for everyone to wake up and listen and pay attention. The whole world—well, the whole of Israel—will stop what they are doing and go out and listen to his words and climb down into the Jordan River to be baptized.

If you wanted to know, if you wanted to be able to say definitively who was the best person ever to live, it was John. Strange, stark John, out in the wilderness, shouting. His father's song of praise is lyrical and opulent compared to the cutting, biting judgments of John. The song paints a lovely picture of God's action in the world, and then John comes and no one can believe it. Then Word himself comes, and there's an outcry of anger.

Not According to Plan

And she gave birth to her firstborn son and wrapped him in swaddling cloths and laid him in a manger, because there was no place for them in the inn.

LUKE 2:7

The modern mother would never get away with this. You can't give birth in the presence of a lot of farm animals, and why would you want to? You want the birth of your child to be warm, and clean, and perfect. Why else do you fill out that long Birth Plan in the days before the baby is scheduled to make his appearance? You fill it out and give it to the nurses and midwives who smile with gentle condescension and shove it in a cupboard, because they only give that to you as a lying ruse to make you think you have some kind of control, some ability to plan.

Well, guess what? You don't have control—not in birth, not in anything. Mary's immediate and alarming yes to God was a yes that meant that no plan she made would ever be anything more than shoved in a cupboard. And it wasn't about discovering God's perfect plan for her life. She wouldn't have wanted to know in advance, at the point of saying yes, that the plan included giving birth to a baby far away from her own mother, in obscurity and discomfort, and then having that baby grow up into somebody who publicly announced the overthrow of Israel, and then was arrested and killed as a curse—The Curse.

Simeon

And Simeon blessed them and said to Mary his mother, "Behold, this child is appointed for the fall and rising of many in Israel, and for a sign that is opposed (and a sword will pierce through your own soul also), so that thoughts from many hearts may be revealed."

LUKE 2:34—35

Mary and Joseph, obedient and faithful in all matters of the law, wrap up the very new baby Jesus in a tight bundle and travel the short distance from Bethlehem to Jerusalem to ascend the sharply rising steps of the temple. They are so poor they only have a couple of doves to give as an offering for their baby. They deliver up their sacrifice in the proper way. But then, as they turn to retrace their way, an old man stops them, picks them out of the crowd, takes hold of the baby, and cries out in praise.

He can die happy, he says, because he's finally seen with his own eyes what he's been waiting for his whole life. I'm gonna go all cliché and just pause and ask you what you've been waiting for, with great longing, your whole life. But don't feel too bad when you stop, really think about it, and discover that Jesus wouldn't have been your first answer. Of all the many thousands of people in the temple that day, only two people stopped to notice the Savior of the world. So maybe you didn't catch on earlier in your life, or maybe you don't care that much now: there's still time. You still have time to see the wonder of your salvation, to cry out, "Finally!"

LUKE 2:22–52

The Voice from Heaven

And the Holy Spirit descended on him in bodily form, like a dove; and a voice came from heaven, "You are my beloved Son; with you I am well pleased."

LUKE 3:22

It's nice sometimes, to hear the person who loves you say it publicly, so that other people can know about it too. I never like saying out loud to anyone how I really feel about them because I'm afraid of being needy, of losing a sense, usually imagined, of control over myself. If I confess that I love someone, I've given them the power to hurt me, to reject me.

For centuries and centuries God kept saying to Israel, "I love you." He said it boldly, loudly, and sometimes it made him sound needy and desperate. Israel looked back at God and said, "Meh," and sometimes, "I know," and when things got really bad, "No thank you." And it was heartbreaking, awful. Loving someone who doesn't love you—a spouse, a child, a friend—is a devastating place to be. It's amazing that God endured it for so long.

But Jesus rises up out of the water, and God the Father announces, "I love you" in tones so deafening everyone else can hear it. And the earth gives a shuddering embarrassed groan and turns away. But Jesus expands and fills his lungs with joy and steps out of the water to begin a long and tragic journey of perfect love lived out in perfect obedience. And this is also pretty amazing.

Leviathan

And Jesus, full of the Holy Spirit, retuned from the Jordan and was led
by the Spirit in the wilderness for forty days, being tempted by the devil.
And he ate nothing during those days. And when they were ended, he
was hungry.

LUKE 4:1—2

There was the woman, all those years ago, with the man, helping him to tend the garden. His ego was as delicate as the tiny porcelain teacup you might hold in the palm of your hand. One false move and it could shatter in a million pieces all over the garden floor. He was supposed to care for her, too, even as he worked the garden. He had only one command to teach and to obey: "Don't eat from the tree that is in the midst of the garden." But, like the burden of trying to keep hold of one's car keys, of listening to and talking to his wife while paying attention to everything in the garden, when the serpent came to do battle, he stood by as she fought and lost, and then he took hold of her ruin.

Are you wrestling with Satan in the course of your sin-addled life? Are you trying to do your own job and everybody else's? Or are you avoiding responsibility altogether? Are you lonely? Ill-equipped? Beset? Do you feel like it's your job to combat all the evil?

Step aside. A new man has entered the arena. Though the lush landscape lies wasted, though wild animals circle, though you have no strength, though the devil exults, yet this strong man will stand in your place, will do down Satan, will endure the consequences of your hunger, your pride, your discontent.

The Hole in the Roof

. . . but finding no way to bring him in, because of the crowd, they went up on the roof and let him down with his bed through the tiles into the midst before Jesus.

LUKE 5:19

It's not what you would call an expensive house. It is comfortable and convenient. It keeps out the heat and cold, and you look forward to coming back to it when you've been away. After all, it's yours. If you didn't like it, you would make adjustments. It is, then, a touch horrifying to find the entire town trying to stuff itself in. The maximum occupancy is, maybe, twelve—not Everyone. The crush of humanity produces a sort of mob stubbornness. No one listens to you when you beg, "Please be careful with that." As you stand mashed against the wall, anxious, dust begins to sift down from the roof. You look up to see more and more dust, and then bits of clay brick, falling, falling. Someone is deliberately beating a hole in your roof. It grows bigger and bigger so that you can even see who is doing it. Before long, it's huge, like the size of an actual person. And then—can it get any worse—suddenly a guy, who would be holding tightly onto his mat if he could move his arms, is lowered down, and comes to rest right smack at the feet of Jesus. Really? They couldn't wait till Jesus left the house? What kind of desperation is this? Jesus speaks to the man, and the man gets up and rolls up his mat and walks away. And then there's some shouting between Jesus and the Pharisees. And honestly, now you have a huge hole in your roof.

The Good Soil

"As for that in the good soil, they are those who, hearing the word, hold it fast in an honest and good heart, and bear fruit with patience."
LUKE 8:15

Hope you aren't Bad Soil!

Just kidding. The fact that you are struggling along trying to read the Bible at all, or even just a book about the Bible, that alone proves you're not bad soil—probably.

But don't think about it like that. Don't sit there worrying about yourself, what kind of soil you might be. Consider the strange quality of this soil, that it produces "a hundredfold." No ordinary soil wakes up in the morning, finds the seed scattered all over it, and produces that kind of abundance. Just like it was so strange for Isaac, after trying to pass off his wife as his sister (a strange family habit), to reap a hundredfold in the land of the Philistines. The "good soil" cannot be some verdant moral quality inside the person.

The soil and the seed are both about God. God prepares the ground. When there are rocks that have to be a split apart, he does that too. He is the grain of the wheat that falls into the ground and dies. The Word itself produces the harvest. When you're washing the dust off your feet at the end of a long day, or digging in the dirt in your garden, turn it over in your soul and wonder about the power of God to make the soil and the wheat both so sure, so abundant, so rich.

"Which of these three, do you think, proved to be a neighbor to the man who fell among the robbers?"

LUKE 10:36

And everyone sits around in painful embarrassment, because the Samaritan was supposed to be hating the Jewish man who fell by the wayside. He was supposed to keep walking, the way everyone else kept walking. The fact that he didn't makes everyone in the crowd feel bad. Hating each other—not necessarily with the emotions, but certainly in word and deed—is what we do; it's who we are in our inner beings. When someone acts in love, when someone puts herself out on my behalf in such a way that I am in debt and can't think of a way to even things up, it doesn't usually make me feel happy or grateful. It makes me anxious and uncomfortable.

And this is what is so irritating about Jesus. He is unfailingly kind and loving to such a measure that you cannot pay him back. Even though you might try, you won't be able to. When you are hateful to him and those around you, he nevertheless does good to you and for you, so that the debt keeps building.

Anyway, you're not the Good Samaritan. You're the man lying by the side of the road, and sometimes you are the other guys walking by. Jesus is the Good Samaritan. You can know this is true by trying to be the Good Samaritan for a while, until you collapse by the side of the road, half dead from the effort.

LUKE 9:1–10:37

But the Lord answered her, "Martha, Martha, you are anxious and trou-
bled about many things . . ."
LUKE 10:41

Oh yeah. I am anxious and troubled by just about everything. I am on my feet all day, trying to calculate the length of a task commensurate with its importance and its proximity to every other task. I flit, or, more often, trudge from one thing to another, dealing with the constant interruptions that characterize the kind of life I lead. I have a bunch of kids and a smartphone. Those two things prohibit me from thinking any single thought for more than thirty seconds.

Honestly, how is a person like me supposed to cope with Mary over there, sitting down to enjoy the company and the teaching? Mary, who drinks deeply from the well of Scripture every morning, and I know that because I saw her on Facebook, her children all clustered around her as she read to them from the Bible.

I guess I could just stand here, hands covered in soap suds, looking at my mountainous piles of dishes and laundry and cry about it. I guess when Jesus says, essentially, "Stop it," I could try to understand the words coming out of his mouth. It's not that I'm never supposed to wash the dishes, but that if Jesus is physically sitting in my living room, maybe I could pare back the menu, or not worry about ironing the tablecloth. Maybe I could pour myself a glass of something and sit down to hear what he is saying. Maybe, as I'm anxious about so many things, I could ask Jesus to help me with some of them.

The Found Coin

"And when she has found it, she calls together her friends and neighbors,
saying, 'Rejoice with me, for I have found the coin that I had lost.'"
LUKE 15:9

It's been an intolerably long day. Nothing went right from the beginning. Every time you started something you were interrupted. Everything you attempted was a failure. As twilight crept over the brow of the hill, you yearned to put your weary feet up, you were counting the minutes and the tasks, trying to rush along because you knew you were going to collapse into a heap. So, when you discover that one—and you only have ten at this particular moment—of your coins is missing (and you count them over and over just to be certain), all you can do is stand there in a heady, adrenalin-fueled panic.

Light the lamp because darkness falls swiftly. Put everything away. Put everyone to bed. Take up the broom and, with all the concentration you can summon, search. That one coin is necessary. It cannot be lost.

"Have I wearied you?" God asked many, many books ago. Not that he gets tired, not that he needs anything. He has searched for you, he has gone to the ends of the earth to look for you and to find you, like a lost coin. But he also is the coin. Don't give up until you find him. You cannot live without that one thing. You may have all the other coins, all the other things in place, but if you lose that one coin, him, you will not be able to go on.

The Rich Man

> *"He said to him, 'If they do not hear Moses and the Prophets, neither will*
> *they be convinced if someone should rise from the dead.'"*
>
> LUKE 16:31

If I could lift only one detail from this remarkable parable, it would be that the rich man doesn't want to be in Abraham's bosom. He doesn't ask to leave the place where he is, he asks for Lazarus to come to him in his place of torment, or rather hell. He wants an illusory drop of water on his burning tongue. He does not want his tongue to be cool forever. He would like Lazarus, after a lifetime of misery, suffering, isolation, pain, and loss to leave his comfort and consolation and come into hell to bring him what barely amounts to a single ice chip. And then, when he finds out that his desire is impossible, he wants Lazarus to go back to earth, back to his humiliation, to tell the rich man's family what happens when you die.

But what happens when you die should have been no surprise to the rich man. Why do you suppose that people who avoid the question of God their whole lives face real fear as death approaches? It is because we know, deep down, for true, that this isn't all there is. There is an accounting. And not only so, we have several thousands of years of Scripture to confirm this inner knowledge.

The real tragedy is that, as Jesus says these words, he knows he's going to be the one who comes back from the dead and that those who didn't believe the Scriptures before, won't believe him even if they could see his actual body.

Anything Good

Nathanael said to him, "Can anything good come out of Nazareth?"
Philip said to him, "Come and see."
JOHN 1:46

The answer is supposed to be no. No, of course nothing good can come out Nazareth, that foul, provincial backwater. What is Nazareth? It is small. It is too hot. It is full of religious fanatics and poor farmers and fishermen. And there's a family up there that, you know. Well, I mean, they didn't get married soon enough. I don't want to say more, but you probably get my meaning.

Which is kind of a funny objection, as if all the other places of the world are respectable and pure. As if not every family is hiding some grotesque secret. As if all brothers everywhere aren't inclined toward unforgiving hatred. As if animosity isn't nestled in every human breast.

Putting all that aside, of course—your justifiable objections and the way you don't want to taint yourself by association—you might as well go and see. Uncross your fingers, peel open the eyes of your soul, and discover in that backward offensive place the only thing good that ever was, the only good in the whole world, the only true perfection ever. Something good does, in fact, come from Nazareth.

Jesus alone is good. Perfect even. And his goodness, embarrassing as it is for everyone, is worth going to look at, examining carefully and honestly. Go on, go look. Nobody thinks you're that holy anyway.

Happily Ever After

When the master of the feast tasted the water now become wine, and did not know where it came from (though the servants who had drawn the water knew), the master of the feast called the bridegroom . . .
JOHN 2:9

You had a whole year to prepare for this day. What on earth had you done with it? Your excuses teeter and fall into the abyss of the truth—the failure of one of your fields, the illness of your sister, the fact that you blew off valuable work time in the winter. It wasn't just that you mismanaged your finances, you didn't pay attention to the details of the wedding feast. There is no one to blame but yourself. Which you will do, hoping it will ease the humiliation you get to take with you into your new marriage.

So, of course you don't want to look at the master of the feast. You cower low in your chair, hoping he will be too drunk to notice that there's no more wine. Every crushing moment of your whole life runs through your mind on a loop. You have not met the eye of anyone important to you for two whole days.

You slouch down, your eyes on the ground. You want the day to be over and for death to come. And then, as a still, cool breeze wafts over the feast, you look up, and into the sparkling, astonished eyes of the master. He is holding out both his hands and laughing. Somehow, you have served up the best wine anyone has ever tasted.

JOHN 2

Delivered in the Dark

> *For God so loved the world, that he gave his only Son, that whoever*
> *believes in him should not perish but have eternal life.*
> JOHN 3:16

The more complicated a religious system, the better. The more you can tease out the rites and rituals of a group of people, the more fascinating they are.

Nicodemus, creeping up to Jesus "at night," was hoping for some profound, transforming insight to enhance what he already knew, some special information that would explain the incomprehensible behavior of this unremarkable man, who, nevertheless, in a very short time had overturned not only the marketing tables in the temple, but the very religious order upon which his life as a strict Pharisee was founded.

God, who loved his own creation, gave the person he most adored—his own Son, who is God also—to buy back that creation from death, to open the door to life that doesn't end when dirt is flung down on a casket.

Nicodemus, as smart as they come, doesn't get it. He doesn't want to endure a second spiritual infancy, he doesn't want to be helpless, dependent on God any more than you or I do. It would be nicer if he could do something, say something, be something. He skulks along behind Jesus in the shadow, considering this alien love, this life that might never end. Then, as darkness falls over the face of this perishing world, when the love of God was that moment overturning the cosmos, when the Truth was hanging in darkness on the cross, Nicodemus rushed headlong, like a newborn babe, into that very light.

Give Me This Water Always

The woman said to him, "Sir, give me this water, so that I will not be thirsty or have to come here to draw water."

JOHN 4:15

It is a major hassle to brave the blazing noonday sun in order to avoid all your neighbors and frenemies who always manage to get in a dig about your questionable life choices when you go to the village well to draw your water too late in the day. You might as well go now. By the time you get there, you're parched.

You set down your heavy jar and nod to the stranger sitting there, singularly ill-equipped to get water out of this ancient well for himself. He's not from here. Looks like he's from the vile north. When he asks you for water, you could spurn him, but you pause, and obligingly lower your bucket down into the cool depths. By the time you have hauled it up again, sweat prickling the back of your neck and spine, your whole world has toppled over.

Not only have you had a drink out of the true well—lapping up the word of life—but the deep pain of all the broken relationships cluttering up your soul have been healed, bathed in cool, refreshing, eternal water. You tell this strange man to wait, and you rush back to your own village, the very one from which you have been estranged almost your whole adult life. You knock on every door, you talk to every neighbor, the cup of living water spills out, runs over, and restores you to your family and people again.

The Bread of Life

Jesus said to them, "I am the bread of life; whoever comes to me shall not hunger, and whoever believes in me shall never thirst."

JOHN 6:35

My husband hates it when I, placid and cheerful mere seconds before, suddenly snap at him. When we were first married, he would yell at me in the most disconcerting way whenever this happened, apparently because, or so he says, I was yelling at him. Now he doesn't say anything. He just disappears and comes back with a plate of something, usually cheese, olives, or, when things are really bad, bread. Turns out I'm hungry. That's all.

Imagine never being hungry. Some of the trial of being human would disappear if I, or any of us, were never hungry. It seems like life might be easier. But look what I would miss! This sudden fall into hunger and desperation, as with all the other parts of the created order, is so that I will understand that I need God. It's not that God needs me, but that I need God. I cannot carry on in even the most basic way without him. The fact that I do carry on without him, that it seems like I'm doing fine, that I can just pop off to the store and buy whatever I want, is really only me shoving off the day of sudden and tragic collapse into a spiritual hunger that lasts forever. Better that I eat of him now, depend on him now, cry out to him now, before it's too late.

The Light of Life

Again Jesus spoke to them, saying, "I am the light of the world. Whoever follows me will not walk in darkness, but will have the light of life."
JOHN 8:12

Light, bread, water—these are the most basic elements of life—excepting the *main* one. You *can*, I suppose, try to make God fit into the margins, after you've sorted out the basics.

Like that old gimmick—fill a jar with the biggest rocks, the things that really matter, and then add in the smaller rocks, the things you want to do but aren't necessary for survival. And then what comes next, sand? Can't remember. Try doing that little exercise in the dark when you're hungry and thirsty. Light and bread and water are the big rocks that have to go in first, but we have these things so easily that we don't worry about them. They are a given. And God, who is the biggest rock, is optional.

Jesus comes and says "I Am the Light." I don't just provide the light; I *am* the light. If you don't have me, you live in darkness and obscurity. You can't do any of the things you expect and count on doing without light. You can't read or cook or work or walk or function. You are like a completely blind person, living in deep darkness, trying to orient yourself in time and space groping along with your hands, trying to hear what you can with your ears. If you don't have Jesus, if you don't know him, that's who you are.

JOHN 7:1–8:30

Before Abraham

Jesus said to them, "Truly, truly, I say to you, before Abraham was, I am."
JOHN 8:58

And they rose up to stone him because "I Am" is the name God revealed to Moses out of the burning bush. Everybody understood very well that Jesus was claiming to be God. And there he was—a man—standing before them. They filled their lungs with rage and picked up stones and then were confounded because he disappeared from them and went on to the next thing.

God—whom no one wanted—insisted on revealing himself to Moses, insisted on saying his name, and insisted the people know it. And, when the world had roiled itself into a rage, he himself came, he came as a man, he came and said his name to men. I Am. I hold everything together. Without me, you are not. You don't exist. You don't breathe. You don't eat. You don't live.

It's so offensive. You, no matter how much you structure every moment of your existence around yourself, are, at the final moment, a speck in the hand of the One who was and is and is to come.

But it is a hand that bled, a hand that was stretched out. Because you, O Speck, were of value enough to first create, and then to save. Put that stone down and form the better word in your mouth: "Thanks."

JOHN 8:31–59

The Open Door

*So Jesus again said to them, "Truly, truly, I say to you, I am the door of
the sheep."*
JOHN 10:7

The shepherds would take it in turns to lie across the door of the sheepfold
at night as a protection against thieves and predators. That one shepherd,
lying there—probably wrapped up in a cloak, hopefully dozing lightly—was
all the hope the sheep had of safety in the danger of the night. What were
they going to do? Save themselves? Fight the lion? Do down the wolf? If
trouble came, all they could do was cry out, pathetically bleating for the
shepherd lying there across the door to wake up and apply his stick.

But Jesus doesn't just lie across the door, He *is* the door. You can't go
in or come out without him. You can't go out of the fold to find pasture,
to drink water, to live, without him leading the way. And you can't go in
at night to safety without him showing you the way back. It's best if you
look deep inside yourself and discover yourself not to be a unicorn, or a
leopard, or a cheetah, but a bony, stubborn, not-that-beautiful-to-look-
at-non-European-sheep. Such a sheep errs and strays. Such a sheep is
foolish and prone to disease and trouble. And, most importantly, such a
sheep cannot continue living in security, cannot get the food and water
necessary, without Jesus, the Door. It might feel humiliating, at first, but
honestly, it's the safest way of life you can imagine.

JOHN 9:1–10:10

The Sheep and Their Shepherd

"I am the good shepherd. The good shepherd lays down his life for the sheep."
JOHN 10:11

Many false, evil, deceitful shepherds have climbed into the fold to steal and destroy the sheep over the many centuries of human existence. These shepherds sidled up who knew the weak foolishness of the sheep, eager to devour their fat, complacent minds, to eat up their flesh. There are still some among us now. Some wear muscle shirts and twist the Scriptures. Some are ready to receive your "seed" donation online. Some have re-defined important words like "love" and "Jesus." Others have perfectly shiny smiles and amazing hair and raise their Bibles in the air, promising you your best life this minute. They all feed themselves out of the pockets of the lost.

Considering these bad shepherds, you may start to lose your temper. But your wrath is nothing to the white-hot rage incited in the heart of the Good Shepherd. No, the Good Shepherd doesn't feed himself on the sheep. He lays down his life for the sheep. He rescues them. He saves them. He feeds them. He does everything for them. He doesn't hold them up to some measure and make them meet some mark of goodness. He doesn't kick them out of the fold for the evil they bring in. When they sell themselves to the beast, he buys them back, in his own blood.

Though He Die

Jesus said to her, "I am the resurrection and the life. Whoever believes in me, though he die, yet shall he live . . ."

JOHN 11:25

If there's one thing that equalizes everything, it's death: we'll all die, sooner or later. And here, Lazarus has died too soon. Unbelievably, Jesus does not rush to the bedside of his friend. He waits until Lazarus has died. Even though it is a great injury to Mary and Martha who knew that he could do something, could heal Lazarus, Jesus waits on purpose until Lazarus is in the grave.

The accusation, "If you had been here my brother would not have died," is basically, "How could a loving God let this happen?" The trouble is that the asker of this question, however it is phrased, is as dead as the person in the grave. Sure, she might be walking around, talking, breathing, doing stuff. But if she hasn't put herself in the hands of Jesus, then she is dead. Or he. It's not just Martha asking this question.

So, Jesus waits. He waits because at exactly the right moment, just like for Lazarus, he raises the dead. First he raises your heart. He takes away the dead stone and gives you a true, feeling, beating heart. And then, on the last day, he gives you your whole self—alive, body and everything. He is the resurrection. His is the life that does this.

It's Not the Journey

Jesus said to him, "I am the way, and the truth, and the life. No one comes to the Father except through me."

JOHN 14:6

All of us are trying to get somewhere, even if it is only to the grocery store. I, for example, am always trying to arrange my life so that I will end up in a golden pool of happiness, where all my troubles are inconsequential and my house is clean. This destination is always slightly beyond my grasp, but I work hard at it, because I know that it is the kingdom of true happiness.

It is not surprising that lots of us like to use Jesus as the way of getting from one place to another. If Jesus is the way, he can take me where I want to go. He can maybe get me a job, or a house, or a pile of money so I can have some stuff that will definitely make me happy. He said it himself: I am the Way.

It is a terrible disappointment, then, to discover that when he says he is the Way, he also means that he is the Destination. He is what you get. No wonder that so many people strike off looking for a different path.

In the same way that wherever you go, there you are, when Jesus is your way, he is also there, hassling you. And that can be a pain if you don't like him. You go through the door, you take the piece of bread, you look for a drink of water, you light a lamp, and then, you're still just left with . . . him, and yourself. Maybe he should also offer cake.

The True Vine

"I am the true vine, and my Father is the vinedresser."
JOHN 15:1

When you were the vine in that beautiful vineyard, planted in such serene loveliness, do you remember? You turned rotten. You went wild. You turned sour. And rather than let you carry on in recklessness and rebellion, thinking you were good when you were really evil, the vinedresser thought it better that the vineyard should be torn down, the watchtower destroyed, and wild animals let in to devour and destroy. And so it could have continued on forever—you a devastated and ruined vine, abandoned and helpless.

Yet the vinedresser mourned the loss of the vineyard. He was jealous for the vine that had once been so lovely. The vineyard and the vine weren't meant to be forever thrown away. And so he came and restored the vineyard. In the place of the rotten, rebellious vine, he planted the True Vine, a vine that would never be corrupted or diseased.

Then he found you and grafted you on to that perfect, healthy vine. You grew together so closely that you became a living part of the true vine. His life began to flow, even to the very ends, all the way to the outer reaches of your limbs.

It's hard, now, to tell where his life stops and yours begins, as it should be. The fruit that grows on this vine, is it yours? Is it his? When it is plucked and pressed down into the cup that flows over, the taste is exquisite. The master of the feast laughs with joy.

JOHN 15, 16

Your God and My God

Jesus said to her, "Do not cling to me, for I have not yet ascended to the
Father; but go to my brothers and say to them, 'I am ascending to my
Father and your Father, to my God and your God.'"
JOHN 20:17

In a thousand pages and a thousand years the ruined garden gave way to a
desolate field, to the wilderness, to a broken city, to exile from home and
family and people. Is it possible that *this* is a garden once more? It is not
hidden in the naval of the world, that protected paradise where men and
women were irrevocably sundered from each other, alienated from their
God and married to death in the unbreakable union that leaves women
standing alone, grief-stricken, looking into the grave over and over and
over and over. And men too.

What are these words—*your God and my God*? The last time they hung
in the air they fell from the mouth of a young woman, like a seed into the
ground, germinating over a hundred painstakingly recorded generations.

Is this the moment they spring to life out of the rocky soil of this public
garden? Does this man undo that ancient divorce? Does his glorious life
destroy death?

Can his God be my God? His Father, my Father? Can we never be divided, separated by the chasm of misunderstanding and death that isolates
me forever? That long-dead woman "clung" to her life, to the one who
wanted to be called "bitter" because of all she had lost. This living woman
needn't cling because nothing will ever be snatched from her again.

You Know That I Love You

When they had finished breakfast, Jesus said to Simon Peter, "Simon, son of John, do you love me more than these?" He said to him, "Yes, Lord; you know that I love you." He said to him, "Feed my lambs."

JOHN 21:15

You might not think of trying fish for breakfast, but you should some time. White fish, freshly caught, filleted to remove the bone, grilled straight over hot coals, sprinkled with some rough salt, nestled right inside a crusty loaf slit apart—you stand over the fire and savor it, burning your fingers and your tongue.

Polishing it off it when you've been awake all night, struggling with the nets and yourself, caught in a silent loop of self-loathing, guilt, and hope mean that its flavor is lodged in your soul. You'll be able to recall its fragrance no matter what else happens to you.

And lots will happen. Because you do love him. You've always loved him. You've always desperately wanted him to know you, even when you couldn't stand yourself. You are willing to go to the grave, as you will do, painfully, brutally. Onlookers will wonder about your fanatical attachment to this person still so reviled by the world.

Yet you were dead and now you are alive. You were lost and now you are found. You were hungry and now you are full. You were alone, yet now you possess the love of your Savior and your friend. And the whole world will see how much *you* love him.

He's Coming Back

> ... and [the angels] said, "Men of Galilee, why do you stand looking
> into heaven? This Jesus, who was taken up from you into heaven, will
> come in the same way as you saw him go into heaven."
>
> ACTS 1:11

So many of the questions asked in the Scriptures are sort of ridiculous. Like when the women go to the tomb, lugging all their spices, and the angel asks, "What are you doing here?" I mean, what do you think they're doing? Is the angel asking because he wants real information? Can he really not tell that they have come to a grave to look at a dead body?

I always imagine the disciples turning around to these angels and complaining, "What does it look like we're doing?" Here was Jesus, chatting away with us, and now he's gone up on a cloud, which, from a regular human perspective, is not at all what we expected. Indeed, nothing that has happened over the last three years has been what we expected.

At least the angels tell them what is going on: he's going away, and he's going to come back. You can't possibly know when he'll come back. It'll be the same way, though, but from above. Don't stand there craning your neck—it won't be for a while. The disciples straggle away full of the disappointment they have come to know so well.

And every Christian for 2,000 years has gone on wondering whether to keep being disappointed, or to stop and stare at the sky. We wait. And wait. And read the Bible another time. And measure the earthquakes and the evil in the world, and wait.

Seeker Sensitive

". . . this Jesus, delivered up according to the definite plan and fore-knowledge of God, you crucified and killed by the hands of lawless men."
ACTS 2:23

The Father is God, Jesus is God, and, as lots of people know, the Holy Spirit is God. The Spirit's main task is to convict the world of sin and bring them to the Son, who, through his work on the cross, restores them to fellowship with the Father. It might be alluring to hope that Holy Spirit does his own thing, that has some kind of job that isn't directly related to whatever it is the Son and the Father are up to.

Uncomfortably for many of us, the Holy Spirit is peculiarly anxious that sinful people, through the hearing of the word, cling to the Son, who delivers them up safely into the presence of the Father. That happens here by the near violent dispatch of Peter into the street to be heard by the assembled throng. The words the Spirit puts in Peter's mouth sound awfully like an accusation of the crowds: that these very ones, hearing this exact sermon, each in their own language, are guilty of the death of Jesus. It's not exactly seeker sensitive.

It's not mean though, however you might feel about it. Because 3,000 people hear this judging accusation and their hearts are cut, are broken open. They, rather like the Ninevites, weep, and believe, and cling onto Jesus for the salvation of their souls and bodies and everything.

Now when they saw the boldness of Peter and John, and perceived that they were uneducated, common men, they were astonished. And they recognized that they had been with Jesus.

ACTS 4:13

One of the extraordinary things about Christians is that they're not that much better than any other kind of person. It's easy to look at a Christian, as you might some modernist art, and say to yourself, "Well, at least I'm as good as that, better even," and then go on your way, comforted in the knowledge that you're basically fine. So, the Christian person is not good. What is it, then, that makes a Christian markedly a Christian?

Peter and John, still hanging around Jerusalem after the Ascension and Pentecost, trying to organize and handle the work Jesus left in their hands, are still unsophisticated. They still talk like they are from Galilee. They still chew their food in the same way. They still have the same mannerisms. But now they can't stop going on about Jesus. They are the annoying born-again variety that can't shut up about religion, even at Christmas dinner, who go around not only asking about the eternal destination of everyone at the table, but then offering advice and bringing Jesus into the conversation. They are all Jesus-y, all the time. They smile too much. They are too cheerful. And, in Peter and John's case, they are aggravating to the authorities because all kinds of ordinary people are listening and repenting, flinging themselves on the mercy of Jesus.

Try Not to Lie

When Ananias heard these words, he fell down and breathed his last.
And great fear came upon all who heard it.

ACTS 5:5

It should have been the perfect scam. You sell off your stuff—in particular that valuable plot of land no one knows anything about—but you keep back a small portion, and then you come, with all humility and simpering, to lay the money at the feet of the disciples. You smile a crinkly smile, nod at all the Christians gathered there, and murmur about how it was nothing, anyone else would have done the same.

If you tried this trick now, in an ordinary small-time church, cutting a nice fat check and placing it in the hands of the pastor, you'd probably get away with it. Even if you said, "Look, I sold everything, and here is all the money," even if you were lying, even if the pastor could tell, you would probably get away with it, at least until you died and had to face Jesus.

Why would you, though? What's to be gained by giving money to a church anyway? Times have changed. If you want to get credit from anyone, you had better donate to a GoFundMe where everyone can see how much you've given when you click the link.

Still, it's foolish to lie, even if you get away with it. I suppose you think God is stupid and can't see or doesn't care. But he does see. He does care. And when you deliberately try to deceive him, he may not kill you right then . . .

I mean, what I'm trying to say is that repenting, asking Jesus to forgive you and cover you with his redeeming blood is a good idea.

ACTS 5, 6

And Stephen said: "Brothers and fathers, hear me. The God of glory appeared to our father Abraham when he was in Mesopotamia, before he lived in Haran . . ."

ACTS 7:2

By now the church is monstrously big and filled with loads of poor people. Everyone is needy in one way or another, but these new Christians aren't embarrassed to admit it. And there's trouble brewing: the Greek-speaking Jews and the proper Jerusalem Jews have all joined up together, but they look down on each other, and they've brought this attitude with them into the church. Every day, as everyone shares everything in common, the church takes special care of the widows and those with greater need. And the Greek-speaking Jews find themselves being put second, and sometimes being passed over.

So the apostles, rather than stopping everything to make sure everything is perfectly fair, appoint seven young men to take over the distribution of food. And one of them, Stephen, turns out to be a fiery preacher, so that the number of believers continues to grow. Then he preaches an offensively long sermon, recounting to the elders of Israel their own history, beginning with Abraham, as if they didn't know anything about it. It's like when you arrive in church and the pastor stands up and you realize the text for the sermon is the entire Bible. "Turn to Genesis," he says, and you know that he's going to make it all the way to the book of Revelation.

Anyway, don't be so worried about offending your friends and neighbors with the good news of Jesus Christ. What's the worst that could happen? Someone could throw a rock at your head? You're going to die sometime anyway.

Salvation by Social Awkwardness

Then Philip opened his mouth, and beginning with this Scripture he told him the good news about Jesus.

ACTS 8:35

One of the worst parts about the Christian life, I think, is having to talk to strangers. I am what you'd call "shy." I would rather die than talk to someone I don't know. Which means I wander hopelessly around in a grocery store, or drive a hundred miles in the wrong direction, because I can't bear to ask for help or directions. It is therefore deeply uncomfortable to be sometimes commanded, for the sake of the gospel itself, to talk to people to whom I have not been properly introduced.

By my calculations, it would have been weird for Philip to wander up to a parked chariot and interrupt the person quietly reading. You can't go into the library, accost the person settled by the window, and interrogate him about how well he understands the words right under his nose. *I* couldn't anyway. Which must have been why God did not think of me specially for this bizarre evangelistic moment.

"Then Philip opened his mouth," says God and Luke, but who doesn't wonder if it wasn't more like, "Then God pried open his jaw and made the sound come out of his throat against his will while he died a little inside." Not that I don't believe the Bible. Maybe Philip is actually an extrovert (shudder).

It seems like Philip and this Ethiopian person never see each other again in this life, so maybe the awkwardness, if any, was soon forgotten.

300 Sight Regained

And immediately something like scales fell from his eyes, and he re-
gained his sight. Then he rose and was baptized . . .
ACTS 9:18

The scales fell from his eyes . . . heh. Sorry. It's not a joke. It really happened. Paul, or rather Saul—who held everyone's coats while they stoned
Stephen in that back alley, who had taken it upon himself to go all over the
world rounding up Christians and intimidating and killing them, whose
very name struck fear into the hearts of every single believer—this same
Saul, clutching his special orders in his righteous fist, is struck down by
a bright, blinding light. He hears a voice, sees Jesus—whom he may even
recognize by sight, having probably been around during the events sur-
rounding the crucifixion, which wasn't that long ago—falls off his horse
and discovers that he can't see anymore.

The thing is, he's never been able to see. The fact that he can't physically see now is just a more obvious way of realizing that he has never
been able to spiritually see. Had God not knocked him off his high horse
and appeared to him, convicting him of the truth—that Jesus is God—
he would never have done anything other than go on being blind. What
a mercy for all of us that God knocked Saul over with his resplendent,
eye-opening mercy.

301 Delicious

And there came a voice to him: "Rise, Peter; kill and eat."

ACTS 10:13

I have always heard this described as a capacious picnic blanket, coming down from heaven, and Peter finally getting to eat bacon and shrimp.
Better yet, bacon-wrapped shrimp, with just a hint of cayenne and maybe
a little sauce . . . But the word *kill* kind of casts a shadow over this otherwise delicious picture. The sheet is full of live animals, crawling around,
like a fascinating lobster tank where you can pick the one you want to take
home along with a pound of lemons and a pound of butter. Except that all
the creatures in the big sheet are not what Peter wants to eat, or to touch.
They are all the stuff that would turn his stomach and make him retch at
the thought.

Mercifully, it's just a dream. The sheet is taken up to heaven and then
Peter is directed to go to the house of a man who has already killed all
these creatures, and eats them pretty happily, though probably with olive
oil rather than butter.

All the commandments against eating certain kinds of food were meant
to make you understand that the body, however carefully preserved in holiness, was still the dwelling place of the heart, and that heart, no matter
what you eat, is deceitfully wicked. So, once Jesus came and cleansed the
heart, and made it truly clean, you wouldn't have to worry about eating
wrongly, because the dream is over and the reality is here. Just hand me
another garlic-butter-soaked snail if you would. Delicious.

And when he knocked at the door of the gateway, a servant girl named
Rhoda came to answer.

ACTS 12:13

Poor Rhoda. A sweet girl, you know, but so prone to doing the wrong thing. If anyone's going to break that new pot, or accidentally throw a whole cake's-worth of flour on the floor, it will be her. In shock, hearing Peter's voice, she rushes headlong to tell the gathered prayer meeting that he's okay—forgetting, as it were, to open the door to him. I would kick myself for a lifetime, especially as it's the only thing she gets to be known for. *She* is the person in the Bible who panicked and left Peter standing outside in the deserted street.

It's the best kind of praying, that praying without very much faith. There she was, with a group of other anxious Christians, begging God to take care of Peter. So far, being a Christian was a good way to get yourself killed, especially for those Christians who talked out loud, like Stephen, or James. And Peter had been in trouble before, so everyone is so anxious for him.

"Why be anxious?" a modern prosperity preacher might say. "Just ask with faith." But, well, all the faith in the world won't keep you alive if God wants you dead. And which is it? Does he want you to suffer this time? You pray, feeling pretty sure that this time is death.

So when God answers your prayer, you can't believe it. You're so surprised you go down in gentle infamy. And Peter goes out into the night to a safe and quiet place to get some rest.

303 Trust and Obey

While they were worshiping the Lord and fasting, the Holy Spirit said, "Set apart for me Barnabas and Saul for the work to which I have called them."
ACTS 13:2

I wish the Holy Spirit would be this clear with me. "Go do this," I wish He would say, "and everything will be wonderful." Instead, I have to labor away through the Bible, feeling like I'm in the dark, not always sure which way to go.

But I shouldn't complain. For one thing, the Scripture is not that hard to understand. So far we've been able to see together that People are Evil and God is Good. I don't really need to have him say it to me audibly. If I take the trouble to read it, and then read it again, and then again, and then again, all the time carrying on living my ordinary, quiet life, being repentant and sensible and realistic about myself, God will arrange the circumstances of my life the way he wants them, without having to tell me about them first. It's not very glamorous this way, but it's a lot safer. God talked to Paul all the time and look how much he had to suffer.

No, give me providence over an audible voice every day of the week. It turns out the same in the end. You're not going to do something that God hasn't accounted for. He's not hiding in a cupboard whispering at you, waiting for you to figure out what he wants you to do next. He's there plainly on the page.

ACTS 13:1–14:7

The Meeting in Jerusalem

After they finished speaking, James replied, "Brothers, listen to me."
ACTS 15:13

The gospel has gone out into the far reaches of the known world. Jesus said it would, and so it has. "Go," he said, "taking the good news with you to Judea, and Samaria, and to the ends of the earth." And when Jesus tells someone to do something, he does it for them and through them by the Holy Spirit, not leaving it to chance, like the way, if I want a child to clean a room, I have to actually make the little hand pick up the block, though very gently, and put it, me and the child together, into the block bin. A person whom Jesus has called to do something, can't help ultimately doing it. It's not that the Church didn't care about the ends of the earth, but they didn't know how to do anything about it. Jesus himself, through the Spirit, brought about the obedience he required.

And so the ends of the earth are there all together in the Church, and the Church has to cope with them. Peter and James and Paul and the others get together in council in Jerusalem, and after much discussion, accept what has already happened. Even gathering together, as they all do here, they are not acting on their own, they are not making their own decisions. They are doing what the Holy Spirit is directing them to do.

ACTS 14:8–15:35

And there arose a sharp disagreement, so that they separated from each other. Barnabas took Mark with him and sailed away to Cyprus . . .

ACTS 15:39

And forever after this, all of us, trying to lighten things up, would point out how the gospel then went in two different directions rather than only one, and that was very good. And it was. But nevertheless, there was this sharp disagreement. Paul and Barnabas vociferously disagreed with each other, and neither of them gave an inch. And that's just not very nice. Christians shouldn't disagree with each other publicly about anything. It is unseemly. It doesn't further the gospel. It's bad form.

Or not. Maybe it's okay to sharply disagree about how the mission of the church should be carried out. Maybe it's okay to disagree about the order of service. Maybe it's okay to think the other person is totally and completely wrong. Of course, you can't both be right, but time will suffice to tell who was right about what and who was wrong. Of course, Paul could have been more patient with Mark and Barnabas. Of course, Barnabas could have refrained from getting his back up. These two are sinners just like you and me. They could have worked harder on reconciliation.

Nevertheless, observe that all the time the gospel goes out. Don't, as I like to do, lurk around the edges of public disagreement and snark passive-aggressively. Go ahead and join the fray.

ACTS 15:36–16:10

> And after she was baptized, and her household as well, she urged us,
> saying, "If you have judged me to be faithful to the Lord, come to my
> house and stay." And she prevailed on us.
>
> ACTS 16:15

Diversity is currently all the rage, but it is by no means a modern human innovation. Its origin is actually divine. Paul's trip to Philippi, like so many of his adventures, is legendary for the extremes to which the Holy Spirit will go to bring different kinds of people together. Jew and Greek, slave and free, man and woman—these, as the letters will tease out, were the great divisions of that day. You wouldn't walk into a synagogue, smile beatifically and say, "You know what this place needs? More Gentiles." Neither would you go to the Areopagus and lecture everyone about letting slaves make speeches, or women.

But the Spirit isn't interested in diversity *for the sake* of diversity. When Paul flees Philippi, leaving behind a Roman jailer and Lydia, an affluent female Jewish entrepreneur, as the pillars of his tiny church, he isn't trying to make the church relevant or cutting edge, or even better able to preach to the world. God chose to shove those two people together, picking out peculiar personalities and idiosyncrasies and cultures and commanding them to love and forgive each other. For though we are alienated from each other through animosity and selfishness, yet Christ unites us in himself, the visible sacrament of the way we are reconciled to him, the ultimate stranger.

But go on, steal our great idea. We also have much to say about forgiveness and would be happy to give you that also.

ACTS 16:11–17:34

[Apollos] began to speak boldly in the synagogue, but when Priscilla and Aquila heard him, they took him aside and explained to him the way of God more accurately.

ACTS 18:26

I wish I could have had dinner with Priscilla and Aquila. A cozy affair on the roof, lanterns dotted here and there, perfect roast lamb with garlic and mint, wine flowing in abundance. Priscilla must have been the sparkly, fascinating one who chattered away and waved her arms in the air, getting up mid-sentence to rush into the kitchen to see if the stove was really off and then coming back and picking up the thread as if nothing had happened, so that you always thought of her name first. And Aquila probably sat back and smiled, but then would lean in suddenly with some life-shattering insight, pulling everyone back onto the subject.

I can't imagine that Apollos even knew what hit him. Except that he enjoyed a gorgeous dinner and stayed out way too late and came away with so many pieces of the gospel having fallen into place that hadn't before been quite within his grasp.

And then they all rush off to the next call and miss each other but then are totally thrilled when they occasionally bump into each other around the Mediterranean. That's the missionary way. Long periods of exhausting, discouraging work punctuated by shrieks of joy when you run into a kindred soul.

Death by Preaching

And a young man named Eutychus, sitting at the window, sank into a
deep sleep as Paul talked still longer. And being overcome by sleep, he fell
down from the third story and was taken up dead.
ACTS 20:9

There you are at the end of a long day, wedged into the open window trying to catch the faint breeze outside. Up at dawn, a drink of porridge-like
gruel, back-breaking work, and then straight to church, which is on the
third floor of some rich, luxurious compound. And Paul, of whom you
have heard plenty, is in town. He is short, balding, and his voice isn't
quite loud enough for the room. Some seem to be hanging on his every
word, and others are catching and hanging on to every second or fourth.
But despite your knowing—and kicking yourself to stay awake—the incredible honor of hearing this man speak in person, you cannot keep your
eyes open.

Every time you're sure it's over, it turns out he's just introducing another subject. Eventually, the heat of the room, your own fatigue, and the
strain of trying to hear send you straight to sleep. And because of your
position in the window and the depth of your fatigue, when you fall, you
die. Could happen to anyone, except this time it was you. You progress
toward the bright light and see all your dead relatives . . . just kidding.
Who knows? Unlike some, you don't get a book deal. Paul toddles down
the steps, picks you up, raises you from the dead, pats you on the head,
climbs back up and, and—unbelievable—keeps talking. You find a new
spot, not in the window, and prop your eyes open.

It Heats Up

Then all the city was stirred up, and the people ran together. They seized
Paul and dragged him out of the temple, and at once the gates were shut.
ACTS 21:30

Being seized and beaten was Paul's peculiar spiritual gift. It happened to him all the time. If you saw him, you would think he had a fascinating past, because he did, in fact, have one.

I always imagined that Paul must have had an anxious stone in the pit of his stomach over the many weeks leading up to this moment, knowing that something was going to happen, but not being quite sure what. But as soon as the crowd began to rage and the temple gates slammed shut, his anxiety flew away and he got his own back in the thick of the conflict, not waiting for whatever bad thing that was coming next. However bad it's going to be, it's a relief when you finally get to face it. Of course, Paul is much holier than I am, so maybe he never really felt anxious beforehand.

So began his long pursuit of justice which culminated in a perilous journey to Rome and, although it's not recorded here, an audience with Caesar. Paul got to speak of Jesus to everyone everywhere—in season and out of season, in times of peace and conflict, when it made him friends and when it produced enemies. He was single-minded, devoted, loving of Jesus and his Church to the bitter—but really glorious—end.

ACTS 21:1–22:29

It's Too Plain

For what can be known about God is plain to them, because God has
shown it to them.

ROMANS 1:19

Paul wanted so much to go to the church in Rome, and he eventually did,
but before then, being the apostle that he was, he got busy and wrote them
a letter. If you sat down to write to someone you longed to see, *people you*
haven't even met, you might not do it this way, though. The opening lines
are devastating. They get the letter and—bam!—have to toil through it,
wondering what sort of person Paul is, to say so boldly whatever it is he
is saying.

But then, after you've shrieked in horror, torn it up, and flung it into
the fire, consider how carefully the Roman church kept hold of this letter—copying it meticulously and sending it around to all the other churches. Which means that when they read Paul's indictment against humanity,
rather than getting angry, they were struck to the heart. They saw themselves condemned and flung themselves on the mercy of God, the very
God Paul describes. They did not, as I recently heard, say, "I really don't
see myself in this text." Don't say that. You are described here. You have
suppressed the truth about God, as have I. But don't stop there—read the
whole letter.

The Presumption

Or do you presume on the riches of his kindness and forbearance and
patience, not knowing that God's kindness is meant to lead you to
repentance?

ROMANS 2:4

God, whether we like or not—have I said this before?—is the judge of all things. He knows the thoughts of each heart. He knows and sees actions, and all the parts and complexities of every action. Nothing escapes his notice. This being so, the way we carefully wrap ourselves in protective cloaks of self-justification is really the most foolish thing any of us can do. I wake up in the morning and try to set myself up to be better than somebody—anybody. There's got to be somebody out there worse than I am. Only there's not. And it's better for me to judge myself harshly and truly—to look at myself as I really am rather than as I want to be—so that when God judges me, it is not a terrible shock.

The fact that God has waited so long and hasn't come back and blasted us all with the judgment we deserve is a great kindness. He is giving us time, lots and lots and lots of time so that we have the space to realize how bad we are, what a wretched mess we have made of everything, and then fling ourselves on his mercy. His waiting kindness is meant for salvation. What is it that everyone says? "Judge not, lest ye be judged?" No, no. Judge yourself. Before the sure and coming judgment, judge yourself by God's holy perfection.

The Counting

That is why his faith was "counted to him as righteousness." But the words "it was counted to him" were not written for his sake alone, but for ours also. It will be counted to us who believe in him who raised from the dead Jesus our Lord . . .

ROMANS 4:22–24

I always get sweaty when I come up against the word "count." I'm terrible with numbers. Whenever I'm asked to count anything, I have to do it many, many times because the numbers don't fix themselves in my mind. I have to do it and then double-check over and over because I'm sure I've made a mistake.

Abraham is told by God that he's going to have as many offspring as of the grains of sand on the seashore, and as many as the stars in the heaven. And every Sunday school teacher gets to tell all the little children to go out sometime and count the stars in the sky. Just try. Make a go of it. You won't be able to. You can't hold a number that size in your head.

Just like you can't really hold on to your own goodness. It will slip through your fingers like sand blown out of your hand by a blustering ocean wind. You can't count up your goodness and bring it to God and have it be enough. If you count yourself up to him, you will come up short. So, he counts his goodness out to you, out of himself. And then it is not a thousand grains of sand, it is one stone, a cornerstone. That one stone weighed, comes out sufficient, plenty, perfect.

Enough with the Death

For one will scarcely die for a righteous person—though perhaps for a good person one would dare even to die—but God shows his love for us in that while we were still sinners, Christ died for us.

ROMANS 5:7—8

It can get sort of tedious, reading and thinking about death all the time. How many times can it come up between Genesis and Revelation? I suppose someone has counted and a quick google search would tell the tale. The problem, I think, is that death is the sort of thing that happens to oth-er people, until it happens to you. Then, of course, it is awfully personal.

Some people choose to die for others. They decide that a cause or a person is so worth it that they sign up. Lots of people die in war for the sake of others. And many doctors and nurses put their lives on the line when infectious diseases without cures sweep over the world. In both cas-es, those willing to die are so high-minded they do it even for strangers, people they will never know and may never see.

But Paul is right, I don't know anyone who would go ahead and die for someone really wicked. Go through the worst section of the worst prison and pick out the murderer-child molester—that's not who you think of dying for when you sign up to defend your country. But that's who Jesus had in mind when he went to the cross.

314 Slow Motion Win

So I find it to be a law that when I want to do right, evil lies close at
hand. For I delight in the law of God, in my inner being . . .
ROMANS 7:21—22

So goes the interior dialogue of the Christian. Having committed your
way to Jesus who brings you out of death and into life, you are faced with
death everywhere you look. What seemed ordinary and fine before now
bears a whiff of decay and grief. No matter where you turn you discover
within yourself bitter motivations, unkindness, anger, the overpowering
desire to set someone else straight, and, of course, deep regret. When you
try to shellac it with goodness, with the Spirit, deep down you feel terrible
and mad at yourself. Going to church makes you feel sad, especially when
you think about Jesus. All your friends and relations think you are too
hard on yourself and start trying to make you feel better.

The problem is that God's goodness is so pervasive; his mercy and his
love overtake you so much that you want to be good, and when you cannot,
you feel sorry and unhappy about it. You battle away, helplessly, feeling
more and more evil as you go, but looking less and less so. People think
you are fine and upstanding and begin to ask you to pray for them. So you
do, but you know your body of death, and cling ever more tightly to the life
and goodness of Christ.

You Were Once A Slave

For you did not receive the spirit of slavery to fall back into fear, but
you have received the Spirit of adoption as sons, by whom we cry,
"Abba! Father!"

ROMANS 8:15

This is awkward—Paul likening me to a slave. At the time he chose this word it had the whole range of connotations and meanings that it has today. "Slave" is not a neutral word—it is entirely negative.

You, he says, were a slave to sin. You were bound, both against your will and by your will, to sin, to death, to evil. You couldn't do anything but wrong. Even when you thought you were free, you were not. When you thought you'd like to do good, as a person owned by evil, you could not but do evil. You were chained up, owned, bound under its destructive power.

And then God remembered you. He turned his face toward you and paid for your life with his own. You were made free, released from the power and tyranny of sin. You belong to him. You can rightfully do good as his slave now. Except that he doesn't treat you like a slave. He makes you a child, his own child. But a lot of the time you go on acting like a slave—not his, but still the slave of evil.

In the spirit of being grateful, notice with me that God has taken and transformed the fallen and corrupting categories of slave and slavery to show us something about the soul. How great the contrast between adopted son and bound slave! How great a mercy that I would be changed from one kind of person to the other!

It's Going to Be Okay

And we know that for those who love God, all things work together for
good, for those who are called according to his purpose.
ROMANS 8:28

This has to be the whole world's favorite Bible verse. Let me get out my list and see what good things are being worked out for me. Surely this must be a divine treat box, offered up for me to rummage through until I find a delicious pastry or a new car.

When actually, and most disappointingly, the way this works is that you, the Christian, having been called out of darkness and into the light, having been rescued out of the pit and set on green grass, having been spit out of the belly of the whale—I could go on but it's probably starting to be tedious—you look around and find yourself just as beset by darkness and trouble as ever. It seems like the light is constantly about to flicker out. You go to bed weeping as usual. Clearly, good is not about to win.

But now—and this is so great, but also exasperating—God is using all those unhappy experiences to some good purpose that you can't see yet. You have no idea how they will turn out. You wonder if God is doing anything. Everything within and without is suffering and trial. But all the while he is providentially working out his will and purposes in the world and using you to do it. It's all fitting together perfectly, even the bad stuff, even the awful disappointments.

Is Christ Divided?

Is Christ divided? Was Paul crucified for you? Or were you baptized in the name of Paul?

I CORINTHIANS 1:13

It sure looks like Christ is divided. The further we go from the cross, the more divided we seem to be, both in physical proximity, and in theology. Division is everywhere—little walls of conflict, some low, easily climbed over, some so high they cannot be scaled. Therefore, the world concludes that Christ is of too many minds. Or they don't bother to think about him at all, except to point the finger and notice the obvious fact that Christians are terrible sinners.

But Christ isn't divided, whatever mess his body the Church is in. He lives, he endures the division and sin with patience, so that some might be saved. He is himself. And though we are likened to his body, we are not yet his glorified body. The Church is his broken, bleeding body, beaten, hurting. When the world looks at the Church they see the shame, the reproach, the judgment of sin. And in this we are all united. The greatest division, between God and man, is illuminated, blinding the world, so that the world looks away.

Is Christ divided? No more divided than bread distributed into baskets to feed the world. No more than water poured out to quench the believer's thirst. No more than the fruit on the vine. No more than the body carved up and sent to all the people of Israel, convicting them all at once of their wicked rebellion. No more than single drops of blood, dripping out onto the parched, barren ground.

318 The Shame

*But God chose what is foolish in the world to shame the wise; God chose
what is weak in the world to shame the strong...*

I CORINTHIANS 1:27

I like to take this verse as a comfort, rather than as the humiliation that
Paul intends. Well, I like to take it as the comfort I need on the days when
I am failing, which is about half the time. On days when I'm doing bril-
liantly, I dislike it and try not to look at it at all. And sometimes, a sliver
of the time perhaps, I find that I am not the foolish being used against the
wise, nor the weak against the strong, but that I am the "wise" and God
has used someone I thought "foolish" to shame me.

Shame is such a tricky business. It is the opposite of what I want for
myself. I want to go upward into glory and honor. I want God to recognize something in me that is worthy of praise. I flinch when I look at the
shame of the cross. The humiliation—the unbearable disgrace of a man
weighed down with all my offensiveness. How could it be that I had, and
have, so much ugliness? That God chose me for himself—when there were
so many better, wiser, more interesting people—is a humiliation to the
world. It isn't something I can boast about, because I am the weak fool.

I CORINTHIANS 1:18–3:23

The Leaven in the Lump

Your boasting is not good. Do you not know that a little leaven leavens the whole lump?

I CORINTHIANS 5:6

A little sin goes a long way. It wraps itself around everything. It infiltrates the whole batch of dough, leaving no single part unaffected. There isn't any way to get rid of it, though the people of Israel were supposed to try to eradicate it from their houses before Passover. Over time elaborate ceremonies grew up for the removal of leaven. A household would wash everything, scrub the kitchen, extracting yeast even from the air, if possible. Of course, they couldn't. If you've ever made sourdough bread, you know this is true.

So it is with sin. A little goes a long way, and you can't ever completely get rid of it. Then why—this being the case, and its power being so immense and destructive—would you go out and find it and bring it in on purpose? Because it makes life taste better? Because you think you will overpower it with the good that you dredge up from somewhere inside you? Or maybe through the Spirit? Maybe you will overcome sin through the Spirit.

Better not think so highly of yourself and your abilities in the first place. Flee from sin. Confess it when you discover it in your pocket, or your screen, or the back corner of your thoughts. Call out to Jesus for help. You can't do anything without him.

The Temple

Or do you not know that your body is the temple of the Holy Spirit within
you, whom you have from God? You are not your own . . .
I CORINTHIANS 6:19

The people of Israel, camping placidly in their rows of tents, in the shadow of the mountain, watching the tabernacle of the Lord take shape day by
day, were never able to understand their own hearts and minds and what
kind of God, what kind of love, was making a home with them. They stood
far off and tried to make it out. Later they built a great imposing stone
structure—a temple—glittering with intricate floral detail. It was to be a
home for the ark—a box made of wood, overlaid with gold, adorned with
two golden cherubim, the footstool of God, the seat of his mercy. The box
sat in that immense building and the people drew close but did not quite
understand.

You are like that tabernacle. You are made of stuff—atoms and mol-
ecules and cells and hormones. You would probably like to look better
in one way or another. You know you should take better care of yourself.
You wish the parts that ache wouldn't. You wish you could think kinder
and purer thoughts. Confronted with that ancient temple, you certainly
wouldn't understand any better than anyone else. And now that God has
come to make his home in you, it's fine that you don't really get how it
works, how he can be so close, and you can still be such a wreck.

That's a Lovely Hat

That is why a wife ought to have a symbol of authority on her head,
because of the angels.
I CORINTHIANS 11:10

The Corinthian women were pretty sure they had ascended to such a lofty spiritual state that there wasn't much difference between them and the angels. They no longer worried about the base infirmity of their own flesh. They were so exalted they didn't even need to dress according to their stations in life, or their culture or anything. They had written to Paul to tell him how fierce and beautiful they were, along with the rest of the church, but Paul has word from other sources that tell a rather different story.

And so Paul writes them back and tells them to keep their hats on, to both look and act as if they are under authority, and of their husbands no less. You can hear the murmuring as the letter is read out in church. Our husbands haven't done anything worthy of any so-called authority. Or, have you met my husband?—you can't possibly know what you are asking of me. I'll let him have authority when he can find his car keys by himself.

If Paul had been there, he would have told them all to simmer down. You're not as spiritually together as you think you are, and your husband isn't as incompetent as you think he is. And everyone can see that you're not angelic, witness your throwing away that perfectly fine hat.

You Still Aren't Worthy

That is why many of you are weak and ill, and some have died.
I CORINTHIANS 11:30

If you meander up to the communion rail—or maybe in your church they pass the bread and wine around in little trays and everyone takes and eats and drinks all at the same moment—and you are overwhelmed by the great gift of Jesus, that he gave all of himself, his whole body, his whole life, everything that he held by right, that he laid it down and died so that you, ruined and sinful as you are, can be restored to fellowship with God and all your friends and relatives, then you don't need to worry about getting sick and dying because you have already died to yourself. Jesus' own death has made itself real inside you. Your heart bears the marks of his suffering.

If, on the other hand, you go forward to take the bread and wine—or sit and eat and drink—hanging onto a quiet, hidden bitterness against God, that he has acted unfairly or unkindly to you, that he has not attended to you as you believe he should, that your neighbors have wrongfully offended you, then you have not yet died, and so this warning is for you, that death still awaits. Don't waste any more time. God's great kindness is for you, he has given all of himself, withholding nothing. Let all the bitterness and resentment die as you eat his broken body.

The True Love

Love bears all things, believes all things, hopes all things, endures all things.

I CORINTHIANS 13:7

Sure, I'll just do that. In fact, let me read the whole chapter and just re-place the word "love" with my own name, just to depress myself and make you laugh.

Or . . . remember . . . there you were, sitting under your glorious mel-on plant, conveniently shading you from the intense sun while you waited for God to destroy the city of Nineveh. You didn't even remember that you'd disobeyed him in such a catastrophic way that you nearly died, by drowning. He rescued you and gave you another chance. And so you did what he wanted, but you did it grudgingly, angrily. So angrily that God asked you a question. Do you remember? He said, "Do you do well to be angry?" And you knew the answer was supposed to be a resounding, "No," but you weren't feeling it.

Love is the counterpoint of anger. It isn't a feeling. It's a choice, an act of the will. It's what God does for us when we are sitting under our green leafy vines muttering and disobeying. We are the "all things" that he bears, that he endures, that he hopes for. It's not your name that goes in the place of love, your name is the object of the Love. You can't love like this. But God can and does. He is patient with you, and kind. He doesn't fail. Get out from under that vine and leave the anger there when you do.

The Dithering

Was I vacillating when I wanted to do this? Do I make my plans accord-
ing to the flesh, ready to say "Yes, yes" and "No, no" at the same time? As
surely as God is faithful, our word to you has not been Yes and No.
II CORINTHIANS 1:17

It hasn't been going well between Paul and this intransigent congregation. Letters have traveled back and forth. Accusations have been lobbed
across the Mediterranean. Paul even cancelled a planned visit because he
knew it wouldn't go well. And meanwhile, while they fail to sort themselves out, Paul's work in Asia has been so terrible that he "despaired of
life itself." If anyone had expected their best life now, they were sorely
disappointed.

It seems the Corinthians have insinuated that Paul can't make up his
mind, that he is making decisions about where to go and what to do "in
the flesh," which is a nasty thing to say, especially since his physical flesh
is so battered and beaten.

What I like to do, myself, is to dither around, trying to make up my
mind without really praying about it, but mainly consulting my feelings.
But then, when I pick wrong and end up having to back up and do the other thing, I say that it was God's fault. I felt "led" to go one way, and then
the other, and how was I to know. When really, I could own my bad decision. I thought I wanted to do something, but then I changed my mind. If
I were honest, of course, I wouldn't have to blame God for anything, but
that's not quite as much fun.

When the Veil Lifts

And we all, with unveiled face, beholding the glory of the Lord, are being transformed into the same image from one degree of glory to another. For this comes from the Lord who is the Spirit.

II CORINTHIANS 3:18

You remember all those generations ago, how in the wilderness you survived the horror of the golden calf, even after you threw some of your own gold into the pot, dancing furtively along the edges of chaos. By grace you happened to be far enough away from those who were consumed by the fire of God's wrath. You anxiously crept back to the darkness of your tent and wondered if you would ever be able to see what God is really like.

Then Moses had to go up and down the mountain, and then, when God came down into the very camp where you were, and Moses stood before him in the tent of meeting, whenever he came out, his face shone like the blazing bright morning sun. You could not bear it, and so Moses covered his face so that you could hear what he was saying. He veiled his face, and some of what he said filtered through the veil, though not much.

Well now, all these years later, the glory of God is displayed brightly in the broken body of the Son. The Spirit of God has lifted that heavy veil. The light—not from Moses, but of the very glory of God—shines straight on you, transforming you "into the same image," that is of Christ.

Better Than a Tent

For in this tent we groan, longing to put on our heavenly dwelling, if indeed by putting it on we may not be found naked. For while we are still in this tent, we groan, being burdened—not that we would be unclothed, but that we would be further clothed, so that what is mortal may be swallowed up by life.

II CORINTHIANS 5:2–4

There is a horrible nakedness about some clothes. Rather than elevating—or even just shielding—the soul from the cold wind of reality, or the elements, or other people's opinions, those clothes actually expose the defenselessness of the person.

The battle against nakedness, or its embarrassing embrace—the unconsidered efforts to cover up too much or, more usually, not enough—each point to the fact that it's not supposed to be like this. We aren't supposed to be unhappy in our bodies, and we aren't supposed to struggle into ugly clothes that intensify the chronic misery of material existence, trying to pretend we're happy when we're not. Cloaking the self in body positivity, or even just body neutrality, is like sitting in a soaking wet tent in a thunderstorm eating an uncooked can of beans while insisting that the sun's out and we're dining in a three-star Michelin restaurant.

But there is a hope. There is something to look forward to, to groan for, to be impatient about, like waiting for closing day on a new house—a comfort and satisfaction you can only dream of now. Everything that fits well today is an exquisite reminder of the glory to come.

The Lord Loves a Cheerful Giver

He who supplies seed to the sower and bread for food will supply and multi-
ply your seed for sowing and increase the harvest of your righteousness.
II CORINTHIANS 9:10

It's very wicked, of course, but it is awfully easy to get caught in a mindset
of poverty in the Church. The vestry or elder board sits around bleakly,
looking over the accounts, collective brow furrowed. Eventually someone clears a scratchy throat. "So, should we pay the pastor or the electric
bill?" More weak coffee doesn't make the dilemma go away. Sometimes
the money just does not roll down like water, even when everyone is invit-
ing their friends on Sunday, and trying to make eye contact with strangers
in the grocery aisle.

Paul spends almost two whole chapters encouraging the Corinthian
church to be generous, to remember how much they have and to open
their hands—not just for the sake of practicing the spiritual discipline of
giving, but because the Christians in Jerusalem are starving. The way he
expects God, "who supplies seed to the sower and bread for food," to supply food for Jerusalem is by way of Corinth, and all the churches in Asia.
Which means that some people in the Church are very poor, while others
are well off, perhaps even rich.

In other words, this isn't a magical promise about the state of the
crops. The "harvest of righteousness" includes those with plenty digging around in their cupboards and giving what they find to those—even
across the world—who have nothing. In this way the whole body of Christ
in every place, not just the local gathering, is provided for through the
power of the Spirit.

II CORINTHIANS 8, 9, 10

To Keep Me from Becoming Conceited

So to keep me from becoming conceited because of the surpassing great-ness of the revelations, a thorn was given me in the flesh, a messenger of Satan to harass me, to keep me from becoming conceited.

II CORINTHIANS 12:7

I know someone who claims to hear from God all the time, to be swept up in visions and shown the very "heart of God." This person is uncor-rectable, having wandered away from the Church, so sure of being right about what God is saying, though it directly conflicts in many points with almost all of the Bible, that this person won't countenance any other opinion. Conceit, incidentally, doesn't even begin to describe the kind of attitude this person has developed as the years have gone by. The result is foolishness and alienation for all the people in this person's sway.

It's so interesting that Paul twice repeats that phrase in one short line—"to keep me from becoming conceited." Since he was an apostle, and often heard directly from God, even being caught up to glimpse a vi-sion of heaven itself, God went ahead and told him exactly why he was suf-fering the persistent harassment of Satan. He didn't have to guess. God came straight out and told him.

If it's dangerous for Paul to go from "strength to strength," to get what-ever he wants, to have life go smoothly and painlessly, how much more important is it that you should suffer, that God should afflict you, that you should know your own weakness, that you should endure various kinds of humiliation.

II CORINTHIANS 11:1–12:10

You Are Still Very Weak

For the sake of Christ, then, I am content with weaknesses, insults, hardships, persecutions, and calamities. For when I am weak, then I am strong.
II CORINTHIANS 12:10

This doesn't mean that when you are weak, you are actually strong—that somehow inherent in your weakness is some kind of hidden strength that will pop out if you just suffer enough or work harder. Maybe your true, gritty strength will be revealed in some kind of "weak moment"—no, a thousand times no. The more Paul was beaten and insulted and persecuted the more beautiful he did not become. In fact, he died alone, in prison, separated from his friends, much like the failure that Jesus was seen to be, hanging out there on a cross, bleeding and dying.

The strength here isn't your own. It never was and isn't going to be. The strength is God's. It is Jesus, bearing the weight of the sin of the world on his shoulders. The strength is the cross. It is the perfect death of the perfect One. When people see you enduring unspeakable suffering, they should not be able to remark on how strong you are, on how well you are bearing it. They should be amazed because they know you are weak, they know you chronically do the wrong thing and react the wrong way, and so are surprised to see an alien strength appear in your broken body. They should be able to see that someone has come to help you, to lift you up, to carry you along. When they ask you about it you can easily say that it is Jesus, that his strength is being made perfect in your weakness.

330 That Wasn't A Good Angel

But even if we or an angel from heaven should preach to you a gospel contrary to the one we preached to you, let him be accursed.

GALATIANS 1:8

Unfortunately, because reading the Bible frequently feels like such an exhausting and unrewarding exercise that few people bother with it, plenty of angels have been able to come along and preach all kinds of different gospels. Every few hundred years a spectacular "angel" dupes another biblically-illiterate "prophet" into starting a new religion, always with a vague, faux-respectful nod at Jesus and the Bible. In between those fantastical religious manifestations all kinds of regular biblically-bored Christians look everywhere in the world but here for information about God. Most of us don't need an angel, we can mess it up all on our own.

The gospel—that Jesus came to earth to be my perfect substitute; that I was swallowed up by sin; that he absorbed all that sin and carried it to the cross; that He died a humiliating and shameful death; that he was buried; that he rose again on the third day in his own body; that he sits on the right hand of the Father, bringing me to the attention and concern of that same Father; that he brings my anxieties and griefs into the presence of a perfectly holy God because paid, in himself, for all the stupidity and foolishness and evil—well, this gospel is just not that exciting. And so, please, give me lights and wings and a new, weird "sacred" text.

33¹ The Foolishness

Are you so foolish? Having begun in the Spirit, are you now being perfected by the flesh?

GALATIANS 3:3

It's kind of an unfair question. What else does Paul expect I'll do? If I can't perfect myself, then really, I'm going to be most unhappy. Give me a good, solid, comprehensive list of guidelines. Set me going on the right path. Give me enough time. I'll get there, I will. I will totally get there. I just needed a little Jesus kick-start—said practically every Christian ever. Though not with words, never with actual words, it's never necessary to use words. My manner of life speaks loud enough by itself.

Beginning by the Spirit—that is, being brought back to life from spiritual death, and then, as the life is beginning to settle in and take hold, as the stink and stench of death begins to dissipate, to grab it back and say, "I'm good now, thanks"—is utter foolishness. You who died in your own sin, who rejected the source of your own life, but who, nevertheless, by the mercy of God were restored to life and health, will you really be able to carry on keeping yourself alive? The answer is no. You shouldn't stop and think about it too long. And when, as you are struggling along in your own power to be "good"—good enough for yourself, good enough for the world, good enough for God—you should stop. Because you can't. And the more you try, the more you play the fool.

What Happened?

What then has become of your blessedness? For I testify to you that, if possible, you would have gouged out your eyes and given them to me.
GALATIANS 4:15

It's hard to get someone's attention back once it has strayed off to something more interesting. And there are so many interesting ideas and people out there. They make all kinds of promises, mostly about how special and beloved you'll be if you follow that new, exciting path.

Oh, sure, you do have to make some adjustments to your life, but that's part of the charm! Like, you might have to climb Mount Everest once a week, or its spiritual equivalent. Or you might have to adopt a boatload of orphans. Or you might have to heal this broken world with your good ol' lovin'. Or you might have to buy a new wardrobe made from recyclable hemp and only eat grain from a certain South American country. Who knows? You'll probably be able to buy some cool virtuous stuff and also go on an expensive retreat. If it heals your soul, it will be totally worth it.

Jesus, in comparison, is *démodé*. Besides, there's no way to tell if you're getting "better." The more you read your Bible, the unhappier you feel. The more you love your enemies, the more irritating they become. The vaunted "freedom" of your life in Christ feels narrow and confining. And meanwhile all the rest of the world is having a great time on Twitter.

Goodness, says Paul, you used to be so grateful for the gospel. You would have given me your very eyes if I had needed them. What happened?

333 Can I Actually Have a Different Job?

For we are his workmanship, created in Christ Jesus for good works,
which God prepared beforehand, that we should walk in them.

EPHESIANS 2:10

This is so great until you really delve into what counts as "good works." As long as it's something obvious, like curing cancer, of course we would all be on board with the sort of fateful destiny idea that God would pick out one single amazing person and enliven his mind, or train her fingers to do this remarkable thing. And, sure, lots of Christians do remarkable things that clearly God prepared for them. But that doesn't let us mediocre types off the hook. God has prepared good works for us, too.

Like, maybe you got through the day without descending into total despair. It could be that you prayed through a panic attack. Maybe you endured the night with no electricity because the country where you live turns it off without warning. It might be that you gave some of your food away and went hungry. Or perhaps you refrained, with all your might, from gossiping. It was that first moment you believed in Jesus and kept believing even when all your friends backed away from you. It was absolutely those fifteen years of going to the nursing home every day and watching your husband or mother or friend's mind slip away from you.

"This is what you prepared for me? From before time? You must be kidding," you will often complain, discouraged, overburdened by other people's needs and your own failures. "Yep," says God, "you are my workmanship."

334 Can You Bear It?

... so that Christ may dwell in your hearts through faith—that you,
being rooted and grounded in love, may have strength to comprehend
with all the saints what is the breadth and length and height and depth,
and to know the love of Christ that surpasses knowledge, that you may be
filled with all the fullness of God.

EPHESIANS 3:17—19

The fact is, you don't really have the wherewithal to grasp the depth, let alone the breadth or height or length of any of it. The distance between God's perfection and your sin is a chasm with one of those threadbare rope bridges that snaps when you get to the middle. You can't leap over it, or paddle around it, or comprehend how vast it is.

But, as I've said a couple of times, you were meant to understand. Just because you can't doesn't mean that God doesn't want you to know the vast extent of his love. This is a prayer; Paul is praying that you *will* be able to grasp it.

You have to have Jesus living in your heart (to lean heavily on a tired cliché) through faith. You have to screw your eyes shut like a little kid and ask for something that, on the face of it, is impossible: for a perfect God to make himself at home in you, for a holy God to move in and make room for the weight of his love.

You could get all schmaltzy thinking about this great love. But keep in mind, the fullness of God is best expressed in the stark vision of a cross standing against a storm-laden sky. The fullness of God is seen best in the abandoned man hanging there to die for you.

It's What Brings Us
Together Today

*This mystery is profound, and I am saying that it refers to Christ and
the church.*

EPHESIANS 5:32

How can the chaotic hassle of two troubled, basically dysfunctional people, trying to make life work in the same space, trying to make decisions
together, trying to raise children maybe, trying to negotiate the anxiety of
money, trying to figure out how to take care of their own parents, trying
to figure out what to eat for dinner, refer to Christ and the Church? There
should be some more composed picture, some Edenic tableau, shouldn't
there? Maybe God is confused. Maybe he said that marriage was a profound mystery so that we wouldn't get too close.

Except that in the Bible, the word mystery is used for something that
God is going to show you that you hadn't seen before, something that was
hidden, but is now obvious. All marriages before Jesus were hiding the
secret of Christ and the Church. Then he came, and now we can see and
understand what they were, and are, for. Marriage was invented to show
us how God relates to his people. It's not only about the two people caught
up in the middle of it. It's about God loving us, the Church. It's about him
not giving up when it gets ugly. It's about him not cutting and running
when we fail. It's about him dying to protect and care for us. It's not *People
of Walmart*, it's *Apartment Therapy*.

Jesus Did It

Do nothing from selfish ambition or conceit, but in humility count others more significant than yourselves.

PHILIPPIANS 2:3

Who even does this? My own efforts to be unselfish and unconceited for more than a few minutes are probably enough to metaphorically kill me. How could God make such a broad, universal, all-encompassing command? Doesn't he see how impossible it is for me to count another as more significant than myself?

If you walked in my shoes for 200 yards, maybe you'd be fooled. After all, I clean, I make soup for the sick, I teach Sunday school for children, I listen to other people talk about their problems, but all the time I am mostly thinking about myself and how I feel about it and if anyone is noticing. The fleeting moments of loss of self-consciousness—where I do not consider myself but am wholly and completely caught up in the other—as soon as I draw a breath the moment is gone.

But, look! There is one who did this. He did not count equality with God something to be grasped. He counted your significance and did not think of his own, even though he is the only one in all of space and time who could be counted significant at all. Whenever you start thinking about yourself, try thinking about him. Gets your mind off the problem and onto the solution.

Six Feet Tall and Blond

Let your reasonableness be known to everyone. The Lord is at hand . . .

PHILIPPIANS 4:5

You have probably noticed this by now, but God generally commands people to do what they cannot do. The stuff that they *can* do, he doesn't say anything about in particular. So, he doesn't say, "Don't forget to eat that delicious bowl of butter noodles!" because you won't forget. But he does say "Work for your bread!" because you will be deeply inclined not to do that. He doesn't say "Be happy!" because every fiber of your being is inclined in that direction. But he does say "Be joyful!" and worse, "Don't be anxious." But those are nothing compared to this line that often gets skipped over.

"Let your reasonableness be known to everyone." That's the equivalent of God commanding me to be a supermodel. Become six feet tall and blond, he might as well say, and then join the Royal Ballet. My goodness, reasonableness? Please, Lord, send someone else.

Remember all those ages ago when he said, "Come now, let us reason together," and Israel was all like, "Meh . . . I'm fine." If he had told them to do it, they couldn't do it. So he did it for them. Which is what happens here. "The Lord is at hand"—I don't have to be reasonable all by myself. I don't have to dig myself up out of my own anxiety. I only have to give myself to Jesus, and he accomplishes it inside of me while I kick and scream.

And you better believe, it is as amazing as if I turned suddenly into a supermodel.

And he is before all things, and in him all things hold together.
COLOSSIANS 1:17

We're talking about Jesus here, in case you were wondering. And not just any version of Jesus—not Republican Jesus, or Granola Jesus, or Commie Jesus, or Give Me Money Jesus, or Increase my Borders Jesus, or any other culturally-palatable Jesus. This Jesus is the Son, the second person of the Trinity, a member of the Godhead, of one substance with the Father and the Spirit, the Word through whom creation sprang into being, the coal that touched the lips of Isaiah, the white-haired vision that troubled Daniel, the One who walked with Adam and Eve in the cool of the day, the person who ate dinner with Abraham, the hand who hid Moses and Elijah in the clefts of the mountains, the Rock that was struck and the water that flowed forth, the pillar of fire by night and the cloud by day, the One who heard Hagar, who wrestled with Jacob, who moved as a firepot between the cut up animals . . .

The One who took on human nature in the obscure humility of the womb, who came to look into the eyes of his people, to speak to them, to redeem them.

You can't have the cosmos, your own breath, the movement of your fingers, the thoughts in your own mind, without him. Everything is held together by Jesus. Nothing happens without his knowledge and permission. Warm, cuddly, long-haired, Movie-Star Jesus with well-groomed beard, crushing the head of the serpent under his bloody feet, ruling over the cosmos, keeping you alive by his own will.

COLOSSIANS 1, 2

339 The Ultimate Discouragement

Fathers do not provoke your children, lest they become discouraged.

COLOSSIANS 3:21

Parents sometimes wander into church and peek through much-finger-printed windows into my Sunday school rooms. They inquire about what we offer for children, when we meet, and about the curriculum we use. I give little tours and invite the children themselves to come and look at all the curious items I have that help me talk about the Bible to the smallest people in the kingdom of God.

Children, on the whole, are delighted with Jesus. They know that he is strong and good and trustworthy, and that when they are in trouble, they have only to ask for help and he will come. How they know flabbergasts most grownups, long removed from the deep joy that comes with wandering through a flower-laden garden, or eating a juicy peach, or trying to count the stars.

But then my bright smile generally fades, because when it comes to actually bringing children into my carefully arranged rooms, prepared especially for the least of these, the parents utter a lot of exasperating excuses. "Well," they might say, "she likes to sleep in on Sunday. It's the only day we get to sleep in," or, "his soccer game starts at noon, and it takes half an hour to get there, and it's in the opposite direction."

I'm exasperated, of course, but not nearly as much as the little child who goes rushing headlong into life, without pausing for at least one joy-filled, quiet hour on Sunday, to bow before the Lord of life, to be fed on the word, to meet the Shepherd whom he has seen from afar off, whom she heard calling her name.

It's Inevitable

While people are saying, "There is peace and security," then sudden destruction will come upon them as labor pains come upon a pregnant woman, and they will not escape.

I THESSALONIANS 5:3

I love that "sudden destruction" is likened to childbirth. Ask me how I know. I'm sure that's not what Paul means. He loves the woman in labor analogy, not having had to experience it himself.

It's the inevitability that matters, the not being able to escape something no matter how much you wish that you could. You go along saying, "Everything is fine," but it's not true and just when you least want it to be true, everyone will see that it was never true.

Jesus will come in glory, not just the quiet resurrection appearances to his friends, but so that the whole world can see only him. And when he comes, there won't be anything that anyone can do about it. The baby grows and grows, and when your body finally kicks into labor, there isn't any way you can avoid it: you have to give birth. It is inevitable. In the same way, Jesus coming back in glory is inevitable. It will happen. In the meantime, like a pregnant woman, we are all pretty angry and uncomfortable, stuck in a situation that can't go on like this forever, enduring all kinds of discomfort and pain, wanting it to end but being pretty scared of the moment when it does.

34.1 Keep at It

As for you, brothers, do not grow weary in doing good.

II THESSALONIANS 3:13

This is the verse for everyone who picked up this book because it had "worn-out" in the subtitle. Weariness is the name of the game. You work really, really hard, collapse on the couch and fall asleep instead of going to bed, and when you wake up in the morning, you get to do it all again. After a while it's easier to grab the potato chips as you walk by, or skip the workout, or just get in the shower without trying to pray. You yourself erode, incrementally, with fatigue and bone weariness.

This is partly because doing good is so much harder than doing evil. If you want to become tired, try doing that which you should do, eat that which you should eat, say that which you should say, think that which you should think, feel that which you should feel. The effort is exhausting.

Fortunately, Jesus is coming back. The end is surely coming. There will be a judgment and a setting right of everything by God on the last day. If you lift up your countenance to contemplate the end of the world, you may find an imperceptible strength come into your weary limbs.

But also, don't worry, if he doesn't come back right away, you at least have the sweet release of death to look forward to. Put down that cookie, and call that difficult person at church to find out how she's doing.

342 The Childbearing

Yet she will be saved through childbearing—if they continue in faith and love and holiness, with self-control.

I TIMOTHY 2:15

Some people think this is my life verse because I've had six children. If anyone is going to be saved, I guess it's going to be me. Except for the "if," because if you've had children, you know that the child uproots all the ugliness in your heart and splays it out on the kitchen counter so that everyone can see it. You didn't have faith, love, holiness, or self-control before you had children, but you thought you did, so at least now you know that you really didn't.

So then, how can you be saved? Well, one woman gave birth to a child. She held him in her arms and loved him. When he was all grown up, she watched him die—the Savior of the world—and then he was laid in her arms again. That's the biggest way that women are saved through childbearing, because of the child she bore. Everyone is saved that way. But also, in some small way, every woman who gives birth—who bears in her body the life of another, who, as she brings forth that child, is able to taste the suffering of the one who bore in *his* body the sins of the world, giving life where there should have been death—must die to herself. She experiences, not just in her mind and her heart, but in her very body, the business of counting someone as more significant than herself.

I mean, men can experience it to but not in the same way and so it's harder. Too bad for them.

343 It's Okay to Know

. . . always learning and never able to arrive at a knowledge of the truth.

II TIMOTHY 3:7

It is out of fashion for Christians (and pretty much anyone) to be certain about anything. If you arrive at a definite conclusion about something, especially any religious matter, there's probably something wrong with you. You obviously haven't really considered all the options. You haven't read the whole world wide web. Worse yet, you might even be a hater, maybe even a bigot. How dare you know something for certain. You must, with all the certainty you can muster, announce that you Don't Know.

Happily, prevailing fashions, along with the cosmos, will eventually all pass away. And so, even though you will definitely lose the respect and admiration of the world, you should still go looking for the truth. And once you have found it, you should grab on and know it, no matter how costly to your self-perception, your way of life, or your plans for the future. Luckily, the truth is not just an idea. It is a person. It is Jesus. Not only can you know about him, you can know him. You can fasten your way to his. You can actually arrive. And even if everyone is angry with you along the way, in the long run, knowing him will be worth all the trouble.

The Cretans

> One of the Cretans, a prophet of their own, said, "Cretans are always
> liars, evil beasts, lazy gluttons." This testimony is true. Therefore rebuke
> them sharply, that they may be sound in the faith . . .
> TITUS 1:12–13

It's okay because a Cretan said it. Really, it's okay—Paul is just quoting a
Cretan. IT'S OKAY. I mean, I realize, especially in the day that I type this
out, that this is not okay. No one is allowed to say anything like this. No
one is allowed, with a few strokes of the keyboard, to categorize an entire
group of people one way.

Or we could say, yes, he can. He absolutely can. No one needs to faint
on the couch. What have we said all along? Take away the word Cretan
and substitute the name of any people group, all people groups, and all
individuals everywhere. This statement is true, and, being Scripture, is
useful for correction and rebuke. All of us are always liars. We lie about
everything, most especially our true standing before God. And as for being
an evil beast, come over to my house at the witching hour of four o'clock,
when I am trying to make supper, and everyone is screaming. Walk in and
see me become the person described here. Then watch me sit back and
eat too much of what I cooked, and be too tired and lazy to clean it up.

Titus must rebuke them so that the word of Christ might take root in
their hearts, so that they will stop lying and become nicer. So also with
you. And, I guess, me as well.

The Slave and the Master

Confident of your obedience, I write to you, knowing that you will do even
more than I say. At the same time, prepare a guest room for me, for I am
hoping that through your prayers I will be graciously given to you.
PHILEMON 21—22

If only Paul had written a sharp little letter telling Philemon how bad he
was for owning a slave at all. He could have gone into all the evils of slavery and enumerated the great benefits of not owning slaves in the first
place. The great scandal is that God decided, through his Son Jesus, by
the power of the Holy Spirit, to save both the slave and the slave-owner,
making them brothers, members of his own body. Neither one of them
got to claim to be the victim. They both were forgiven and saved.

If I were Onesimus, I would go to Paul and say something like, "I've
been praying about it, and I just don't think Philemon and I can work together. Too much water under the bridge. Know what I mean? I feel called
to serve the Lord in Antarctica." And if I were Philemon, I would write to
Paul and say, "Of course I want to work with Onesimus. I do value him so
much. I just think the power differential is too great. I think it would be
better if we had some space. Also, I prayed about it."

How mean of Paul to send the slave back to the master and command
them to work it out as brothers in Christ, and then tell them he'll be coming along shortly, to see how they are making out.

The Sword

Let us therefore strive to enter that rest, so that no one may fall by the same sort of disobedience. For the word of God is living and active, sharper than any two-edged sword, piercing to the division of soul and spirit, of joints and of marrow, and discerning the thoughts and intentions of the heart.

HEBREWS 4:11—12

Once, a few years ago—okay, still—I gave up taking a "day off" every week. There's too much work to do. The only way to get it done is to work all the time, sometimes even on Sunday. You might be shocked to learn that this life choice has only increased my workload, rather than lessening it. Then, in a fit of rage, I tried reading the whole book of Hebrews, figuring that if God really wanted me to rest, he needed to figure out a way for it to happen.

Trouble is, real rest takes work, especially on the most "restful" day of the week—Sunday. The people of Israel, when they entered the Land of Rest, had to first kill everyone off, which sounds pretty stressful, actually. They had to "strive" to enter that "rest"—two words which do not sound well together, especially with the specter of death looming.

And death is looming up because the word of God comes along like a sharp, two-edged sword—not unlike the sharpened blades my two sons got for Christmas. "Be careful!" we shout. But the sword which is the word of God which cuts to the heart is not for death. It brings life, revealing all the futile striving that keeps you from the eternal rest of God.

HEBREWS 1:1—4:13

The Comfortable Chair

But when Christ had offered for all time a single sacrifice for sins, he sat
down at the right hand of God . . .

HEBREWS 10:12

When my children were young, I barely got to sit down, except when I was
nursing a baby. As soon as I thought I'd done all the work and collapsed
in a chair, I would remember six things I should have done, so that if I
did keep sitting, I could only do it by feeling guilty. Now I sit all the time
in front of my computer but still feel bad about how little I accomplish.

The nature of human work is futility, is never finishing anything, is
having to do the same tasks over and over and over. This is the way the
priests worked in the temple before it was torn down. In the Holy Place
and the Holy of Holies, there was no place to sit. The priest could never sit
down because his work was never finished. As soon as he had sacrificed
one animal for someone's sins, that person would go and immediately sin
some more, on the way out of the temple. He'd have to come back with yet
another animal.

But Jesus, whose blood is enough for every sin committed by every
person for all time, after offering himself up as the single sacrifice, sat
down. He doesn't need to hurry, busily accomplishing tasks that will immediately need to be done over again.

Sometimes, as you are feeling discouraged, slumped in your chair,
pondering the work that lies before you, cast your mind's eye up to him
sitting because all the work is completed forever.

Couch to Eternity

Therefore, since we are surrounded by so great a cloud of witnesses, let us also lay aside every weight, and sin which clings closely, and let us run with endurance the race that is set before us . . .

HEBREWS 12:1

Every so often someone will try to pressure me into running a 5K. Running in events like these, is one of the ways that a lot of us make ourselves feel like we're "doing" something against disease or other kinds of worthy causes. It's also, apparently, a great way to kick-start a new weight loss program. You start training for the "race" and then maybe, when it's over, you'll keep running, or walking. I don't know—I am unwilling to try. Especially with anyone watching. Especially while holding weights.

Except the writer thinks you should actually put the weights down before you start running. And the people watching you aren't judging you for being fitter than they are. Nor are they impressed with your virtue. They themselves have already successfully run the race. They are sympathetic, delighted by your efforts, sure of your success.

Though you, in the middle of it—and really, you have no way of knowing whether you are in the middle, or near the end—feel that there is no finish line, you are just slogging it out with no real knowledge of how long you have to endure. When you feel like that, it's okay to slow to a walk, and look up at the crowd, or cloud if you will, and see that you really haven't got that far to go.

Just a Suggestion

For if anyone is a hearer of the word and not a doer, he is like a man who looks intently at his natural face in a mirror. For he looks at himself and goes away and at once forgets what he was like.

JAMES 1:23—24

I'm sorry to say that I do this practically every day. I look in the mirror and then I walk away and completely forget what I look like. And it happens with the Bible as well. I read the Bible and see that I'm a sinner and then spend the rest of the day explaining to everyone around me that I'm not that bad, adding up all the good things I've done to present to God as justification for my great virtue. If no one in my real life notices, I post some pictures on Instagram and immediately feel better.

While I'm doing that with my crummy, hypocritical, dark heart, I'm yelling at my kids or taking offense at strangers on other parts of the internet. The great thing, though, is that I do feel sort of bad about it when I discover that that's what I've been up to.

Really, though, this verse is for people who read the Bible and don't even care. Or worse, people who don't even read the Bible. Those bad people. For real, James is a good book for people who just need to get a clue and not be so hypocritical and evil. If you know anybody like that, maybe suggest it to them.

350 So, What Are You Saying?

And the tongue is a fire, a world of unrighteousness. The tongue is set among our members, staining the whole body, setting on fire the entire course of life, and set on fire by hell.

JAMES 3:6

I read recently that the invention of safe spaces from, not for, but *from* free speech is the sanest thing ever. I was complaining about all the young people of today, shouting at them to get off my lawn, reminiscing about how anyone used to be able say anything and we could all deal with it, when I stumbled across an explanation of this phenomenon. It's true, back in the day, you could say something audibly and it might be hurtful, but it would disappear. No one had the ability to repeat that thing in a forum where other people could screen shot it and keep it forever.

If you want to encounter a "world of unrighteousness" there are whole sections of the internet where you don't even have to click that much. One glance will show it to you. Either through the witty use of a keyboard, or the little record button, it's possible to "set on fire the entire course of life," which is rather a comprehensive way of putting it.

Some sensible younger people demand to be kept safe from this kind of inferno, even at the expense of enduring mockery from their unwise elders. Of course, there is also the option of just never saying anything you could ever regret. Which seems to be what James is suggesting, though with rather more hyperbole than required, even for the internet. Man, was he on Twitter? What on earth?

35¹ You Can't Know the Future

. . . yet you do not know what tomorrow will bring. What is your life? For you are a mist that appears for a little time and then vanishes.
JAMES 4:14

At the beginning of the week, I like to hand draw on a tiny bit of thick paper a little calendar for myself. I make the grid and mark the days and then, with a fine tipped pen, I write in my appointments and obligations and plans. I write what I intend to make for dinner every day, and what rooms I will clean. I make long lists of people I will call and emails I will write. Then I put this piece of paper in my pocket and carry it around for the week: a scrap, a thin, papery burden that cannot be pried out of my hand, no matter how cold and hard and dead it makes me to cling to it. In the middle of the week, when all my plans are ruined, I react as though I am being killed. James may think that I don't know what tomorrow may bring, but I think he is crazy. I know what tomorrow will bring, and therefore I must get through my whole list today. If I don't, the cosmos may come crashing down. Certainly, everyone will blame me.

Perhaps you are more circumspect about yourself and your plans. Perhaps you have a proper understanding of your own importance and the true extent to which you control the outcome of your days. If you do, I'm totally happy for you. Really, I am. I just want you to know that.

Kept in Heaven for You

... to an inheritance that is imperishable, undefiled, and unfading,
kept in heaven for you ...

I PETER 1:4

My inheritance from my grandmother included an accordion that I didn't know how to play, so that it went to live with an aunt. No one really has time to learn to play the accordion I've discovered. In addition, I and all the other grandchildren each received an allotment of giraffes. My grand-mother had a thing for wooden giraffes. She couldn't walk by one without buying it, and as she lived for most of her childhood in Africa, and knew lots of people who would never visit without bringing one as a present, it meant that the twenty grandchildren each inherited ten. I have mine propped in my window and they occasionally are knocked on the floor and bits of them chip off.

Of course, the little giraffes were barely any consolation to me when she died, though I clung to them furiously. I couldn't believe she would go away. I couldn't believe I would be left here without her, staring at the little wooden line of long necks and spindly legs.

The inheritance here in this verse is actually the other way around. Instead of dying and leaving all your junk to your children, what happens is that you labor along, breaking and destroying whatever it is you touch, and all the time, God is guarding, protecting from anything that could possibly spoil it, your eternal life with him. The moment you close your eyes in death you step over the threshold to an inheritance that doesn't just remind you of something you loved but is the very thing that you adore now.

I PETER I, 2

The Glittering Jewels

Do not let your adorning be external—the braiding of hair and the putting
on of gold jewelry, or the clothing you wear—but let your adorning be the
hidden person of the heart with the imperishable beauty of a gentle and
quiet spirit, which in God's sight is very precious.

I PETER 3:3—4

Observe me running wildly around on a Sunday morning, adorning myself with hair gel and mascara, trying to make sure that all my children
look sweet and presentable, tying hair bows and soothing the one who
cannot bear the seam of the tights to come up over her toes. Watch me
as I berate myself for eating a bagel during the week so that my church
outfit doesn't fit as smoothly as I'd hoped. Wince when you see me writhe
in embarrassment when someone tells me I look nice and instead of just
saying "thank you," I make that person feel guilty for trying because I, I of
all people, do not feel satisfied with myself. Honestly, if it really were all
about my appearance, no one would ever be my friend.

If the outward adorning is all there is, none of us would have any relationships with anyone at all. There has to be a hidden person of the heart.
There has to be—even if it is under several layers of screaming—a gentle
and quiet spirit. When you dig down and find it, it is a balm and a rest to
all the raging, whether it is your own or someone else's. Seriously, just try
to think about Jesus for a few minutes. It totally helps.

354 Get a Handle on Yourself

For whoever lacks these qualities is so nearsighted that he is blind, having
forgotten that he was cleansed from his former sins.
II PETER 1:9

Take a moment to read through the list in verses five through eight. You've
been saved, says Peter, you've been given everything. You don't lack anything. Then he launches into an appalling listicle of impossible things.
(That's the technical theological term: "things.")

Supplement, that is, add, to virtue—which is being a fine, upstanding
person, not given to notorious sin that ruins your life and everybody else's—
knowledge. And what is knowledge? It is knowing both about God, through
the Scriptures, and relating to him as you would to a person. And then add
to knowledge self-control. Get a handle on yourself. Don't give way to every
whim or impulse. Try to get yourself under some kind of regulation. And
then when you've got self-control down pat, add to that steadfastness—the
grit of digging in your heels and not being blown away by every new thing
that comes along. And to steadfastness add godliness. That's right, try to be
more like God. Try to like the things he likes and do the things you think
he would like you to do. And when you've managed to become more like
God, add brotherly affection, which is having a kind sincere care for those
around you. And when you've got all that down, add love.

Why? Because if you don't, it will be like that time when you went into
a room and couldn't remember why, or tried to read a book without your
glasses on, or woke up and forgot to go to church on Sunday morning. I
know! Why would you do that?

No Cosmic Deck Chair

*The Lord is not slow to fulfill his promise as some count slowness, but
is patient toward you, not wishing that any should perish, but that all
should reach repentance.*

II PETER 3:9

I am a big fan of slowness in theory. I am all about trying *not* to rush on
to the next thing, to be deliberate, thoughtful, not just flying along at
some insane speed. Of course, that is well-nigh impossible, because the
more people you add to a household, the more you find yourself rushing. Hepzibah wanted a dance lesson, which doesn't *exactly* conflict with
Ludovic's soccer practice . . . Blink and you're in the vile minivan, hur-
tling down the highway, late to everything.

Meanwhile God takes his sweet, sweet time. He takes ages to do anything. When you pray, it feels like you're speaking into a silent void. While
I rush from the store to home and back out to soccer and then back home
and then out to small group, all the time it seems like God is probably
watching me, leaning back in his cosmic deck chair, sipping lemonade.

Nevertheless, he is not slow. He is patient, which is not the same
thing. He hasn't dug in his heels like a recalcitrant child determined not
to face the school bus. He is not me, pretending I can't really hear my
whole family railing that we are already half an hour late. He is patient,
which means that he knows when the good time to do something is, and
he will do it then. Meanwhile he is in the car, and at the soccer game, and
in the small group, in my very heart lest I perish as I run my feet off.

356 Happy Clappy

And we are writing these things so that our joy may be complete.

I JOHN 1:4

Complete joy sounds great, doesn't it? It would be really nice to have some joy in the daily outworking of life. Really, I'd even settle for some mediocre happiness. Or even just not being totally dissatisfied with everything all the time.

But that's the problem, I'm willing to settle, to make do with a temporary, fleeting happiness that I can work out for myself with a four-dollar cup of coffee or a new pair of shoes.

"If you could have anything in the world," a child once asked me, "what would you have?"

"A perfect handbag," I said, without pausing to consider. If I could just have the perfect bag, I would be perfectly happy. John looks at me down the corridor of time and despairs, knowing that happiness is a waste of my time.

Happiness cannot be had in such a way that it endures. It has to be joy, a joy that comes through suffering, through need, through desperation. People experience joy when they thought they were dying, but then they discover that they aren't going to die after all. Joy is found when, after enduring unendurable pain, the pain is removed, or strength is given to bear it. It's not something you can get for yourself, even if you work really hard. Joy is the gift of the rescuer to the one who was sinking into the pit of death. So, if you're not feeling too happy, don't worry about it. Joy will come if you fling yourself into the arms of Jesus.

You're Still Here

Everyone who goes on ahead and does not abide in the teaching of Christ,
does not have God. Whoever abides in the teaching has both the Father
and the Son.

II JOHN 9

One of the surest marks of a true Christian is how long he hangs in there.
Or she. Or you. If you feel all the time like chucking it and going on to
something more interesting, if you sit in church and long instead to be
out in a green, vaulted cathedral forest, if you cringe as the music and
praying goes on and on, if you find yourself bored to tears by the Sunday
school lesson, it doesn't mean you're Not Saved. It means you're just like
everyone other Christian struggling along.

It's not that you have to like it, the teaching and fellowship of Christ;
it's that no matter how much you feel like you can't endure it, you actually
do. You abide. You bear with it. You go on showing up and doing the best
you can, even when you stand outside of yourself wondering why you keep
coming back, especially when it's so weird and Christians are so weird.

The person who "goes on ahead" is not advancing to anything better.
That person is not experiencing enlightenment. That person isn't discovering anything precious. That person is abandoning a great salvation,
a saving that God works out amongst people who do hateful things to each
other, sometimes even with sticky smiles plastered on their faces. But it
is God who does it, which means you can't always tell how it is going day
by day. Therefore, abide. Hang on. Bear with it.

358 The Church Needs Jesus

So if I come, I will bring up what he is doing, talking wicked nonsense
against us. And not content with that, he refuses to welcome the brothers,
and also stops those who want to and puts them out of the church.

III JOHN 10

The Church has always been a turbulent place. Mixed in amongst all the
true believers are many people who, for lots and lots of reasons, just want
to wreck it. They don't really believe, or they want power and influence,
or they read a foolish book and get some wacky ideas, or they are lazy and
don't want to do what the Scriptures command in the matter of getting
along with other believers. During the sermon they sit there and think of
who else ought to be hearing it. And lots of times beleaguered believers
wonder why Jesus doesn't prevent these kinds of people from coming in
the first place.

No, instead of supernaturally dealing with those who stir up contro-
versy or lead the sheep astray, Jesus wants the Church to try to cope with
it. He wants true believers, while trusting him, to defend against error, to
call out false teachers, to practically care for those preaching the truth, to
sharply expel those who are not. Gear up for battle, in other words, join
in the fight, even though it is painful and messy.

In It to Win It

Beloved, although I was very eager to write to you about our common
salvation, I found it necessary to write appealing to you to contend for the
faith that was once for all delivered to the saints.
JUDE 3

Every time the Church gets sort of comfortable and settled and happy about things, she should probably begin waking up in a cold anxious
sweat. The fact is, the Church is caught up in the same battle God has been
fighting since Adam and Eve wiped the sweet juice from their insolent
lips. God is in a war against sin, both inside each individual Christian,
and in the church itself. Little battles are being fought all over the pews.
Not to mention all the sin outside of the Church, bashing at the doors,
hoping to get in. Christians can't, therefore, be really comfortable people. Sometimes you just have to put down your bulletin, or your post-
church muffin, and enter the fray.

When someone walks up to you at coffee hour and says, "I really think
Jesus is a big meanie and how do we know he was God anyway," instead of
nodding and backing away, take a big sip of coffee and say, "It's true that
Jesus can be abrasive, especially against sin, but did you know that we can
know both from history and the remarkable evidence of Scripture itself
that God really did come in the person of Jesus to rescue you from yourself? Would you like to read the Bible with me some time? Maybe we could
meet for better coffee than this mediocre church swill." In other words:
Contend, Enter the Fray, Be a Little Bit Stubborn.

360 The End

"As for the mystery of the seven stars that you saw in my right hand, and the seven golden lampstands, the seven stars are the angels of the seven churches, and the seven lampstands are the seven churches."

REVELATION 1:20

The Church around the world is such a mess. Every day it seems I hear about some new bad thing, some error a pastor has fallen into, some abuse perpetrated upon the faithful. Either Christians are being persecuted from the outside, or they are being foolish and divisive on the inside. It's easy for me to want to let myself off the hook. "Look," I could say to Jesus, "I'm small potatoes, I can only do this little bit of evil. Cut me a break." But he is cutting me a break in these first few chapters of Revelation.

He could wait until the end to judge and then destroy the whole world at one go. It would be totally within his rights. But in his mercy, he is judging the Church now, while there's still time. When he takes a lampstand away from a church, he is judging that congregation before the end, which means all those Christians can repent.

If I read the chapters and discover that I have lost my first love, or that I've fallen into heresy and error, or that I've compromised with the world, I have time to turn around. Jesus doesn't let the Church go up in the ball of smoke and fire at the end. He judges her, he cleanses her, he brings her through. As you read though these last remaining terrifying, chapters, keep your eyes open. When you get to the very end, the Church will still be there.

Lift Up Your Head

Then the kings of the earth and the great ones and the generals and the rich and the powerful, and everyone, slave and free, hid themselves in caves and among the rocks of the mountains, calling to the mountains and rocks, "Fall on us and hide us from the face of him who is seated on the throne, and from the wrath of the Lamb. . ."

REVELATION 6:15—16

It's hard to imagine the powerful of the world so terrified that they beg for the mountains to cover them, to protect them from the face of the God they don't believe in. Interestingly for me, as it stands now I'm the one that's afraid. I'm both afraid of God and afraid of all the mighty of the earth who are free to kill and destroy me, knowing that there isn't anything I can do about it. It's hard to read the news and not be covered with fear and grief. But just like Mary, who, in the discovery that she would carry the Savior of the world in her own flesh, saw afar off the bringing down of the mighty from their thrones, I can ponder the certain promise of the corrupt rulers of today and tomorrow cowering under the earth. I can pick my perilous way through this dangerous world, waiting for God to do what he is going to do.

And when he comes and lights up the sky and everyone runs to hide, begging creation to close in and cover them, I can lift up my head and fix my eyes on the glory that is finally revealed—my strength, my shield, my ever present help in times of trouble—come at last to vindicate himself.

REVELATION 4, 5, 6

Nobody Puts Baby in a Corner

Then the dragon became furious with the woman and went off to make war on the rest of her offspring, on those who keep the commandments of God and hold to the testimony of Jesus. And he stood on the sand of the sea.

REVELATION 12:17

Not even Satan gets to put Baby, I mean the Church, anywhere, let alone in a dark, overlooked corner. Seriously, this is the biggest, grandest, most thrilling story from which every successful epic narrative or dated rom-com has ever spun its thread.

There's a dragon. There's a knight on a white horse. There's a beautiful woman. There's a battle so great that the number of the slain pile up all over the desert floor. There's suspense and drama and nail-biting. There's pure Goodness against foul Evil. Every time you think it must be at an end, a sudden twist drags the suspense out further. If you wanted to make a movie, all the special effects ever invented wouldn't give even a bland taste of the astonishing scope of drama and violence.

Except that it's not a fairy tale. It's not the summer blockbuster dream of a great screenwriter. It's the actual story of humanity, battling it out against God, picking the wrong side in the war, having to turn and accept the good and true before it's too late. For all the blood-drenched scenery, the panoramic camera angles, the fantastic dancing and singing numbers, the heart-stopping suspense, there are thousands of interior moments where you can zoom in on the face of each character and watch them choose which way to go. At the end, the heroine (Baby) flings her arms wide with sheer joy.

REVELATION 12

363 The Microchips

. . . so that no one can buy or sell unless he has the mark, that is, the name of the beast or the number of its name.

REVELATION 13:17

I saw that creepy video of those cheerful employees willingly reaching forth their wrists to the company boss so he could implant them with tiny microchips. The chips not only gave them access to the building but also contained their IDs and their bank information, so the employees could easily buy snacks in the breakroom without having to worry about a wallet or purse or anything like that. The boss looked really happy and so did all the employees—I mean, of course they did. I bet they were crying on the inside. The comments were epic. Best two hours I've ever spent online.

I get it, it's creepy. Will we ever get to the point where we have to promise to adore Satan or starve to death? Could happen. There's no good reason to think it won't eventually.

But I feel bad for Satan. Because God takes his law and without any technology at all, indeed, through the powerful, invisible work of the Holy Spirit, he writes that law on the mind of the believer, he traces it in the heart, he moves and strengthens the hands. This work is inexorable, shadowed through centuries of devoted worshipers binding little boxes to their foreheads, wrapping memorials around their arms, yet now inscribed on the soul of the believer by God himself. Satan just can't compete. He has to fearmonger and go into the tattooing and microchipping business. Sad.

Our Eyes Beheld

Then I saw thrones, and seated on them were those to whom the author-
ity to judge was committed. Also I saw the souls of those who had been
beheaded for the testimony of Jesus and for the word of God, and those
who had not worshiped the beast or its image and had not received its
mark on their foreheads or their hands. They came to life and reigned
with Christ for a thousand years.

REVELATION 20:4

Here's another piece of the puzzle. As we go along in human history, more and more events from our perspective fall into place. Isaiah looked up and saw a young woman bearing a miraculous child. Jeremiah had a glimpse of the ark being taken out of the temple. Even farther back in long ages beforehand, Jacob pictured a vine and a colt. Now John, seeing the true end of time, beholds an eerily contemporary vision of violence—the souls of those who had been beheaded for the testimony of Jesus and the word of God.

Sometimes I wake up in the middle of the night in a sweat and think about all the deaths of Christians going on right now, far away from me, but not that far. And I think, "This is so insane, so random." Until I come here and discover that I'm not the first one to see it. It's in the plan. God isn't losing track of anyone or anything.

Don't be downcast and covered with woe. The judgment of the world is drawing near, in the same way that its salvation appeared, suddenly, so long ago.

365 Back to the Beginning

And I heard a loud voice from the throne saying, "Behold, the dwelling place of God is with man. He will dwell with them, and they will be his people, and God himself will be with them as their God. He will wipe away every tear from their eyes, and death shall be no more, neither shall there be mourning, nor crying, nor pain anymore, for the former things have passed away."

REVELATION 21:3—4

You made it! Rub the sleep out of your eyes, stretch your tired neck, pour another cup of whatever you like best, order in another pie, and flip back to the beginning. You can't just read it once. You've got to keep reading it over and over and over until you hear his voice and feel his very hand wiping away the stray tears, the heartbreak, the frustration, the fatigue, the weariness, and yes, even the anger.

Until that moment, the words of this book, the Bible, are the source of your consolations. Until that moment—when the war is over and you have collapsed into a heap of relief, your body made perfect, your mind uncluttered and untroubled, your heart relieved of sin and evil, when you look up into the very face of the One you have waited for so long—until then you need this book. You need the word that gives life and carries you along. You need the correction and rebuke. You need the strange, grief-laden stories that show how God comes into the room and opens up the windows and opens the door and lets in the light and warmth and feeds you with his own self. Don't put it down. Whatever you do, don't stop reading it.

REVELATION 21, 22

Acknowledgements

This book wouldn't exist without the temper tantrum I threw on Facebook one day, when I, having tried to plow through another devotional book, declared that I wished I could write a book called *Sarcastic Devotionals for Angry People*. My first word of thanks goes to all my friends who clicked "like" on the post and said they would definitely buy that book for the title alone.

Second, I would like again to thank Jessica Snell and Joshua Barber who brought it into being by shoving me along and teaching me how to write a book at all. And I would like to thank Ned and Leslie Bustard for taking up the task and pushing me to overhaul it and freshen it up.

Third, I would like to thank my mother who read the whole thing again the second time with a ruthless and unwavering eye, and who laughed when she was supposed to. And my father, who baked so much bread during the coronavirus pandemic that I had nothing to do but sit, eat, and edit. And I must thank my child, Aedan, who thought of the name, and all the rest of them who always look upon my tortured existence with a bemused air. And I must thank Matt, who tried to distract me from editing with legion YouTube clips.

And finally, I must thank all the people who already love this book, and who wrote me so kindly to say it was helpful, and who spurred me on to bring it back into being. Hopefully now you will not need to sell your firstborn to Amazon to get a copy. Oh! And, of course I must also thank God, without whom there would be nothing to write about.

COMING SOON

Other books that nail it . . .

GODLY CHARACTER(S): INSIGHTS FOR SPIRITUAL PASSION FROM THE LIVES OF 8 WOMEN IN THE BIBLE

". . . these 'great eight' propel you towards habits of godliness—putting you in a place to receive grace and fall more deeply in love with your savior—and that in His love you might be re-shaped and re-formed."
—Robert William Alexander, author of *The Gospel-Centered Life at Work*

DEEPER MAGIC: THE THEOLOGY BEHIND THE WRITINGS OF C.S. LEWIS

". . . a treasure trove of systematized information—a must for every C.S. Lewis fan, and all the rest of us who should be."
—Norman Geisler, PhD

A BOOK FOR HEARTS & MINDS: WHAT YOU SHOULD READ AND WHY

"Curators of the imagination, stewards of the tradition, priests of print, [Hearts & Minds Bookstore has] always done more than sold books: they have furnished faithful minds and hearts. This book is a lovely testimony to that good work."
—James K.A. Smith, Calvin College, author of *You Are What You Love: The Spiritual Power of Habit*

THE BEGINNING: A SECOND LOOK AT THE FIRST SIN

". . . a very readable and engaging discussion on the nature and consequences of the original sin using the biblical accounts as his primary authority."
—The American Journal of Biblical Theology

DON'T PLANT—BE PLANTED: CONTRARIAN OBSERVATIONS ABOUT STARTING A CHURCH

"Michael Crawford . . . is a consistent source of wisdom and contrarian thinking. I have been immensely blessed by his wisdom and writing. I highly commend this book to you. Read it and re-read it!"
—Brian Howard, Vice President of the U.S. Networks for Acts 29

GOOD POSTURE: ENGAGING CURRENT CULTURE WITH ANCIENT FAITH

"I couldn't recommend this book more highly. Please read it cover to cover. Please share it. And please, for the love of God, start living it."
—Scott Sauls, pastor and author of *Jesus Outside the Lines*

SquareHaloBooks.com